Achieving understanding
intercultural encounters

LANGUAGE IN SOCIAL LIFE SERIES

Series Editor: Professor Christopher N. Candlin

Language and power
Norman Fairclough

Discourse and the translator
Basil Hatim and Ian Mason

Planning language, planning inequality
James W. Tollefson

Language and ideology in children's fiction
John Stephens

Linguistics and aphasia
Ruth Lesser and Lesley Milroy

Language and the law
John Gibbons

Literacy practices: investigating literacy in social contexts
Mike Baynham

The cultural politics of English as an international language
Alastair Pennycook

Fictions at work: language and social practice in fiction
Mary Talbot

Critical discourse analysis: the critical study of language
Norman Fairclough

Knowledge machines: language and information in a technological society
Denise E. Murray

Achieving understanding: discourse in intercultural encounters
Katharina Bremer, Celia Roberts, Marie-Thérèse Vasseur, Margaret Simonot and Peter Broeder

Achieving understanding: Discourse in intercultural encounters

Katharina Bremer, Celia Roberts, Marie-Thérèse Vasseur, Margaret Simonot and Peter Broeder

LONGMAN

LONDON AND NEW YORK

Longman Group Limited,
Longman House, Burnt Mill,
Harlow, Essex CM20 2JE, England
and Associated Companies throughout the world.

Published in the United States of America
by Longman Publishing, New York

First published 1996

ISBN 0 582 086450 CSD
ISBN 0 582 086442 PPR

British Library Cataloguing-in-Publication Data
A catalogue record for this book is
available from the British Library

Library of Congress Cataloging-in-Publication Data
Also available

Set by 8 in 10/12pt Palatino
Produced by Longman Singapore Publishers (Pte) Ltd.
Printed in Singapore

Contents

General Editor's Preface

The heritage of this remarkable book is made clear in the acknowledgements of the authors, as is its specific focus and research context. As part of a major, possibly the most extensive interlingual and international study of second language acquisition so far undertaken, the research drawn on and described here has both important documentary and disciplinary significance. It provides a record, in considerable detail, of the processes of one important part of a multi-dimensional intellectual endeavour, funded by the European Science Foundation, and now published through Cambridge University Press, the base data from which are being made generally available to researchers and must constitute the single most extensive archive of second language acquisitional data internationally. As a consequence of this project, researchers will thus be enabled to draw down data for a wide range of future studies, both second language acquisitional and more generally interlingual in focus.

Notwithstanding this overarching project context, this latest book in the *Language in Social Life Series* is much more than a particular record of one important sub-project, however extensively treated and carefully documented. I would like to argue in this Preface for the significance of the book as a document about the conduct and engagement of empirical linguistic research, whether such research has the processes of acquisition as its focus or not. In doing so, I am both justifying its placement within this Series and arguing for its messages to be more widely canvassed among linguistic and language educational communities and beyond these professionals to that more general audience for whom language competence presents both opportunities and barriers to personal livelihoods, rights and opportunities.

For such a wider readership what then is the key frame of reference for the book? How might one best begin? The clue lies in the title with its emphasis on *achieving understanding*. The authors (and indeed their interlocutors) view understanding not as a product to be gained or lost, not as something that is inherent and guaranteed given favourable conditions, but always subject to uncertain and conditional processes directed at variably framed subject-matters; an objective with contesting interpretations and varying contexts of negotiation, multiply purposed, and involving always unequal cooperative and conflicting partnerships, with alternate and contested assessments of its achievement. In the words of the authors, 'understanding is a dynamic public and cooperative activity in which both sides are actively engaged', mutually constructed through the active engagement of participants' inferencing processes within encounters.

Given this diversity, how then can one best embark on understanding *'achieving understanding'*? Here the key is to begin with exploring the human relationships which are so distinctively and fully voiced throughout the text, and to identify cooperation and collaboration as the metaphors which unite researchers with their interlocutors, and, if understanding is ever to be achieved, minority speakers with those in the majority. Only such a mutual perspective can permit the reader to address the central questions that constantly recur throughout the book: *who* is involved in such interactions, *where* and under what circumstances, *how* and with which resources, *why* and with which purposes, over*which* matters, and to *whose* interest and advantage?

It will be useful to explore how each such question engages the central characters of the book: the minority ethnic workers, the majority group members, and the researchers themselves, multilingual, ethnically diverse and coming from different research traditions as they are also. For the first time in any detail and extent in the second language acquisition literature we confront participants from a range of different linguistic and cultural backgrounds engaging with majority language speakers outside of the instructional setting and collaborating with researchers in the exploration of their own language learning circumstances and their own local negotiations of meaning. The result for the reader is a richness of interaction and data that permits a novel focus; one less directed at a summation of acquisition, the quantum of what is learnt, and more at the dynamics of acquiring and its dependence on understanding, on personal strategies, social presuppositions and the exigencies of local context. Here the partnership between the researcher participants and the 'informant' participants is criterial. Notice how *interlocutor, interactant* and *partner* are the terms which have replaced the traditional *subject* of research and how this changes categorically their mutual rights and responsibilities and enables novel access by both to processes which are mutually under question.

Throughout the book, the *where* and circumstances of context are interwoven with the data, offering the opportunity for grounding the careful and full interpretations that are proffered. What is important here, though, is that the presentation is not merely in terms of an interpretive gloss, however intricate, on some locally contextualised but rather accidental data, though these will be novel for many whose exposure to date has been restricted in the main to the 'native-non-native' interactions of the classroom. Much more satisfactorily from an explanatory perspective, the authors provide insights into the conditions of production and, especially in this book, the conditions of interpretation of discourse, both those of the interlocutors and those of the researchers. In a manner which is especially insightful for future research, the authors' relate the local to the overarching and informing historical and social conditions which govern the discourse of both minority and majority participants. In doing so they offer, again for the first time, a way of broaching in second language acquisition studies the difficult and tenuous connections between the micro and the macro conditions of discourse, acknowledging how ethnicity, culture and more generally the social are inescapable factors in such research, whether it draws its data from the street or from the academy. In the same way, the explicitness of the authors about their own research methods and processes, the tensions and compromises that had inevitably to be made, represents another influencing context on the data and its presentation. Researchers also are engaged in achieving understanding.

I have already alluded to the book's concentration on processes. It will be important to see these not so much as experimental constructs focussing on strategic behaviour under controlled conditions, but rather the *how* of meaning-making against the influences of shifting schemata, orientations and, above all, of social and discourse roles. This dialogue between the social, the linguistic and the cognitive anchors acquisitional studies even more firmly to expressions in the contexts of use, but in this book, innovatively, at length and over whole events. Respecting once more the interplay

of researchers and their minority and majority speaking interlocutors, we may trace through the often interlingually and
interculturally written chapters, a process of exploratory research
which provides evidence of how such rich partnerships can provide elaborated analyses. It is not only the distinctive perspectives
of the providers of the data that need constantly to be borne in
mind, there is also the process of collaboration of perspectives
among the researchers, quite designedly characteristic of this project by the way, where different traditions on research, empirical,
philosophical, social, augment the analyses displayed.

Addressing the issue of purposes is always problematic, since
purposefulness is in large measure the reader's prerogative. There
are, however, distinct clues throughout the book as to the stance of
the researchers, *why* the book has been written. In the opening and
concluding chapters we have as clear and telling a statement of
research premises, objectives and epistemologies that one might
expect axiomatically to find but which is all too often not so explicitly and conscientiously displayed. More than such a statement *a
priori* however, are the clues that a diligent reader can discover
throughout the book's chapters of how such purposes are themselves subject to dialogue and change, how negotiating them was a
part of the research, not something cut and dried in advance.
Indeed, it is precisely here that the activities of this sub-project need
to be debated against those of other sub-projects in the whole
research endeavour. Partly because of the particular histories and
traditions of the researchers, partly because of their unique research
question, new dimensions were grafted onto the original design,
dimensions which in my view radically reinterpreted its own purposes and achievable objectives. In this way, this research
documented here provides another contesting yet productive voice
in terms of which the other project research outcomes can be evaluated. Speaking here of *voices*, it is to their greatest possible credit
that the authors have not only respected those of their interlocutors,
but linked them to particular orders of discourse. The case study
data allows the identified personalities that populate the book to
tell their own understanding stories, not just in their own terms but
explanatorily to the reader through the triangulation of documented ethnographic discussion. None more poignantly than Tino,
whose:

> . . . auch wenn ich spreche besser deutsch – welches beruf gibt es?
> *even if I speak better German – what job is there . . .*

sums up not only the conditions of learning but also the conditions of living.

In so saying, Tino refocusses the reader to the *what* and the *which* of subject-matter in such research. It moves the reader beyond the actualities of the described data to make the crucial link for both researchers and interlocutors between *purposes* and *advantage*. Such as statement emphasises that learning to communicate in another language is not just a matter of becoming a better, more autonomous language learner. It links his achievement of under-standing, however partial, to a more general responsibility for the consequences of achieving such understanding in terms of access to rights and goods in an increasingly bureaucratised and com-plexedly discoursed society. Nor is such achievement and such a link only the objective of those who do not speak the majority lan-guage as a mother tongue. It is everybody's business. The chapters focussing on obviating misunderstanding, with their message of joint responsibility, but especially that of the majority language speaker, make this plain. If we succeed, we all succeed, minority language speaker and majority language speaker alike, but the pur-poses of such success, however constrained, must be to open access and ensure equity, not merely to demonstrate personal competence. This is where this book has a message which extends its readership beyond those concerned with second language acquisition or the analysis of spoken discourse more generally. Focussing on the par-ticular instances of successful and unsuccessful communication and on the significant texts of a society are not enough. For living, inter-locutors need to be able to make the connections between such individual expressions of a society and the institutions that give rise to them. Social institutions like the family, the workplace, the school, the community centre, the local offices of government, the hospital or the clinic, the institutions of commerce and employ-ment. These are the true locations for the contexts of situation I spoke of earlier and which give meaning to the texts so richly dis-played here and in such linguistic diversity. They indicate strongly where our research sites ought to lie. Such institutional contexts are, of course, not just physical locations, they are places where people discourse and draw purposefully on their resources and their methods to persuade, to show solidarity and cooperation, to compete and to exercise power. Communication is not only a risky business, it is never neutral. If this is so, we can go on, as this book does, to ask what the issues are that give rise to such discourses and what are the obstacles to achieving understanding. In each case there will be a host of living issues depending on particular events, many necessarily remaining silent, the personal and undisplayable property of the life histories of the interlocutors, both minority and majority. What we can identify through these pages, however, and more generally, is that certain central social issues of contemporary society affect us all regardless of particular contexts of use, issues of gender, generation, rights and obligations, race, class and, above all, power. More especially, they affect us through their discursive expression. So in focussing on the particular, the individual cases so carefully introduced here, we ought not to fail to make the underlying connection to the issues which ultimately give rise to the need to achieve understanding, nor forget to honour the central tenet of the book, which is the participatory nature of such an achievement.

Exceptionally, I would like as General Editor, to use this opportunity to convey my personal thanks to the authors and their interlocutors, not only for the book, but more especially for the several years during which I was associated at Lancaster as a consultant to the UK group of this multilingual and multiproject research. Having experienced the struggles that they document here, having worked in part on these data, I came through them to share an approach to the analysis of discourse and to its significance for the understanding of the social which can now, in a different place and at a different time, make necessary and sensible the connections between talk and living, between discourse and polity.

Professor Christopher N Candlin
General Editor,
Centre for Language in Social LIfe,
Macquarie University,
Sydney, Australia

Acknowledgements

We should like to thank the European Science Foundation for supporting the original research project on Second Language Acquisition by Adult Immigrants. In particular we would like to thank the Steering Committee of the ESF project chaired by Sir John Lyons and subsequently by Professor Georges Lüdi. The following served as members of the Committee: Professors A.Aksu, D.Coste, N.Dittmar, W.Levelt, B.Norberg, R.Lo Schiavo and D.Slobin.

We would also like to thank our many colleagues on the ESF project, both central co-ordinators at the Max Planck Institut für Psycholinguistik, Wolfgang Klein and Clive Perdue, and colleagues in Göteborg, Heidelberg, London, Paris, Aix-en-Provence and Tilburg.

Our very special thanks go to the informants on the project who for two and a half years gave up much of their time and from whom we learnt so much, especially to the following who appear in this book: Abdelmalek, Abdullah, Andrea, Angelina, Berta, Çevdet, Ergün, Fatima, Gilda, Gina, Ilhami, Leo, Madan, Mahmut, Marcello, Mohamed, Paula, Ravinder, Santo, Tino and Zahra.

'Es geht hier, dass muss man betonen, nicht um den Fall der Erlernung einer fremden Sprache bei sich, in einem Zimmer, mit einem Lehrer, mit der Rückendeckung all derer, die in der eignen Stadt zu allen Stunden des Tages so reden, wie man's immer gewöhnt war; sondern es geht um das Ausgeliefersein an die fremde Sprache in **ihrem** Revier, wo alle auf ihrer Seite stehen und zusammen und mit einem Anschein von Recht unbekümmert, unbeirrt, unaufhörlich mit ihren Worten auf einen losschlagen. Es geht auch darum, dass man weiss, man bleibt, man fährt nicht mehr zurück, nicht nach einigen Wochen, nicht nach Monaten, nicht nach Jahren.

So liegt einem daran, alles was man hört, zu verstehen; das ist, wie jedermann weiss, zuerst immer das Schwerste.'

'Here, and this has to be emphasised, it is not a case of learning a foreign language at home, in a room, with a teacher with the back-up of all those who, in one's own town, at all hours of the day talk the same way one's always been used to: but it's far more a matter of being abandoned to the clutches of the foreign language on its own territory where everyone else is on its side, not on yours, and where they all gang up with every appearance of being in the right and with not a care but unerringly and continually rain blows upon you with their words. It is also a matter of knowing that you are here to stay, that you're not going back, not in a few weeks, not in a few months, not in years.

And so, your attitude to everything you hear is bent on understanding; and that, as everyone knows, is initially the most difficult thing of all.'

(Canetti, 1976. [our translation])

'I think that in order to attain self-fulfillment one must be brave enough to hover at the brink and to fall at times.'

(quotation by Roger Bissiere)

'"Je ne comprends pas". Il l'a osé. Il a pris sur lui de courir ce risque. Un risque énorme et pas seulement pour lui. Que l'autre maintenant brusquement se taise et appuie sur lui ce regard chargé de commisération, de surprise, qui le repoussera doucement, le rejettera dans les ténèbres, qu'il s'enveloppe de silence le temps de reprendre ses biens, ses paroles éblouissantes, de les enfermer, pour toujours inaccessibles, dans un coffre-fort dont il ne révélera pas le chiffre, et celui qui s'est montré indigne de recevoir de telles richesses, et moi, et nous tous, indignes comme lui, serons comme lui réduits, pitoyables cerveaux en peine, à errer nostalgiquement autour, à jamais dépourvus, indigents.'

'"I don't understand." He dared to say it. He decided to run the risk. An enormous risk and not only for him. Let the other now suddenly fall silent and fix him a look full of commiseration and surprise which gently rejects him, throwing him back into the shadows. Let him shroud himself in silence, allowing himself the time to take back what was his, his dazzling words, to shut them up forever out of reach, in a safe and hide the key. And then he who had shown himself not worthy of receiving such riches, and me, and all of us, unworthy like him, we will be like him, pitiful minds in torment, reduced to wander around, nostalgically, forever deprived and needy.'

(Sarraute, 1980 [our translation])

'The hand must venture into the unknown, it must remain alive to the danger it is courting, it must sense the brink.'

(quotation by Roger Bissiere)

ONE

Background to the understanding project

Celia Roberts

1.0 INTRODUCTION

This study is an analysis of processes of understanding in interaction between minority ethnic workers and majority group members. It charts some of the means by which participants achieve understanding and discusses some of the telling problems in understanding which occur between the majority speakers and those with limited experience of the majority language. It also raises questions about the nature of intercultural communication in providing conditions and opportunities for creating change in such unequal encounters.

Over the last thirty years the major cities of most Western and Northern European countries have been transformed from monolingual to multilingual environments. As a result, issues of ethnic relations and of languages and literacies have been persistently raised along with wider socio-political concerns. The aim of this book is to describe and illuminate some of the ways in which recently-arrived minority groups, with little or no experience of the majority language, learn to understand. And to set this interactive experience within the wider social context in which they are located.

The concerns of this book differ in three main ways from most of the studies in second language development. The focus here is on everyday interaction rather than instructed language teaching, on understanding rather than production and on the interplay of social and linguistic factors, rather than on purely linguistic ones.

Whereas most studies of second language development take the classroom as their context, this study is concerned with how adults manage to learn to communicate in everyday interaction. Minority ethnic workers settled in the industrialised cities of Northern and

Western Europe for economic and in some cases political reasons, certainly not because they wished to improve their competence in a European language. Few have any sustained opportunities for formal language learning, so their developing linguistic competence is constructed out of the kinds of unequal encounters with majority speakers which are a necessary part of getting and keeping work and housing, and of managing one's life. They are in the paradoxical situation of having to communicate in order to learn and having to learn in order to communicate (Simonot 1983, Perdue 1982).

Second language studies have also tended to concentrate on production. We argue here that the development of understanding, both as a process and as a study, is as important as production. Furthermore, far from being a passive skill, understanding is an interactive process which is constantly being negotiated by participants.

Similarly, an interactive perspective forces the researcher to record and interpret, in as holistic a way as possible, the everyday experiences of, and encounters with, the majority which form such a critical element in the social world of newly arrived minority workers. Central to a characterisation of intercultural communication and the problem of (mis)understanding is the fact of racism and the social and linguistic inequality of inter-ethnic encounters. No study of second language development among minority workers can ignore this context.

We also aim in the writing of this study to tackle some issues of representation. So, for example, we prefer to write about minority workers and not language learners and to question some of the formulae and metaphors routinely used in the second language literature. The discourse of this literature assumes a rational, scientific epistemology in which people tend to be abstracted and complex processes are reduced to things. The 'input' metaphor used in second language acquisition is a classic example. It is drawn from the world of machines and is frequently used, unproblematically, to describe potentially understandable language available to participants in the interaction. Such a metaphor tends to mask the complexity of interpretive processes and to ignore or dehumanise the listener.

This book is the result of working together as a group over many years. In the early stages we worked together as part of the European Science Foundation team on Adult Language Acquisition (see below and Bremer et al 1988). Subsequently our own thinking has, to some extent, changed and developed so that we are re-working our original analysis with new perspectives. The remainder of this chapter gives the background to the study from which this book is drawn.

1.1 BACKGROUND TO THIS STUDY

The data for this study was collected as part of a major research project investigating adult language acquisition: **Second Language Acquisition by Adult Immigrants**[1] funded by the European Science Foundation (ESF) 1982–1988. The authors of this book were part of a team researching 'ways of achieving understanding' which was one of the six areas in the original study. This area has formed the basis for this present study.

The project was based in France, Germany, The Netherlands, Sweden and the United Kingdom and two groups of speakers were studied in each country:

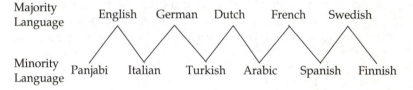

Majority
Language   English   German   Dutch   French   Swedish

Minority
Language   Panjabi   Italian   Turkish   Arabic   Spanish   Finnish

1.2 INFORMANTS

When the original ESF project was designed, the concept of an 'ideal' informant was agreed on. This informant would be relatively young and with little experience of the target language. It was hoped that these factors would allow the researchers to study the process of 'natural' Second Language Acquisition with informants who were not too old to learn and whose learning processes would not be influenced by classroom experiences.

The criteria for selecting informants, therefore, were:

age between 18 and 30
little or no experience of the new language
little formal education in their country of birth
recent arrivals in the country

In practice, these criteria could not be strictly maintained since by the early 1980s immigration restrictions had greatly reduced the number of new arrivals to Western and Northern Europe. A number of the informants selected were over 30 while the Turkish informants in Germany were only sixteen or seventeen. Some informants had settled in the new country for over a year, while others, particularly by the Turkish in Germany, the Finnish and Latin American informants in Sweden and the Latin American informants in France had received over a hundred hours of formal tuition in the majority language. This meant that over half of the twenty-six longitudinal informants had some, albeit very limited, competence in the new language at the start of the data collection.

Typically, informants had completed some six to eight years of schooling. However, the Italian group had all completed secondary education up to fifteen years of age and, by contrast three out of the four Moroccan Arabic speakers had had little or no schooling. Periods of residence in the new country, at the time of participation in the project, varied from nineteen months to one month.

A brief description of the background of one informant, Berta, from Chile, gives a glimpse of her life. Brief biographies of the 18 other informants from whose interactions we draw are given in Appendix A:

Berta

Berta came to France from Chile to join her Chilean husband who had been in the country as a political refugee for a year. She was in her thirties and had had eight years of primary and secondary education in Chile. She had no professional training and no knowledge of French when she arrived. For the first six months, she lived in a refugee centre with her husband and three children aged seven to fourteen, and then they settled in a flat of their own outside Paris.

Her first months in Paris were very difficult for her but she had the will to fight, help her children and better her own social status. From the beginning, Berta seized every opportunity offered to her to work and follow courses in French and vocational training. Her children adapted rather well at school and her sister-in-law having joined them in Paris married a French man. In these conditions, Berta focused on French more and more and her competence gradually improved.

The quest to find ideal informants was based on the assumption that generalisations could be made across informants and, in particular, that correlations could be made between socio-biographical information and language development. Van Hout and Strömqvist (1993) suggest one such general pattern in one particular area of language competence, lexical richness. Younger, single informants and those with relatively more education before settling in the new country tended to score higher on measures of lexical richness.

While this book is based on the informants and so the data from the original project, it has taken a substantially different perspective. Instead of attempting to establish trends that are generalisable, it focusses on *understanding* in the sense of the German 'verstehen' in the tradition of qualitative and naturalistic enquiry. To this end some of the detailed life of informants is related to an interpretive account of intercultural encounters. The case studies and interpretations attempt to bring the informants' voices into the text so that, even in an inevitably limited way, they emerge as people in the text. So, generalisations, correlations of causal variables, quantitative methods and developmental trends have been set aside in order to concentrate on an interpretive and social analysis of interactive contacts between majority and minority speakers.

1. 3 DATA

The data collection methods chosen for the original study were a mix of experimental tasks and naturally-occurring or role-played and simulated interactions and the data was collected over a two-and-a-half-year period. The rationale was to collect data from which generalisations about linguistic and cross-linguistic development could be made over a period of time. The interactional data was included to take account of the nature of intercultural communication.

Data was collected on four key informants from each group of speakers. So, for example, in Britain, four Panjabi speakers and four Italian speakers were studied. Given that the data was collected over two and a half years, more than four informants from each linguistic group were persuaded to join the project in order to maintain the target despite predicted drop-outs. By the end of the project complete data sets were available on twenty-six informants of whom nineteen are represented in this study. [2]

There was a tension built into the design of the project which was also felt at the data collection stage. The project was designed as a systematic cross-linguistic study but it also aimed to describe in some depth the features of intercultural communication which were a daily or potential reality for minority ethnic workers. This tension gave the project strength but it also led to difficult decisions in data collection. In the end the mix of methods alluded to was agreed on. The 'glue' that joined the different sessions together was conversation between researchers and informants. This provided some ethnographic detail and some less structured elicitation.

Given the interpretive and qualitative perspective of this book, much of the data is not perfect. On a continuum from naturally occurring to experimental data, we have opted for the naturally-occurring end. This data was of four types: naturally occurring data collected in participant observation sessions, extended simulations with professionals and 'gate-keepers' (Erickson and Shultz 1982), role-plays with researchers and elicited feedback. Researchers from both the majority and the minority groups were normally present at each data collection session and the feedback sessions were conducted in the informants' first language.

During the pilot year of the original project, researchers had found how difficult it was to collect naturally occurring data. For this reason, the participant observation method was supplemented by extended simulations in which professionals from the majority group – employers, housing officers, counsellors and so on were invited to simulate typical encounters in their professional lives such as job interviews, advice sessions etc.

Data from these simulations became key data because of the continued difficulties of obtaining recordings of naturally occuring events. Many of the recordings of the participant observation data were brief and routine and yielded little evidence, except of the possibilites of the avoidance of extended interaction. In addition, many of the informants found these recorded participant observation sessions so stressful that they were abandoned for ethical reasons.

The role plays were carried out with researchers and consisted of goods or service encounters where the informant has to argue her case or work out procedures. The two most frequent role plays were first, where the informant role plays a customer returning a shrunken sweater to a shop and secondly, in the post office where the informant has to send a parcel or money order back to her home country.

The final type of data used was feedback data (or what was originally called 'self-confrontation'). These feedback sessions were a form of controlled ethnographic elicitation. In some ways, they were similar to the type of introspection techniques known as retrospection or stimulated re-call (Cohen 1987, Ericsson and Simon 1987, Faerch and Kasper 1987). However, unlike introspection techniques, they were not narrowly experimental but part of a more extended relationship built up between researcher and informant over the two-and-a-half years. During this period, much ethnographic information was collected, both elicited and more spontaneous, and researchers also gave advice and help when they could. In the feedback sessions, researchers selected passages from recently recorded interactions. Each passage would be played back once, then a second time at which point the informant was asked to stop the tape and to comment on anything of note. Finally, the passage was played through a third time and the researcher would ask any specific questions they had prepared. These sessions were essential in helping researchers to analyse the processes of (non)understanding and to illuminate some of the intentions in and attitudes towards communication. They also shed some light on the more general ethnographic questions about the experience of the informants.

This first chapter has set the goals of this book within the context of the earlier ESF project from which the data is drawn. Some of the difficulties of using data for a project with a rather different set of intentions from the original research have been raised and these are discussed in more depth in the final chapter. Chapter 2 raises some issues of understanding from a social and discoursal perspective. These issues, which examine understanding, interaction and the notion of context, are then related to questions of data and data analysis.

Chapters 3 and 4 provide frameworks and detailed analyses of the understanding process by focussing on problems of understanding. We start by examining the causes of such problems (Chapter 3) since trying to establish what has not been understood inevitably involves the analyst in working on why it has not been understood. This mapping of some of the difficulties in the understanding process then leads to a focussing on the ethnic minority workers (Chapters 4 and 5) and their responses to problems of understanding. But since understanding (or not) is jointly produced by both interactants (Chapters 6 and 7) it is necessary to chart the ways in which the majority and the minority speakers together negotiate some level of shared meaning. In Chapter 8 we take a more critical perspective as we comment, in retrospect, on our approach and relate the issues discussed in the previous chapters to recent debates in interactional sociolinguistics and critical theory.

NOTES

1. For a detailed discussion of the aims and methods of the ESF project, together with a detailed bibliography of project books and papers, see Perdue (ed) 1993 Adult Language Acquisition: cross-linguistic perspectives, Vol 1 Field methods. The conclusions from the six areas researched are summarised in Volume 2.
2. The data on the 26 key informants has been transcribed and put on line (some 18,000 transcribed pages) and is housed at the Second Language Data Bank (SLDB) at the Max Planck Institut für Psycholinguistik. This data is available to researchers and can be obtained from the European Science Foundation SLDB, Max Planck Institut für Psycholinguistik, Wundtlaan 1, NL-6525 XD Nijmegen, The Netherlands. A simplified transcription system has been used for data in this book (see Appendix B).

TWO

A social perspective on understanding: some issues of theory and method

Celia Roberts

2.0 INTRODUCTION

Readers of books about language and communication are frequently advised that it is a risky, troublesome business. Indeed Erving Goffman goes as far as saying that life may not be much of a gamble but interaction is. That element of interaction that we think of as understanding is as risky and troublesome to write about as it is to achieve.

In writing about understanding, some linguists, following Gilbert Ryle's assertion that knowing *how* is more fundamental than knowing *that*, argue that rather than looking at what is understood or not, we should concentrate on the *how*, the process whereby understanding (or not) is achieved (Brown et al 1994). A few, sceptics, within the world of linguistic theory would argue, along with Locke in his Essay on Human Understanding (1690) that it is not just a question of what may be understood or even how something comes to be understood but *whether* we understand each other when we communicate (Taylor 1992).

In this book we describe some of the ways in which majority and minority language speakers interact and in doing so work towards some degree of understanding. So we focus on the *how*, the processes of understanding but we cannot ignore the *what* since it is only by attempting to analyse local interpretations in turn by turn utterances that we can begin to account for the processes. Nor can we ignore the sceptic's view – whether there is understanding at all. In his book *Mutual Misunderstanding* Taylor (1992) asserts that many of the prominent theories of understanding by linguists argue that communication assumes shared understanding. This assumption is either based on a naturalistic and commonsense view that we know enough about language to believe that if there is shared understanding, there is communication, or a behaviouristic view that people act as if they understand each other and that is justification enough for saying that they do.

While neither position, Taylor suggests, seems satisfactory, even the most sceptical of sceptics would concede that, at some level, the making of understanding has to be carried on under the banner of business as usual. In other words, that a sufficient degree of under-standing is reached for both parties to come to 'a reasonable interpretation' (Brown and Yule 1983). Whether such an interpreta-tion approaches the kind of 'open communication' which Habermas calls for is another matter.

The value of the sceptical approach is to raise critical questions that challenge such comfortable notions as shared understanding or even sufficient understanding by putting them in the wider context in which all communication is asymmetrical given the unequal power relations in society. Within this context, is any understanding shared or is it all contested? Such a critical approach also raises questions around the idea of minority ethnic groups inserting them-selves into the 'host' community by understanding enough to ensure themselves equal opportunities in bidding for scarce institu-tional resources. The critical perspective implied by Taylor's 'mutual misunderstanding' is taken up more fully in the final chapter.

In looking at understanding, therefore, we always take for granted that there is a potential for misunderstanding at many levels; and that both understanding and misunderstanding are founded in linguistic difficulties and imbalances, social and cultural differences and power relations which structure individual encoun-ters in hierarchical ways. (See Coupland, Giles and Wiemann 1991 for a similarly eclectic view but from a more social psychological perspective.)

In this book we draw on a variety of sources including studies of natural second language acquisition from the ESF project, interac-tional sociolinguistics (particularly the work of John Gumperz and his associates), work on pragmatic failure, conversation analysis methodology and critical theory. Aspects of these studies are threaded through the subsequent chapters. But there is also a debt to second language acquisition studies more generally, particularly analysis of native/non-native interaction. This is not the place to survey SLA studies. A number of excellent surveys are available (Ellis 1985, 1994, Klein 1986, McLaughlin 1987, Cook 1991 and Larsen-Freeman & Long 1991).

As these surveys show, the area of understanding has been a relatively neglected one in SLA, nor have there been many longitudinal studies. The three major longitudinal studies of adult migrant workers carried out before the ESF project were concerned primarily with the acquisition of morphology and syntax (Klein and Dittmar 1979, Clahsen et al 1983 and Jansen, Lalleman and Muysken 1981). They also differed from the approach here in attempting to account for acquisition and 'fossilization' through correlation studies in which informants' output was correlated with individual factors such as age and education and environmental factors such as opportunity to use the new language. (See Perdue 1993a for a fuller description.)

There is, however, quite a substantial literature on the adjustments made by majority speakers in order to contribute to minority speakers' understanding and, more recently, on the negotiation of meaning. Early studies drawing on the work in first language acquisition and foreigner talk (Hatch 1978, 1980, Long 1981) were concerned with 'modified input' such as slowing down of speech, restricted vocabulary and fewer grammatical contractions. Later studies developed a 'modified interaction' theory (Hatch 1983, Long 1983b, Gass & Varonis 1985, Varonis & Gass 1985 and see Faerch and Kasper 1986 for a summary), examining the negotiation work between interlocutors and the re-structuring of 'input' that consequently takes place. These studies generally assume the more negotiation the better as a driving force in the acquisition process (but see Aston 1986 for an alternative view).

Although 'modified interaction' studies provide a helpful starting point for looking at understanding, they offer only a partial picture for several reasons. Firstly, they tend to draw on short pieces of data, usually only from informal conversational contexts, taken from a variety of different sources rather than from a body of data. Secondly they are often concerned with modelling misunderstanding in native non-native interaction in terms of rather general choices to do with continuing or giving up on the communication and whether to comment or not on the understanding. This is in contrast to the approach taken here in which local interpretations and reactions are examined in depth and in context in extended extracts. Thirdly, there is little or no ethnographic evidence to support the conclusions drawn – either of a more general nature (based on the knowledge of informants over time) or specific feedback data on the interactions themselves. In the rest of the chapter, we argue for a more social perspective on understanding which takes account of some of these issues.

2.1 IDENTIFYING UNDERSTANDING AND PROBLEMS OF UNDERSTANDING

In the rest of the chapter we discuss the processes of understanding in the context in which minority workers have to cope with problems of understanding in their everyday lives. We outline a conceptual framework which informed our analysis. First we discuss the ways in which understanding and problems of understanding can be identified. We then go on to consider understanding in an interactional perspective and briefly introduce the procedures used by minority and majority participants in attempting to resolve understanding problems. Finally, we draw on some recent thinking on context to describe and account for the ongoing interpretive activities of participants.

Our *framework for analysis* (which has developed out of the work of a number of ESF project researchers including the authors of this book) views understanding as a continuum from, at one end, sufficient understanding for both parties to continue to, at the other end, total lack of understanding (Allwood and Abelar 1984, Bremer et al 1988). In addition, many interactions are characterised by the illusion of understanding (Trévise 1984) in which both sides believe, at least for a while, that they have understood eachother. In other words, misunderstandings occur which may or may not be resolved during the course of the interaction (Gumperz 1982a).

These misunderstandings provide the 'starting point for reconstructing a system of social presuppositions' (Gumperz 1984:143) which account for difficulties in understanding of even apparently simple words and utterances. For example, a Moroccan informant, Abdelmalek, went to a travel agency in Marseilles to buy a ticket for Morocco:[1]

(1)   A: je partir a casablanca, maroc
              i am leaving for casablanca, morocco
       N: par quoi vous voulez partir ↑
              how do you wish to go ↑
       A: [se] beaucoup problèmes là-bas papa malade
              je partir tout de suite
              a lot of problems there father is ill
              i'm leaving right away

(5)   N: je comprends pas là qu'est ce que vous voulez
           où vous voulez aller ↑
           i dont understand that what do you want
           where do you want to go ↑

(Deulofeu and Taranger 1984)

Abdelmalek understands 'par quoi' as 'pourquoi' 'why' and proceeds to explain the pressing reasons for needing to go home. Even
if a native speaker had some difficulty with distinguishing between
par and *pour*, Deulofeu and Taranger argue, they would be very
unlikely to interpret the travel agent's question as a request for reasons for travelling. But in the feedback session later, Abdelmalek
said that he expected to be interrogated by French people in any
kind of a formal encounter. So his social presuppositions were very
different from that of a majority speaker in that he assumed that the
travel agent had the right to ask him about his motives and his personal life. He went on to say, in the feedback session, that he was
deliberately polite and co-operative 'pour s'attirer les bonnes graces
des plus racistes de ses interlocuteurs' (op cit: 107) (to get in the
good books of the most racist of his interlocutors).

An added complication in intercultural communication is that
both sides may have understood the others' utterance in different
ways. So the question is not just, ' Did the minority worker understand or not?' but 'How did they understand each other's
utterances?' (Fritz 1991). We can illustrate the different levels of
non and partial understanding with an example from Madan, a
Panjabi informant in England, when he role-plays a post office
scene in which he wishes to send a parcel of clothes to India:

(1)   N: okay if you send it airmail it will cost you
           nine pounds sixty one
      M: one ↑
      N: air mail
(5)   M: yeah
      N: will be nine pounds sixty one

In this example, Madan repeats the final word 'one' but it is very
unlikely that he has understood the entire utterance except for this
word. This final item does not carry the crucial information load –
the nine pounds is surely more important – but it is likely that the
final word is the most salient to Madan and in his general uncertainty about what has been said, he repeats the word that has been

heard and understood. The subsequent turns do not clear up the understanding problem.

Any attempt to categorise different types of (non) understanding, (the *what*), involve exploring the causes of it (the *why*). It is for this reason that we discuss causes relatively early in this book, in Chapter 3. Any degree of (non) understanding results from a complex fusion of particular, local inferences and general or global knowledge. As listeners try, creatively, to match new information with stored knowledge, they are constantly 'top-downing' from the higher level global expectations, and 'bottom-upping' from cues in the immediate, local linguistic context, such as semantic fields, collocation and syntactic and phonetic knowledge (see Hörmann 1981), and from coherence relations inferred from the sequencing of utterances.

In interactions where the minority worker has little experience of the new language, they will rely on the global and general contextual features typical of such encounters (Klein 1986, Noyau 1984, Deulofeu & Taranger 1984, Trévise 1984, Faerch and Kasper 1986, Wolff 1986, 1989). In the gatekeeping encounters which are routinely experienced by minority workers, this global knowledge is realised as schemata, or specific structural knowledge sets which create expectations about what topics will be raised, how they should be interpreted, and about the different orientations and discourse roles of the participants. As we have seen above in the example of Abdelmalek in the travel agent, these schemata and social presuppositions can readily override cues from the local linguistic context. In much cognitive psychology, the notion of schemata is of fixed knowledge structures. But it is clear from an interactional perspective that schemata are dynamic and constantly shifting (Tannen 1993).

This interplay of schemata, orientations and discourse roles is well illustrated in a contrastive study of two of the Italian informants in Britain, asking about buying property in an estate agents, a typical service encounter (Roberts and Simonot 1987). One informant, Santo, has a number of strategies for making the clerk more customer-orientated and so creating a more equal encounter, while Andrea treats the interaction like a typical gatekeeping encounter in which the majority speaker dominates in both topic and turn-taking.

One of Santo's strategies which helps to maintain conversational involvement is to make general, impersonal comments. These, in turn, elicit helpful comments from the clerk:

(1)   N: then you might get one for about fifty or sixty. +
                or say forty eight sixty something like that
        S: very expensive area anyway
        N: well this/this is expensive this is less expensive

(1)   N: take you twenty five minutes i suppose twenty
                minutes twenty five minutes
        S: anyway for er forty thousand very complication
        N: (yeah you've got a) very difficult + erm even two
(5)   bedroomed flats is not too easy now.

(1)   N: i can't think of anything really
        S: yeah
        N: that would he suitable
        S: yeah i know is not easy for found
(5)   N: no no
        S: okay
        N: might be agents in haringey they might have
                something

By contrast Andrea's strategies are largely reactive and he tends to develop only those themes which the estate agent has implicitly sanctioned:

(1)   N: blackstock road er er that's a one bedroom flat
        A: yeah
        N: its not two bedrooms
        A: mhm

Here difficulties both in understanding and in becoming a conversational partner compound each other. They help to produce a context which not only reflects the social structure but itself becomes a factor that contributes to the shaping of social reality. Contact feeds stereotypes just as stereotypes structure contact. So, in an ethnically stratified society, negative ethnic stereotypes are confirmed and further constrain opportunities for learning.

2.2 UNDERSTANDING AND INTERACTION

The example above clearly illustrates that understanding is an interactive process. Using an interactional sociolinguistic perspective, we can say that it is 'a process mutually constructed in the course of inferencing by all participants in an encounter' (Gumperz 1982a). So, understanding, in the real contexts of negotiation, cannot be separated off from the business of starting, maintaining and leaving the interaction. This means that both sides have to maintain a level of conversational involvement as well as achieving at least a partial understanding. Indeed, Fritz argues that a theory of dialogue ought to be one of the essential ingredients of research in understanding (Fritz 1991).

This has two important implications: firstly, it is frequently difficult to disentangle the means of conversational maintenance from ways of indicating understanding and secondly, since the conversation is a joint activity, the processes of understanding (or not) have to be interpreted by looking at the activity from the perspective of all participants.

This interactive perspective owes much to the studies of learning and language learning by Vygotsky (1978), Bruner (1986) and Wells (1987). It also leans heavily on the theories of Bakhtin (1981, 1984), Volosinov (1973) and their work on the inseparability of language and context:

The organising centre of any utterance, of any experience, is not within but outside – in the social milieu surrounding the individual being . . . Utterance as such is wholly a product of social interaction, both of the immediate sort as determined by the circumstances of the discourse, and of the more general kind, as determined by the whole aggregate of conditions under which any given community of speakers operates.

(Volosinov 1973:93)

Bakhtin's notion of the 'dialogic' emphasises the social nature of language in the sense that an individual's use of language draws on, and in, multiple voices from the social and cultural world around them. A stretch of speech is not the product of a single consciousness but the interaction of many voices brought into focus by an individual's performance. One of the best known exemplars of this is the way in which reported speech allows both the speaker's and the reported speaker's voice to resonate together.

Similarly, in any interaction, an utterance is dialogic in that it takes account of what has preceded it and of what is to come (Bakhtin 1978). Each utterance is made both in the light of what has already preceded it (the *déjà dit*) and in the light of the response that is as yet unspoken but solicited and anticipated:

Se constituant dans l'atmosphère du 'déjà dit', le discours est déterminé en même temps par la réplique non encore dite, mais sollicitée et déjà prévue.

(Bakhtin 1978: 103)

So, as de Hérédia (1986b) has pointed out, understanding is not exclusively reserved for the recipient of an utterance, nor production for the speaker. In the same way, Vygotsky's work shows how language develops as part of an activity system which is created in the interaction between carers and children and their environment. Our notion of understanding, therefore, is of a dynamic, public and cooperative activity in which both sides are actively engaged. (Cooperative in the sense of certain ground rules or maxims (Grice 1975) which have to be followed to allow the interaction to take place at all, but not in any affective sense of participants willingly helping each other.)

The interactive and jointly constructed nature of understanding and misunderstanding is well illustrated in the following extract from an interview between a Dutch housing officer and Ergün, a Turkish worker. Ergün is asked about his family:

(1)   E: ja
            yes
      N: vrouw wel in verwachting ↑
            wife is expecting ↑
      E: jawel
            yes
      N: wel in verwachting ↑
            is expecting ↑
(5)   E: ja wacht
            yes wait
      N: wanneer komt de baby ↑
            when will the baby come ↑
      E: weet ik niet
            i do not know
      N: niet ↑
            not
      E: nee
            no
(10) N: hoe lang is ze in verwachting dan ↑
            how long has she been expecting then ↑
      E: oo misschien een jaar twee jaar [ik]
            oh maybe one year two year [i]
      N: oh
            oh

E: weet ik ook niet < >
      i dont know – me either <laughs>
N: dat lijkt me wat onwaarschijnlijk + nee [kijk]
(15)   *that seems unlikely to me + no [look]*
      ik denk dat je me verkeerd begrijpt
      i don't think you understand me correctly . . .

Here the illusion of understanding is maintained over eleven turns as both sides work through the classic question and answer sequence of a gate-keeping encounter. The misunderstanding finally surfaces and the process of clarification can begin. But in other cases, the misunderstanding may only be resolved at the end of the encounter or not at all. (This example is discussed further in Ergün's case study, 5.3 below.)

Despite the fact that the process of understanding is not a private one, it is largely an invisible one. Although (in the preceding turns of an interaction) there is frequently evidence of whether or not there has been a total lack of understanding, the extent of any partial (non)-understanding is by no means clear. For this reason the *Framework for analysis* focusses on non-understandings and misunderstandings. Often non-specific and indirect clues from the minority worker start the process of clarification which begins to distinguish the understood from the not understood. So examining moments of communicative difficulty acts as 'a magnifying glass', (Trévise 1984) for analysing how both sides come to a partial or sufficient understanding.

This process of clarification entails studying the responses from both minority and majority speakers. These responses are on a cline from direct to indirect. Direct responses are indications that there are or have been understanding problems. Indirect responses are symptoms of non-understanding which surface in the talk. There is no clear response from the minority worker but the majority speaker assumes there is some problem of understanding (see Chapter 4).

The following is an example of a clear and direct response to an understanding problem. Çevdet, a young Turkish worker in Germany, is asked about his childhood in school in a conversation with one of the researchers.

(1)   N: und wie war das in der schule
             das war in dorf die kleine schule ne ↑
             and what about the school
             it was in the village the small school, no ↑

```
      C:   ja+ nicht de/e mein
           yes+ not the/er my
      N:   also ab/ die ersten jahre
           what i mean from/ the first years
(5)   C:   ja die ersten jahre im dorf
           yes the first years in the village
      N:   und wieviel wart ihr da
           wieviel kinder ↑
           and how many were you there
           how many children ↑
      C:   wir ↑ acht kinder < >
           we ↑ eight children <laughs>
      N:   ganz kleine schule
           very small school
(10)  C:   <aa ↑> in der schule ↑
           hundert ich glaube ↑
           <oh?> in the school <louder>
           hundred i think
      N:   oh also ihr wart acht in der klasse oder wie ↑
           oh ok you were eight in your class or what ↑
      C:   nee acht nicht ich habe gedacht wieviel kinder sind sie ↑
           no not eight i thought how many of you children are there ↑
      N:   ach zu hause
           i see at home
(15)  C:   wieviel zu hause ja
           how many at home yes
```

In this example, after an initial misunderstanding, Çevdet is quite explicit about the source of the difficulty: 'I thought how many of you children are there'. This type of metalinguistic comment in which Çevdet openly talks about what he thought the interviewer had meant is, however, quite rare.

More indirect responses to understanding problems are more frequent and more contentious both for the participants and for the analysts. The following example from an interview between a Dutch housing official and Fatima, a Moroccan woman, is much more problematical.

```
(1)   N:   kun je niet zolang bij je vriend gaan wonen ↑
           you cannot live with your friend for a while ↑
      F:   ja
           yes
      N:   bij jouw vader en moeder ↑
           with your father and mother ↑
```

F: ja
     yes

5   N: ja
     yes

F: ja
     yes

N: kun je daar niet zolang blijven ↑
     you cannot stay there for a while ↑

F: ja
     yes

N: totdat er 'n huis is
     until there is a house

10   F: nee
     no

N: (waarom niet?) ↑
     why not ↑

F: ik wil mijn huis
     i want my house

N: waarom? waarom kun je niet naar je ouders ↑
     why? can you not go to your parents ↑

F: daarom
     that's why

15: N: ah dat is/ nee/ dat is geen mooi antwoord+waarom niet ↑
     ah that is/no/that is not a nice answer+why not ↑

F: +ik uh wil uh+vlug trouwt
     + i er want er soon marry

N: jij wil vlug trouwen ↑
     you want to marry soon ↑

F: ja
     yes

N: waarom ↑
     why ↑

20   F: daarom < >
     thats why <laughs>

N: + + en jouw vriend wat vindt die d'r van ↑
     + + and your friend what does he think about it ↑

F: met vader en moeder
     with father and mother

It is not clear from the initial analysis of the data whether Fatima's minimal responses, yes and no, are ways of affirming the negative question: 'you cannot live . . . ' or whether they are simply a means of keeping the channel open so that the interaction can continue, a strategy of 'wait and see' (Voionmaa 1984). Also her formulaic answers to the *why* questions, *daarom*, (that's why) could be a learnt formula to respond to non-understanding or a means of avoiding self-disclosure. In the post-session feedback, Fatima stated that she understood almost nothing that the housing officer said.

The uncertainty that lives in this data is an acute form of the uncertainty in any interaction. What is clear from this kind of data is the degree of responsibility that the majority speaker must take in both pre-empting problems of understanding and in collaborating with the minority speaker in solving problems once they have arisen. The role of the majority speaker will determine the relative success of a particular interaction and, cumulatively, the potential for a motivating learning environment.

The majority speaker's responsibility lies in both pre-empting anticipated problems of understanding (see Chapter 6) and in handling non- and misunderstandings when they have arisen (see Chapter 7). This distinction, although not always as clear cut as it may seem, has been well established in the literature on negotiating understanding and we retain it in this book. In addition to the preventative/post-hoc distinction, managing problems of understanding requires the majority speaker to work at both the utterance and schematic level simultaneously.

For example, in an interview between a French Doctor and Zahra, an Arabic speaker, the doctor makes the new information more predictable by moving the topic to the front of the utterance to give it focus:

(1)   N: et des maladies vous avez eu des maladies
             quand vous étiez jeune fille ↑
             quand vous vous étiez/vous avez déjà été malade
             à part ces grossesses ↑
             and illnesses you had illnesses
             when you were a young girl ↑
             when you/you had already been ill
             apart from these pregnancies ↑
(5)   Z: oui toujours + toujours malade
             yes always + always ill

This strategy functions both locally to make the subsequent utterance more understandable and at the schema level it signals a major sequence about the patient's personal history which would be a routine element in taking case notes on a new patient. This example illustrates one of a number of procedures for preventing trouble by making the following utterances more expectable (see Chapter 6). In the following example, a breakdown in understand-

ing has already occurred and the majority speaker has to attempt
'repair' strategies. (The term 'repair' is widely used and we have
followed this practice but it is misleading to assume that it suggests
any complete understanding is accomplished.)

Angelina, an Italian speaker, now seeking work in Germany, is
being interviewed for a possible job as a kitchen worker or as a
server in the dining room in a large company. The interview has
reached the stage when the interviewer asks whether she would
like to ask any questions about the work. This leads to a protracted
clarificatory sequence. The following excerpt is taken from the
interviewer's second attempt to help Angelina understand that *she*
can ask *him* questions about the job.

(18)   N: < es gibt die arbeit in küche oder saal in der kantine ja>
            there is work in the kitchen or dining room
            in the canteen yes <loudly and clearly>
       A: mhm
(20)   N: und jetzt möchte ich wissen ich mochte wissen ob sie
            fragen haben +
            and now i'd like to know i'd like to know whether you have
            questions
            ja sie fragen mich ob e die arbeit < was weiss ich>
                                              <speeded up>
            yes you ask me whether er the work < i dont know what>
            schwer is ob das lang ist ob das + heiss ist
            is heavy if its long if its hot
            verstehen sie was was ich meine
            do you understand what i mean
       A: <nein> <quietly>
            no
(25)   N: verstehen sie nicht + ja
            you dont understand + well

At line 18 Mr B launches into a new clarificatory sequence in
which he recreates the frame within which the question will be
asked. He then reformulates his question with more explicit content
than on the first occasion but makes it syntactically more complex.
He attempts to shift the agency of the questioner from himself to
Angelina by emphasising 'mich' (do you have questions to ask *me*)
but as yet fails to make his utterances understandable. His lack of
success is not surprising since inexperienced speakers of a new language appear to achieve more understanding if the grammatical
component is made less complex and the lexical component more

explicit. Deulofeu and Taranger (1984) call this 'iconic syntax' (see Chapter 7 for a full discussion).

These examples give some indication of the complex interactive work required by both sides in order to reach some level of understanding. The complexity derives from the interplay of wider contextual factors brought into the encounter and the local contextual features created in it. So, it is to a discussion of context that we now turn.

2.3 UNDERSTANDING AND CONTEXT

While it seems difficult to define the term 'context' in any general way, it is important to take as the point of departure the participants' perspective on context. In other words to get as close as possible to how the participants attend to and organise the language and other interactional features of events as ongoing interpretive frames.

Although distinctions have been made analytically between linguistic and social context, between local and wider contexts, we have found it difficult to make such distinctions. Any momentary (mis)interpretation, even though it may appear a purely perceptual one – as in a misheard phoneme – will be shaped by and help to shape the context of situation.

Duranti and Goodwin (1992) drawing on Ochs (1979) suggest four dimensions of context:

Setting: the social and physical framework in which interactions are set and which is continually created in the talk itself. So, for example, the housing interview or estate agent encounter is in some ways 'there' at the outset but is also constructed by the question and answer sequences which characterise it.

Behavioural environment: the non-verbal communication and use of social space in an encounter.

Language as context: the way in which language calls up contexts and itself provides contexts for other talk.

Extrasituational context: wider social, political and cultural institutions and discourses.

Knowing how much contextual consideration is appropriate to try to account for (non) understanding is always a problem. As van Lier has pointed out: 'Context may be regarded as extending like ripples on a pond, in concentric circles from any particular action or utterance. At some point we will have to draw a line and say: this is as far as we shall look' (van Lier 1988).

Contextual information is frequently potential rather than explicit. In other words it does not appear as readily available to participants and/or is not necessarily relevant and therefore attended to at any one time. So such information will have more or less marked traces on the surface across large stretches of discourse and may emerge or not according to the participants' orientation.

Contextual considerations are particularly significant in intercultural communication because of the reliance on contextual knowledge by the minority speakers. All understanding relies on both context and on decoding the utterance but in inter-cultural communication, where linguistic and cultural resources are unevenly distributed, there is more weight given to the contextual.

It would be misleading, however, to think of context in some static way, in terms of stored knowledge or cognitive schemata. Clearly, as we have suggested, schemata are crucial in establishing expectations, but they only partially account for the social attunement which is constitutive of interaction. In order to account for the interaction in a holistic way – a way that takes account of social relationships, feelings and perceptions – other analytic concepts are necessary. Here, the notion of *frame* developed by Bateson (1972) and used by Goffman (1974) in his frame analysis is particularly useful.

The frame both defines the boundary of an event within an interaction and establishes the focal contextual information needed to draw inferences about it. The *frame* is what makes the difference between the propositional meaning of an utterance or sequence of utterances and the listener's interpretation of the utterance(s). As Gumperz says 'All understanding is framed understanding' (1992a:43), and framing devices signal what is expected at any point in the interaction. *Frame* is a particularly important notion in intercultural communication because shared frames are central to creating the conditions for shared interpretation. Frames signal where interlocutors are in the interactive sequence, what the orientation to this sequence should be or as Goffman says what 'footing' they are on and are markers of assumed social relationships at any stage in the interaction. John Gumperz (1992a) suggests the distinction between schemata which are cognitive structures concerned with substantive knowledge of the world and frames which are interactional devices and constitute part of the inter-action itself.

Minority workers, with little knowledge of the new language, have to manage a bureaucratic encounter in which they are gener-ally ignorant of the schemata associated with it, such as what personal information they are expected to display. But they also lack the sociocultural knowledge to interpret this framed communi-cation or to attune to different frames as they are introduced. A good example of this is Berta's encounter with the job counsellor (see case study 5.1). The counsellor is trying to establish Berta's skills and experiences based on her description of her work in the kitchen. In the part of the interview quoted here, lines 180–193, there are three occasions where a new frame is introduced – at lines 180, 187 and 192.

(180) N: ah ah d'accord et là qu'est ce que vous faites alors ↑
          ah ah ok and there what do you do then ↑

(187) B: oui + eh pour trois mois seulement
          yes + and for three months only

(192) N: quelle partie de/ enfin quel euh + la chef de la cuisine
          vous dit ce qu'il faut faire mais vous faites quoi ↑ les
          plats ↑
          what part of/I mean what er + the chef tells you
          what to do but you do what? the main courses ↑

The first frame is an encouragement to Berta to 'sell' herself by displaying her qualifications and degree of experience. This Berta misunderstands. The second frame is one in which Berta puts her-self on a different 'footing' in which she begins to argue her case for a new and more permanent job. The third frame is introduced by the counsellor, shifting back to the original request to 'sell'. In each case, the relationship between them, the opportunities for (mis)understanding and the overall progress of the encounter depend on the extent to which they share frames.

This general notion of frame has been important in Gumperz's work on context and contextualisation (Gumperz 1982a, 1992a and b). Gumperz's work draws together detailed studies of interactional life, social identity and cultural practices in attempting to answer the question: 'How do people come to make sense of each other and how do these interpretive processes feed into the structuring of social groups and identities?' The key notion introduced here and discussed more fully in the final chapter is *contextualisation.* This is the means by which speakers and listeners construct local meaning together and relate it to the wider context of knowledge, values and assumptions.

Gumperz defines contextualisation cues, as 'constellations of sur-face features of message form ... the means by which speakers signal and listeners interpret what the activity is, how semantic content is to be understood and how each sentence relates to what precedes or follows' (l982a:131). Embedded in this definition is a notion of context and contexualisation as flexible and reflexive (Auer 1992). Context within an interaction is not some fixed set of features, but is dynamic and liable to change. And context is reflex-ive in that language shapes context as much as context shapes language.

This notion of context in turn rests on two basic assumptions: that interactions are inherently indeterminant and ambiguous and that in order to interpret an interaction it is necessary to create it. The ambiguity of interactions means that any utterance can be understood in a number of ways and decisions on how to interpret it are based on notions of expectedness and on the surface features of interaction as they are processed. But the act of interpretation is also part of the process of making the interaction so that as Gumperz says 'understanding pre-supposes conversational involvement' (Gumperz 1982a:2 and see 2.2 above), and so a degree of shared sociocultural and linguistic knowledge. There is, in all this, an inevitable circularity in which context, involvement and interpretive processes are continually acting and reacting on each other.

Contextualisation cues function both globally and locally, draw-ing in taken-for-granted knowledge and creating local, situated meanings. Auer (1992) influenced by Giddens and Hinnenkamp asks how much context is brought along, and how much brought about. He suggests three types of context:

(i) one that is largely 'brought about' in that it is determined by the contextual work itself through script-like patterns, partici-pation frameworks and speaker knowledge of how to relate to the information conveyed.

(ii) taken-for-granted contextual schema which are brought along, usually from knowledge of institutional interactions. However, these brought-along assumptions are subject to negotiation and modification in the way in which the interactants 'contextualise' together so that, for example, unequal social relations may be challenged by more equal speaker roles.

(iii) context parameters which are clearly brought along, such as physical surroundings and features such as gender or ethnicity. Contextualisation can focus or de-emphasise these features but cannot change them.

We can draw together Duranti and Goodwin's four dimensions of context and Auer's three types:

Brought along		Brought about
1. Immediate physical setting	----	Contextual work that creates a behavioural environment
2. Extra-situational discourses		Contextual work determined by patterns, frameworks and speaker knowledge, realised
Features of social identity		through and created in language
3. Institutional schema	--------	Negotiated schema

While attempting to take account of features in (1) our concern with understanding in context focuses on (2) and (3).

There are problems for the minority worker at every level. In the largely 'brought about' contexts, contextualisation work is an enormous additional burden on top of the basic difficulty of segmenting the stream of speech into meaningful units of semantic information. The institutional schema, which is brought along but then may be renegotiated, is likely to be based on the habitual relationships and ways of encountering bureaucracy of the home country, modified by experiences of being a discriminated minority in the new country. Reliance on schema is all the more likely in situations where workers have little knowledge of the linguistic code.

The features of context which are brought along are likely to create stigma. The minority worker, both ethnically and linguistically, will be stigmatised from the start and the difficulties experienced in the interaction serve to reinforce the stigma.

The minority worker is caught in a contextual knot at every turn. Any attempt at interpretation may be hazardous and yet any reliance on brought along schemata is just as likely to cause disruption of attempts at conversational involvement. The mutually reinforcing cycle of interpretive strategies and conversational involvement becomes, so often, a negative cycle since the minority worker cannot get in and maintain the conversation which, in turn, will provide opportunities for developing at least a provisional level of shared interpretation.

2.4 DATA ANALYSIS

Charting the strategies used by majority and minority speakers in intercultural communication poses problems for the analyst. These strategies usually require an enormous amount of interpretive and reconstruction work by participants on both sides, although the minority workers' burden is proportionately much greater. But researchers are also faced with a daunting interpretive task, albeit without the added problem of processing the utterances in real time. Of course, even this is also a problem, since there is no way the researcher can be inside the real time processing of the interactants.

First of all, there is the frequent problem of attempting to judge whether responses are indications of understanding, non-understanding, partial understanding or misunderstanding. This is particularly problematic in long 'linear' sequences (Vion 1986) in which the minority ethnic worker gives only minimal responses such as 'yes' (see 'Fatima' above). Secondly, there is the difficulty of deciding what evidence can be used to judge the degree of understanding.

There are three possible sources of evidence: (i) the analysts' general and social knowledge and their knowledge of the particular world the informants inhabit; (ii) evidence in the data itself in preceeding and following turns; and (iii) ethnographic evidence from the informants themselves. We shall look at each, briefly, in turn.

General and social knowledge

As the researchers became more familiar with informants, they learnt details of their circumstances which the professionals involved in data collection did not. For example gatekeepers' interrogations about family life were all too frequent and were a constant source of understanding problems (and irritations) and were, on occasions, resisted. Researchers, on the other hand, usually met in the homes of informants, were gradually accepted as conversational partners and came to know details of their lives, the conditions under which they were attempting to construct a new life and their perceptions of this process.

But knowledge about the procedures and services in everyday life were also important in disambiguating what were understanding problems or not. For example, Leo, a Finnish informant in Sweden wanted to send a parcel back to Finland:

(1)   N: flygpost eller vanlig befordran ↑
              airmail or normal delivery
(2)   L: flygpost ↑
              airmail

This example looks unproblematic. Leo appears to understand the question. But there are two factors which might encourage the analyst to consider this as a non-understanding. In addition to 'befordran' being a word that Leo is very unlikely to know with his limited Swedish, there is the fact that there are very good mail services between Sweden and Finland. It is unlikely that Leo would opt to send a parcel back to Finland by airmail. But this conclusion rests on high inferencing and needs substantiating from other sources.

Conversation analysis

The second source of evidence lies in the fine-grained detailed analysis of the orderliness of talk. Such an approach, based on the methods used in Conversation Analysis tries to account for sources of 'trouble' by contrasting them with the orderly and systematic way in which people manage to take turns and respond to each other.

Conversation analysis (CA) influenced our work in a number of ways. Firstly, the notion of 'intersubjectivity', the means by which participants come to some understanding of each other in an interaction, was a general influencing factor in our analysis. Studies have shown what rich resources members of a community have to produce orderliness in social interaction and how these resources are used to both accomplish interaction and display their understanding of it (examples of this richness are given in Chapters 4, 6 and 7).

Secondly CA, concerned as it is with talk as creating social order and structure, is one way of connecting the apparently improvised and provisional in face to face interaction with wider social formations. The fine-grained detail of talk and nonverbal communication working together provides insights into the practical reasoning used by participants to make sense to each other and show conversational involvement. These, in turn, are illustrative of the mechanisms used to accomplish everyday and institutional life.

These mechanisms are significant in two ways. The focus on the turn by turn achievement of an interaction is used to trace the (non)understanding process. The extent to which interactants have understood each other is evident in the preceding responses so that the 'invisible' aspect of understanding is brought out into the open, so to speak. Understanding and non-understanding are displayed through the 'responsive treatment' of the 'prior turns' talk' (Schegloff 1984). Atkinson and Heritage emphasise this point: 'The point here and it is a crucial one, is that however a recipient analyses these informings and whatever the interpretative conclusions of such analysis, *some conclusions will be displayed in the recipient's turn at talk*' (their emphasis) (Atkinson and Heritage 1984). In other words there is evidence located in the talk itself of the speaker's interpretative processes.

In addition, the emphasis on the work that interactants must do to accomplish interaction accorded with our insights into how understanding was often (painfully) negotiated. This focus on the interaction as a joint accomplishment reinforced our concern with the role and responsibility of the majority group gatekeeper.

CA offered both general insights and practical guidance on data analysis but its dry and formalistic representation of data (what Moerman describes as 'dry bones clacking together' [Moerman 1988]) draws the humanity out of social interaction. More significantly, the goal of CA is the categorisation of general conversational mechanisms, whereas this study was concerned with the processes of understanding as they were negotiated in each encounter.

There are additional problems in using a CA approach, exclusively, in analysing intercultural communication since researchers use their own practical reasoning abilities to interpret that of participants. This assumes a level of shared understanding between analysts and participants which cannot be taken for granted in intercultural communication. Also this approach does not account for the asymmetry in participants' resources which is such a prominent feature of interaction where the minority worker is inexperienced in the majority language.

An example from the language of CA makes the point. Conversation analysts, routinely, make a distinction between main and side-sequences. In our data there are frequent and extended periods where attempts are made to negotiate a measure of understanding. To represent these merely as side-sequences is to take the struggle and pressure out of them and to assume a symmetrical base which the data clearly does not show. In our data these sequences often become the focal point of engagement for both sides and for the minority worker the very attempt to clarify may create an environment which is increasingly problematic and pressurising. These extended periods of non-understanding and clarification are not so much 'conversation with repair', but 'repair without conversation,' (van Lier, personal communication).

Ethnographic evidence

For these reasons, the third source of evidence, ethnographic information, is also important. Ethnography is the study of the social and cultural practices of a group from an insider's perspective. It is a methodology for attempting to understand the others' world – for getting inside their shoes – and seeing things from their point of view (Agar 1980, Hammersley and Atkinson 1983, Ellen 1984, Watson-Gegeo 1988, Fetterman 1989). Ethnographic methodology assumes a holistic approach in which, as far as possible, all aspects of context are accounted for in the interpretation of data. Instead of the lean, clean methods of quantitative and experimental approaches, the metaphors of ethnographic methods are of thickness and richness as in 'thick description' (Geertz 1973) and of the search to understand 'rich words . . . heavily puttied' with associations (Agar 1992).

Although, as we have suggested above, opportunities for participant observation – the 'lurking and soaking' elements of ethnography (Werner and Schoepfler 1989) were very limited, the longitudinal element of the ESF project meant that researchers met informants regularly and, over time, were able to gradually begin to understand their lives. The ESF project was not an ethnography of minority groups (unlike studies by Wilson 1978, Brooks and Singh 1979, Buechler and Buechler 1987, Wilpert 1988) but the collection of ethnographic material to illuminate the linguistic data was essential.

We were influenced in particular by the work of Gumperz (1982a, 1984) and Erickson and Shultz (1982) in attempting to combine a more general understanding of what it means to make a life for oneself in a new and often hostile environment, with specific, elicited judgements on recently recorded interactions. We have described above these 'self-confrontations' and how they were used. Informants responded to these regular meetings in different ways (see 2.5 below). Some perceived them as opportunities to use English. A few participated more reluctantly but agreed to continue. Many found it difficult to give detailed linguistic comments and, in many respects, these sessions were more illuminating in the way they provoked general ethnographic insights rather than providing any ultimate judgement about what was or was not understood.

These three sources of evidence, the general, the phenomenological, through a CA approach and the ethnographic, interact together in an interpretive framework. No one source comes first or overrides the other if conflicts of interpretation arise. The evidence was used in similar ways to the triangulation techniques used in ethnography, where each data source helps to illuminate the other and deepen the researcher's understanding. The evidence, therefore, from each source is used to come to a persuasive but never final conclusion. We are always left, as analysts, with many of the ambiguities and uncertainties which the participants themselves experienced. But then interactions are not butterflies to be caught and pinned down. In the end, we must be cautious about our conclusions on the understanding process and generous in acknowledging reinterpretations, by others, of our analyses.

2.5 ISSUES OF VARIABILITY

In the previous section we have discussed the case for combining conversation analysis and ethnographic approaches in an interpretive account of understanding in interaction. This combination of approaches is exemplified in the work of Gumperz and his associates in interactional sociolinguistics. This is a case study approach in which each data example is treated, holistically, as representing a microcosm of the larger social patterns which characterise complex, modern, ethnically stratified, urban societies.

In focussing on the specificity of each encounter, Gumperz draws on his own work and that of Dell Hymes in the ethnography of communication: 'Variability is not language specific but situation specific so that the primary unit or domain of analysis is not a language, dialect or code seen as a structurally cohesive entity, but rather a situation, social encounter or speech event' (Gumperz, 1992a:41).

But as Gumperz has also suggested (Gumperz 1982a, 1984, 1992a) the *ethnography of communication* does not account for the *situated* interpretations made by participants in an on-going way. In other words, variability does not only lie in the different elements that go to make up a speech event but in the precise way in which individual interactants make inferences about the other's meaning and adjust their own contributions accordingly. As we have described above this is part of the dynamic, context creating role of interaction. The variability within each encounter therefore arose out of a complex of factors related to the differences among minority workers, among majority speakers and to differences in the interactions themselves and we will look at these briefly in turn.

The mix of motivation and opportunity among individual informants is complex. Some informants, such as Ergün from Turkey and Marcello from Italy combine a stated desire to communicate in the new language with external pressures to do so. For example, although Marcello's work as a waiter in an Italian café brought him into only limited contact with the majority group, he lived with his girlfriend's family. They were of Italian origin, but she was born and grew up in Heidelberg, spoke German like a native speaker and expected Marcello to speak well. By contrast, Mohamed, a young Moroccan informant in the Netherlands who had many contacts with native speakers, including a Dutch girlfriend, and who became a very competent Dutch speaker, did not take any Dutch courses and, by the third cycle, had to be heavily persuaded to continue contributing to the project at all. The range of experiences and mix of motivations that the more ethnographic data illuminated make it difficult to support any simple dichotomies which would account for a high level of competence or for what is generally known by the unfortunate term 'fossilisation'. Schumann's notion of psycho-social distance (Schumann 1978), in which social factors related to the status of the minority community are combined with individual psychological factors such as instrumental and integrative motivation, is not the clear-cut explanatory template it aims to be.

Among the majority language speakers both structural and individual factors are important. Their role and relative power and social distance in what are, usually, gatekeeping encounters frame the whole encounter. Other factors related to the research methods affected their contribution. Professionals who were invited to help in simulations were, understandably, presenting themselves as cooperative whereas encounters in the field varied much more. For example, many informants mentioned that they found the real encounters more uncomfortable. There was also the obvious fact that the cost/benefit factor (Leech 1983) in any simulation is not as great as in a real encounter. In the latter case, it is of real benefit to the minority speaker to understand information or advice. It may be worth the cost in terms of loss of face to go 'on record' with indications of non-understanding (see Chapter 4).

But there was also variability within the simulations. In some instances, the professional would go through a series of interviews in one session and these repeated encounters may have influenced their contribution, possibly making them more impatient and less good listeners or conversely more familiar with informants' patterns of interaction. Also some professionals tried to maintain consistency across simulations while others attempted, as nearly as possible, a naturally-occurring encounter, allowing each interview to develop in its own way.

Finally, the gatekeeper's assessment of the informant's competence in the second language accounted for considerable variability. A pessimistic rating of competence could stem from a generally negative attitude or inexperience. Similarly the gatekeepers' willingness to adjust their own language varied widely both across speakers and even within interactions. For example, in the case study on Tino (see 5. 2) it appears that towards the end of the encounter the interviewer suffers from interview fatigue and despite her highly co-operative strategies throughout most of the session, she simply cannot sustain the level of attention and accommodation necessary.

The great variation within interactions also relates to the task or encounter itself. Data collected in the field obviously could not be controlled, but as we have indicated above, the way in which gatekeeping simulations were handled also varied considerably.

There were variations in the extent to which the simulation was perceived as having a script and the extent to which informants were primed with certain goals or not, for example 'you want to

have a flat'. More generally, there were differences between relatively more precise objectives such as getting a job, and more open
counselling sessions. Cutting across these differences was the
extent to which the encounters involved high levels of abstract and
procedural language, as in Abdelmalek's discussion with a lawyer
where he was seeking compensation after a work accident.

These variables and their relationship to interactional features are
summed up in the table below:

Majority Speaker	Minority Speaker	Task Type
Previous experience with minority speakers	Competence in the majority language	Type of speech event
Ability to assess competence accurately	Motivation to understand	Proximity to reality
Assumptions about data collection exercise	Opportunity to understand	Goals of participants
Ability/willingness to adjust own delivery	Linguistic/ cultural closeness	Degree of abstractedness familiarity/scriptedness
Attitude to data collection/Ability to simulate	Attitude to data collection	
	Interactional Features	
Topic/turn taking Q/A features	The right to speak social distance	Cost/benefit factors

| ↑ | ↑ | ↑ | ↑ |

$$\text{P o w e r} \quad \text{r e l a t i o n s h i p s}$$

NOTES

1. In this volume we have chosen to represent the speech of the informants
   as native-like unless their variety of the majority language causes problems of understanding which subsequently cause interactional
   problems for them. This means that we have transcribed their variety of
   the majority language using standard orthography in virtually all cases
   but have retained features of their variety such as non-standard word
   order. The English translation represents what we believe the minority
   speaker intended to convey. There are always difficulties with repre-

senting speech through transcription (Atkinson 1992, Clifford 1990, Tedlock 1983) and we are well aware of the disadvantages of the decision we made. 'There is no such thing as a "natural" mechanism for the representation of speech,' (Atkinson op cit: 23). Our main reason for not attempting to produce a kind of 'foreign accent' is that it can only feed into stereotypes of how the majority view such talk and its users and detracts from our attempts to let the whole social person come through in the data.

THREE

Causes of understanding problems

Katharina Bremer

3.0 INTRODUCTION

When looking for causes, recent in-depth analyses of intercultural encounters (e.g., among others, Tyler and Davies (1990), Verschueren (1990), Gumperz and Roberts (1991)) have focused mainly on the level of discourse strategies. They are concerned with the lack of shared background assumptions that still form a hidden barrier to understanding where 'purely linguistic competence in terms of command of the languages spoken cannot be held responsible for communication trouble' (Hinnenkamp 1991:91). Since this kind of elementary 'linguistic' level is clearly of major importance in the encounters studied here, our task in this chapter will be to ask in which ways linguistic and contextual elements *combine* as causal factors of non-understanding. This means that we will not be looking for single, simple causes (see Chapter 2). The analysis of typical triggers, reasons and supporting factors for problems of understanding will also lay a kind of groundwork for subsequent chapters which centre on overcoming such problems, and it will give a first approach to the 'nature' of the different understanding problems by exploring their origins. Some conceptual clarifications may be helpful at the start, however.

Possible ways of analysing causes

The analysis of causes can be guided by two different, but closely intertwined questions. One can either ask '*what* was not understood?' and thereby aim at a more descriptive account, which takes as its starting point the linguistic units involved: to differentiate between phonetic, lexical, semantic or pragmatic non-understanding (and this approach will form a useful starting point for the

structuring of the chapter.) Going one step further toward explanation, one can also ask *'why* was it not understood?'.

From the perspective of the 'what?' question, in principle, every
level which contributes to the creation of understanding can also
become a 'cause' of problems with understanding: the *utterance*
itself (whether as stream of sound or individual words or . . .), its
content, the *context* in which it is interpreted (by the listener) or in
which it is intended to be interpreted (by the speaker), the *expectations* of the minority worker which govern the choice of context and
the combination of all these levels resulting in the 'force', the
speaker-meaning related to that single situation. Since utterance
understanding in spoken interaction is relatively 'robust' because of
the extent of redundancy – meanings are expressed on several
levels at the same time and confirm each other – it is rarely the case
that a lack of understanding will be caused by a problematic item
on only one level. (For example we usually have no problems infer-
ring the meaning of a newly coined word someone uses when
addressing us, because other 'surrounding' information enables us
to fill the gap and form a pretty good hypothesis on its meaning.)
And although such helpful 'overlap' is severely reduced for the listener of another language background, 'simple' causes are the
exception there, too. It is in most cases a *multicausal relationship*
(Allwood & Abelar 1984) that can be discovered behind a non- or
misunderstanding.

It has proved fruitful therefore to assume a constellation of several causal factors, which weigh more or less heavily and which are
not all equally accessible to analysis (but there are exceptions, cf. 3.2
below). An early example of this approach in the framework of
ESF-project work on (non-) understanding has been de Hérédia's
analysis (1986) of the genesis of misunderstandings. The failure to
get the meaning intended by the speaker may apparently be trig-
gered by the minority speaker 'mishearing' a sound sequence.
Typically, such a mistake is reinforced by another factor such as the
utterance having been spoken quickly and/or unclearly. Both factors lead to misunderstanding then only when the hearer's expectations steer his or her interpretation in a particular direction.[1] With
such a constellation we cannot speak of *the* cause of a comprehension problem.

In this way of describing the process of misunderstanding the
question of 'why' an understanding problem arises is already
touched on, since through the way an utterance is designed, posi-

tioned, formulated and spoken the speaker has a share in the creation of 'understandability'. In our context this aspect stands in
particularly close relationship to the adjustments the speaker makes
to their own speech or to the lack of adjustments (see chapter 6
below) and becomes especially important if we wish to pursue the
question of how far difficulties with understanding can be avoided.
More recently, the responsibility of the speaker to contribute
towards an adequate interpretation of his or her utterance is
emphasized in the notion that a *contribution* (Clark and Schaefer
1989) to a conversation is only complete when the hearer has
accepted it. (For a discussion of responsibility for understanding cf.
also Dascal (1985) and Gülich and Kotschi (1987).)

But once the language to be understood by a hearer has been discovered as part of the problem, the scope of 'why' questions can of
course be extended to larger contexts. The 'background' for a certain style of speaking may lie in a potentially face-threatening topic,
in conventions of a specific institutional setting, in the preceding
course of the interaction at hand, or simply in the acoustic condition of the situation. In the latter part of this chapter we will try to
trace some of these threads. What will go beyond the scope of our
analyses, here, however, is an extension in the sense of connecting
such regularities of institutional discourse, the minorities' role and
possibilities therein, and the racist power relations of western societies in general – which surely build another level of *causes* for
understanding problems (but see Roberts, Davies and Jupp (1992),
Fairclough (1989), Ehlich (1980, 1992), Hamburger (1989) and
Chapter 8 below).

Perhaps we should not be surprised by the complexities of possible causes of failure to understand – in a way they mirror the
complexity of the process of understanding itself. The fact that the
relationships we discover between specific discoursal constellations
and non- or misunderstanding are seldom that of unambiguous
dependency on each other (i.e. a cause in the strict sense) but rather
that of 'typical co-occurrence' may reflect the non-linear nature of
the understanding process in real time. The components of this
process affect each other and work on each other but not one *after*
another – the process runs 'top down' and 'bottom up' more or less
simultaneously, the preliminary results of interpreting work being
checked continuously against expectations. Or, as de Hérédia puts
it in her analysis of misunderstandings: '. . . ainsi le processus de
reconnaissance des formes n'est pas préalable à la compréhension,

il en fait partie: ce sont les facteurs intervenant dans la compréhension qui sélectionnent une forme acceptable sur un signifiant
plurivoque' (1986:54, our emphasis). *So the process of recognising linguistic form is not a preliminary to understanding, it is part of it: there
are intervening factors in understanding which select an acceptable form
out of a signifier with many 'soundings'* (our translation).

How do we decide what the causes are?

Analysis of incidences of understanding problems has to rely on
the traces they leave in the actual interactive steps – and these
traces are different depending on the awareness the participants
have of their difficulties. This awareness will depend on whether it
is a non-understanding or a misunderstanding.

Non-understanding occurs when the listener realises, that s/he
cannot make sense of (part of) an utterance either because too few
elements in the utterance are accessible (in the extreme case, none)
or because the frame of reference in which they are to be viewed is
not clear – as in a sudden, unannounced topic switch. It is a graded
phenomenon 'which can vary from total lack to a more or less complete understanding' (Allwood & Abelar 1984:28). Since the listener
in these cases is always aware that a problem with understanding
exists, s/he will usually indicate this. The linguistic means used for
indication of non-understanding will contain more or less information on the presumed cause(es) (cf. Chapter 4) which of course has
to be 'filled out' by interpreting it in the context of the whole interactional sequence. Other important sources of information on
causal factors are the characteristics of the utterance to be understood as well as the conversational partner's reaction to an
indication of non-understanding or the effect that an attempt at
clarification (e.g. a partial paraphrase) have, as the examples below
will show.

In the case of *misunderstanding*, by contrast, the listener achieves
an interpretation which makes sense to her or him – but it wasn't
the one the speaker meant. Usually this mismatch is revealed to the
interlocutor very soon after its occurrence, typically through an
'incoherent' answer to the misunderstood question. It is exactly
these answers made on the basis of a 'wrong' hypothesis which
give fairly exact indications of what was understood or not understood by the minority speaker. In some cases, however, the
incompatibility of the listener's interpretation with that intended by

the speaker emerges only later in the analysis. Here, additional knowledge has to be relied on. This includes an assessment of the course of the individual encounter, as well as extensive ethnographic knowledge about the participant's biography and daily life. Two other important sources of help are available as a result of the type of data collected. Firstly acquaintance with the minority participant's variety at various points in time which above all grows out of the experience of one's own conversation with him or her and from a comparison of his/her contributions in different types of interaction. And secondly the possibility to analyse sets of interactions with similar settings and preconditions, which makes it easier to deduce some of the causes 'beneath' the surface of an interview (cf. Ch. 1.3).

In the literature on miscommunication this distinction between non- and misunderstanding is generally seen as a categorical one (for example Gass & Varonis (1991)). In the course of working with the data, however, it has become very clear that this is not always an 'absolute' distinction. Especially for participants with a very limited command of the language they have to communicate in, it seems to be characteristic that there are problems which cannot be attributed solely to one or the other of these categories. They are frequently compelled to make do with insufficient information in order to form a hypothesis about the other participant's utterance and to react on the basis of this tentative understanding. It is very difficult to assess from outside just how aware someone is about the uncertainty of his/her hypothesis. And it would exactly be this kind of awareness that decides whether a failed interpretation was a – well-concealed – lack of understanding or a real misunderstanding.

'Unidentifiable' causes and the limits of analysis

Before trying to give an overview of what we think are the most important constellations of causes in the interactions studied (3.2 below) a qualification is in order. Unlike the description of interactional steps for the management and negotiation of understanding problems in Chapters 4 and 7, part of the data is hardly or not accessible to an analysis of causes at all. This becomes even more relevant if we concentrate on comprehension problems of 'real beginners'. Here we have no or only very rough guidelines for ascertaining what was understood from any one utterance (not to speak of *why* it was not understood).

An example from a conversation with Berta might illustrate the point. The interviewer had just been asking about Berta's husband's job, when this passage occurs:

(1)   T: et tes enfants ↑ + qu'est-ce qu'ils font ↑
           and your children what do they do ↑
(2)   B: quoi ↑
           what ↑
(3)   T: et tes enfants qu'est-ce qu'ils font ↑
           and your children what do they do ↑
(4)   B: *es + en + en el* école *los* trois
           es + en en el school *los* three*

Here neither the form used by Berta to indicate her problem ('quoi ↑', 2) nor the sequence which follows it gives us a hint on what was not understood: we simply do not know why Berta apparently does not understand the question in (1), whilst in response to a repetition of the same utterance (just the pause between theme and rheme is eliminated in (3) she manages an answer.

We can assume that in many instances of this initial phase several elements of an utterance are incomprehensible whilst the odd one or two which are known are identified and understood (cf. Klein 1984, and below 5.2 and 5.3). Actual proof of this only exists in very rare cases, however. (But see the extremely elaborate sequence of negotiation with Angelina in Chapter 7.4.) Some indication of the fact that non-native participants are initially confronted by very 'global' understanding problems are to be found in failed best-guesses, for example. They demonstrate how a response may rest entirely on expectations – usually from contextual knowledge, for example on the activity type, without anything from the linguistic surface of the utterance itself having been understood. Thus when we come to discuss (at least partly) identifiable causes in the following sections, it is worth remembering the fact that a not inconsiderable part – both quantitatively and qualitatively speaking – of understanding problems are being disregarded in this chapter.

3.1 UNDERSTANDING PROBLEMS TRIGGERED BY A SINGLE, IDENTIFIABLE ELEMENT

Although we begin this chapter with a group of understanding problems where just one element of the utterance to be understood can be made responsible, it is only at first sight that this contradicts what has been said before on the layeredness of causes. In the respective sections we will of course take account of other factors that typically co-occur.

Lexical comprehension problems

For several reasons the difficulties we describe in this group seem to be the most unproblematic for both of the participants. Typically they come to light by a correspondingly specific indication of non-understanding since more elementary tasks like chunking the utterance and identifying the relevant lexical item have already been managed by the hearer (see Chapter 4 below; also Broeder 1992: 27 ff).

The following example is from an interview where Mahmut applies for a job in a bakery:

(1) N: uh nou u moet nog gekeurd worden
         ur well you have to have examined
     M: gekeurd ↑
         examined ↑
     N: ja
         yes
     M: wat is dat die ↑
         what is that ↑
(5) N: gekeurd u moet naar arts naar dokter
         examined you have to go to a doctor to a physician
     M: ja keuring
         yes examination

Here, identifying the relevant item and explicitly asking for its meaning is done in two separate steps. In this way a clear and well-limited cause is jointly defined, and the majority-speaking participant thus knows immediately how to tackle the problem, that is by trying to explain the meaning of the word, for example by offering synonyms (cf. Ch. 7.3 below). Another reason for the relative ease with which lexical problems are handled may be that they often are expectable for the speaker. An example from Marcello's interview at the Job Centre may illustrate this. The counsellor is explaining the columns on the registration card.

(1)   N: ihr <u>name</u> ↑ ihr geburtstag ↑ + ihr wohnort ↑ und so weiter
         your <u>name</u> your date of birth your address and so on

    und dann hier das anliegen ↓ # [also sie wollen/]
    and then here your business ↓ so you want/

M: # [anliegen ↑]
                                 business ↑

N: anliegen ↓ das ist ihr <u>wunsch</u>
       business that is your <u>wish</u>

(5) M: ah [ja ja]
         ah yes yes

N: [was sie/] was sie vom arbeitsamt
       what you what you from the job centre

M: ja

N: <u>möchten</u> .
       <u>want</u>

M: mhm

(10) N: da könn' sie also reinschreiben 'ne stelle als dreher und fräser
        so you could fill in there a job as turner and miller

When Marcello interrupts with a repetition to ask for the meaning of 'anliegen', the counsellor was just about to add a paraphrase which would have contained an explanation of the relevant lexical item ('also sie wollen/ so you wish/'). He was probably aware of a possible problem with it – like many experienced professionals he is very good at choosing his words to 'suit' an addressee from a different language background. In his attempt at clarification he then only needs to build on this for further 'work' on the meaning of 'anliegen'.

In the above examples the cause of a single lexical item is picked up very explicitly by both partners. There are many other cases, however, where a very similar trigger of a problem can be assumed but remains more implicit.

(1)   N: sta je <u>al ingeschreven</u> ↑
        are you registered ↑

       M: wat ↑
           what ↑

       N: ben je al meer hier geweest ↑
           have you been here before ↑

       M: nee
           no

(5)   N: nee nog niet
           no not yet

       M: nog niet (. .)
           not yet

Here Mohamed leaves it to the interviewer to decide how to find a somehow simpler formulation of his question. From the means Mohamed uses for indicating his problem, ('what ↑', (2)) it is even not clear whether he himself could identify a specific item causing his non-understanding. Given that the rest of the utterance is short, for the interviewer the item 'ingeschreven' suggests itself as a starting point for clarification – and success of the respective reformulation confirms the interviewer's approach to replace this lexical item. (Some aspects of the interrelations between reformulations and explanation of lexical meaning will be discussed in Chapter 7.3.)

It is not by coincidence that all examples cited up to this point referred to lexical items which do not belong to the vocabulary of high-frequency words. Evidently lexical comprehension problems are not independent of differing degrees of difficulty in general. A common background to this type of problem therefore lies in the topics/subjects of an interaction which demand a more or less 'specialized' vocabulary (cf. 3.4 below). From the majority speaker's perspective, s/he is confronted with the task of finding 'simple words' for the expression of sometimes complex questions in order to choose just the vocabulary that 'matches' the other's language abilities at this point in time. This depends among other things on the opportunity to assess this level, on experience with similar situations and routinization – a question to be taken up again in the analyses.

Misunderstanding caused by 'mishearing' a lexical element

Phonetic problems with understanding are interesting because they show clearly what a strong influence the hearer's expectations have even at the lowest level of the 'bottoming-up' process, that is the *interpretation* of perception. It is a common feature of this category of causes that the hearer perceives one or more phonetic elements differently. This almost always happens in favour of an interpretation which is a possible or – from their point of view – even a more coherent continuation of the conversation than the utterance that has actually just been made.

Dans les cas persistants sur plusieurs répliques, ces interprétations divergentes ne sont pas incompatibles, elles présentent des éléments communs (référentiels, espace/temps etc.) qui entretiennent l'illusion de compréhension, puisqu'il y a coexistence possible des deux interprétations.

(de Hérédia 1986: 50)

When a misunderstanding persists over a longer sequence of responses, these
differing interpretations are not incompatible. They have elements which link to
the previous utterances (referential, spatial or temporal etc.) which give the
illusion of understanding since two interpretations can exist at the same time.
(our translation).

It is, of course, easier for such mis-hearings to take place if the
phonetic quality of the original utterance is blurred as a result of
the speaker's delivery having been fast, slurred or unclearly articu-
lated (see examples in de Hérédia (1986), who also gives examples
of misinterpretations on the side of the majority participant). But
this does not have to be the case. The following example comes
from the beginning of an encounter in which Angelina, right at the
start, had asked the interviewer to speak slowly, and he in response
had made a particular effort to speak clearly. The aim of this first
part of the interview is just to establish basic information about
Angelina's actual situation.

(1)   N: gehen sie zur arbeit ↑
           do you go to work ↑
      A: isch ↑ nee ↓
           me ↑ no ↓
      N: was machen sie ↑
           what do you do ↑
      A: so mit zwei kinder ↓ + kleine ↓
           so with two children ↓ small ↓
(5)   N: ah ja
           oh yes
      A: und e hause kuchen putzen
           and er house cook clean
      N: ah ja
           oh i see
      A: essen (xx) kind die andere kind ↓ viel arbeit ↓
           eat (xx) child the other child ↓ a lot of work ↓
      N: ja ja sie arbeiten im haushalt
           yes yes you do housework (. .)
           [intervening turns about the age of the children]
(10) N: wie/ + wie ist so ein arbeitstag ↑ e was machen sie zuerst morgens ↑
           what what is your working day like ↑ er what do you do first thing ↑
      A: <zu essen ↑ > was ↑   <laughing, amused>
           <to eat ↑ > what ↑
      N: <mhm>   <confirms>
      A   jetz/ heute ↑
           now/ today ↑

N: zum beispiel ja
for instance yes
(15) A: ja ich essen wann mein mann zuhause ne ↑ (. . . .)
yes i eat when my husband home no ↑

Angelina obviously hears *zuerst* (first thing,) as *zu essen* (to eat) as her hypothetical question (l.11) shows. In doing this she makes a logical connection with *her* contribution to the conversational context which is to name the individual practical household chores (6/8). This train of thought is perfectly in keeping with the first part of the question in (3) 'what do you do?'. Her response is thus 'on topic' which is why her conversational partner does not find it necessary to embark on clarification. He accepts the shift of emphasis caused by the misunderstanding and in fact it is not difficult in the ensuing conversation to approach her daily routine from the topic of cooking and eating.

Small phonetic differences often distinguish one word from another. In the following example from Ilhami the distinction between *beschreiben* (to describe) and *schreiben* (to write) is achieved simply through the unstressed prefix 'be'. Since lexical prosody plays a major role in the segmentation and recognition of speech – in most 'slips of the ear' word boundaries are affected (Cutler 1989)[2] Ilhami's misunderstanding is understandable.

(1) N: und was für türkische musik hören sie da ↑ was gefällt ihnen da ↑
and what kind of turkish musik do you listen ↑ *what do you like there* ↑
I: *harrabiks*
N: was it das ↑
what is that ↑
I: <auf deutsch weiss auch net>   <laughingly>
in german don't know
(5) N: können sie's etwas beschreiben ↑
can you describe it a bit ↑
I: <u>wie</u> kann ich schreiben ↑ auf türkisch schreiben oder ↑
how kann I write ↑ *write in turkish or what* ↑
N: nein e <u>erzählen</u> was für musik ↓ das meine ich
no er <u>tell</u> what kind of music ↓ *that's what I mean*

Although it seems a bit odd to him in this connection – as his amazement and checking back demonstrates (6) – the known/familiar constellation of sounds forms the basis of such a strong expectation here that the unstressed syllable is 'not heard'. But in this case too there's another level of cause behind this misunderstanding. Ilhami's reply in (4) that he cannot translate *harrabiks* already indicates that he relates the question 'what's that' (3) to the *meaning* of the word rather than to the object. Seen from this point of view his interpretation 'schreiben' (write) is completely consequential.

Of course not all phonetic problems are misunderstandings. There are also occasions where parts of an utterance are heard differently even if this interpretation makes no (better) sense to the hearer. In the following example Berta forms a hypothesis of what she might have heard. (The excerpt has just been preceded by discussion of whether Berta had ever had a job prior to this one; to which she replied – no, this was the first.)

(1)   N: d'accord ↓ et ça fait longtemps que vous êtes en france ↑
           good↓ and you've been in france a long time ↑
      B: quoi ↑
           what ↑
      N: ça fait <u>combien de temps</u> que vous êtes en france
           <u>how long</u> have you been in france
      B: la <u>personne que</u> ↑/
           the <u>person who</u> ↑/
(5)   N: non <cela fait> combien de temps <separating syllables>
           no how long is it that
           depuis que vous êtes [arrivé en france]
           that you've been in france
      B: [ah *ya ya] si si* huit mois
                          eight months

What is interesting here is that the Job Centre counsellor alters little lexically or syntactically in her reformulation but instead deals with the phonetic origin of the non-understanding by means of clear segmentation. As the example shows, it is of course in most cases the majority speaker who has the best feeling for potential causes, and his or her way of responding to a problem is one of the most important analytical sources for us.

3.2 UNDERSTANDING PROBLEMS CAUSED BY RELATIVE DEGREES OF DIFFICULTY

'When a customer speaks slowly or speaks proper German, I understand better. But when it is dialect or speaking quickly . . .' ('Wenn ein Kunde spreche langsam oder richtig deutsch ich versteh besser. Aber wann ist eine dialekt oder schnell sprechen . . .'). This is Marcello's comment on the ways of speaking that can make understanding easier or problematic after about two years of stay. What it may demonstrate is that also from the minority speaker's perspective both aspects – relative 'simplicity' or 'difficulty' are two sides of a coin.

In the following paragraphs we are not aiming at a comprehensive account of difficulties for participants in face-to-face interactions (cf. for example Fritz (1991)), but only to highlight the most typical constellations where some form of *complexity* led to problems of understanding in the encounters studied. From an analytical point of view it would surely be desirable to keep complexity of *language* (e.g. use of unusual words, sentence embedding etc.) strictly apart from that of *content*. But as Dietrich and Klein (1986) convincingly argue, matters are more complicated:

> . . . the **simplicity of a text** – given a certain content – is not just a matter of simple structural properties such as short words, short sentences, and 'regular' word order, rather it **depends on a complex interplay of its components**: – the structural properties of the language used; – adaptation to the way in which the human mind processes language; – nontextual knowledge on the part of the listener, that is all information (including expectations, assumptions and the like) which the listener may have independent of what is said in the text. (1986:113; our emphasis)

Or, more concretely with respect to our data, for an assessment of the relative difficulty of an interview question at least three dimensions have to be considered: the subject matter it thematizes, the way it is formulated (which encompasses structural properties of the language used **and** adaptation to processing needs as we shall see below), and how it links with contextual knowledge of the addressee (which is interrelated with both of the former dimensions). Since it is inherent in the problem that indications of non understanding are almost always non-specific, we cannot usually expect any help from the hearer's side to distinguish between these levels of complexity.

When we turn to questions of understanding which above all else are caused by an utterance of the majority speaking interviewer being too 'difficult', then even more than for the problems described in the preceding section one has to take into consideration the minority speaker's level of understanding competence at that moment in time in order to attribute causality. This one can only do through an examination of the encounter as a whole and those utterances directly preceding it.

The way of putting it: structural complexity and ellipsis as complementary sources of difficulty

It will come as no surprise that in our data 'difficulty' with the formulation, i.e. the linguistic surface of the language to be understood, can be described from two extremes – on the one hand there is too much information which makes processing difficult, on the other hand there is 'too little' which demands too much inferencing effort. We examine the former group first.

Complex utterances

Typically, minority speakers find utterances difficult to process on a number of levels. Their structural properties tend to coincide with a characteristic style of speaking: they are not only long and syntactically (more or less) complex, but also spoken fast and/or slurred, and accompanied by restarts, self-repair or accumulative use of particles. Both features contribute to making the utterance less accessible for the learner. (We will come back to a discussion of the concepts of accessibility, explicitness and transparency in Chapter 7 below.)

There are different **reasons** why the majority participants in the encounters speak in this way. In many cases especially opaque formulations are motivated by face-threatening topics – for reasons of polite indirectness the interviewer tends to 'bury' what is meant in a series of allusions or hints. For example when applying for an apprenticeship in a garage, the Turkish adolescents who are in fact comparatively advanced, find it difficult to understand a whole series of questions with respect to their school grades. We cite an extract from the respective passage with Ilhami. The preceding topic was how long he would have to attend school before the final exams.

(1)　N:　noch drei monate ↓ e zwischenzeugnis is es schon ma dagewesen ↑
　　　　　three months ↓ er interim report has there been any yet ↑
　　　　　habt ihr des schon ma gehabt ein zwischenzeugnis oder wie/
　　　　　have you all had that yet an interim report or what/
　　　　　wie is da die benotung in der schule ↑
　　　　　what is the grading like in school ↑

I: wie ↑
      what ↑

(5) N: ja ihr habt doch als/e tut als arbeite schreibe ↑ macht ihr des ↑
        well you've all/er do sometimes examination papers ↑ don't you ↑
        so ne arbeit ↑ (un un) gipts die noten eins zwo drei oder [so-]
        such papers ↑ and there are the grades one two three or [so]

      I: [<ja>] <loudly>
                                         yes

      N: un habt ihr da schonmal en zeugnis bekommen
        and have you all got a report yet

      I: <ja> via haben schon gemacht ↓   <in a low voice>
        yes we have got that already ↓

What makes this kind of understanding problem especially delicate for both participants is that clarification forces the speaker to
be more explicit about the topic than he wanted to be. We will come
back to this in section 3.3 below.

Obviously, there is a close relation between this style of speaking
and the question of an 'adequate' adaptation of the majority speaker's speech in general. In some cases (which are not very frequent
in our data, however) speakers simply make no attempt to depart
from their 'normal' way of speaking. So a typical constellation of
causes is found in official settings. The majority speaker is used to
providing information as a matter of routine in her or his professional capacity and sees no necessity, or rather is not motivated, to
attempt an adaptation at any level. A very eloquent example of this
type of difficulty can be found in the information that Andrea
receives at the building society when enquiring about a mortgage.
Having made his initial request, Andrea is told he would have to be
a saver with this building society (or for that matter with any building society) to qualify for a mortgage. He then asks whether his
bank savings might help, and is told that they are run on different
lines and then the following passage occurs.

(1) N: you could do that ++ it is probably/ i mean then + it gives us an
        idea that you can afford to pay out a certain amounts/ amount
        each month

      A: <+++>   <long pause>

      N: you see it would depend how much you are going to pay in i
        mean you could have/ open a share account + its six and a
        quarter percent and thats one way you can pay in and withdraw
        any time

      A: ++

(5)   N: build up share is for regular monthly savings thats for saving up
for (a house) or a car or something but that has to be the same
amount every month you cant pay any more or any less + and
the seven day account is one way you have to start it off with a
hundred pounds but after that you can pay in as much or as
[little as you] want + ya

A: [ya seven twenty five] ++ mm < +++>
<long pause>
its alright thank you ↓ can I take these ↑

What Andrea is confronted with here is a flow of speech where
not only the chunking into utterances and smaller units of meaning
is also mostly left to him, but also the interpretation of what the
(logical) relations between the utterances are. This is asking too
much of him at this point of his stay in England. The fact that this
'hyper-explanation' (Erickson 1982) causes comprehension problems for him only emerges more or less indirectly – there are no
attempts at checking and so no resolutions either.

In other cases, difficult utterances of this kind arise out of a
momentary lapse on the part of the majority speaker who, in a
lengthy encounter, may sometimes flag in adjusting their speech.
Even with those interviewers who, in general, are very good at
adapting to the linguistic means of an elementary learner it is quite
noticeable that after a relatively unproblematic sequence, they tend
to lapse back into a 'normal' manner of delivery. This then again
may cause understanding problems; but on the other hand, it
avoids the risk of over-adapting, and keeps the minority participant
aware what the 'target' level is. (For an example see Tino's case
study, already referred to in Chapter 1.)

Paradoxically, in many cases it is precisely the majority participant's attempt to *prevent* problems with understanding which leads
to especially complex utterances. So whilst the social worker in
Berta's counselling interview (see case study in 5.1) speaks quite
slowly and clearly throughout the encounter, a sequence such as
the following where they discuss hours of work is simply 'too
much' (processing effort) for Berta:

(1)   N: d'accord + et si on vous propose un travail plus que huit heures ↑
ok and if you are asked to work more than eight hours ↑
un travail qui commencerait plus tôt que huit heures du matin ↑
a job which starts before eight in the morning ↑

est-ce que vous/ est-ce que vous accepteriez de commencer plus
tôt que huit heures ↑
would you/ would you agree to start before eight in the morning ↑
avant huit heures ↑ vous comprenez ce que je vous demande ↑
before eight ↑ *you understand what I'm asking* ↑
(5)   B: non non + non
            no no + no

Anticipating comprehension difficulties (and rightly so, for a
hypothetical question, as the section on content and topic will
show) the counsellor offers several self-paraphrases, which are
intended for greater explicitness but make the whole turn rather
long and complicated, since Berta has no possibility of analysing
smaller chunks of it and identifing how the 'modified repetitions'
are related to each other.

Elliptical utterances

Just as there is a correspondence between explicitness and structural and/or informational overload of an utterance so there is the
reverse case with elliptical or condensed utterances, where this
explicitness is lacking. Interestingly it is often the same type of conversational background (where majority speaker's adaptation is
missing or flagging) which provides the other 'extreme' of difficult
utterances. We refer to the contraction of utterances, common in
everyday speech, that occurs through reduction of weak vowels,
frequent use of pronouns or colloquially condensed forms of reference all of which can lead to understanding problems for the
minority speaker.

Both forms of difficulty through the degree of explicitness (i.e.
where it is reduced by elliptical shortness or where higher explicitness means higher complexity) in the interviewer's formulation are
exemplified in the following excerpt from Angelina's job centre session. (Angelina had just succeeded in communicating during a
really stressful clarification that she has got a teacher's diploma but
sees no chance to work in that profession because of her German.)

(1)   N: mhm + für mich isch des halt intressant wie/ sie ham/ weil ich
            jetzt <u>weiß</u> + daß sie
            for me it is interesting how/ you have/ because i know now that you
            schon mit kindern gearbeitet haben + dann gäbs ja vielleicht die
            möglichkeit daß sie
            already worked with children + then there might be a possibility that you

           wieder mit kindern arbeiten + natürlich nicht in der schule +
           vielleicht e vielleicht
           work with children again of course not in school + maybe er maybe ↑
           in nem haushalt in nem privat haushalt
           in a household in a private household

(5)   A: ja
         yes
     N: könnten sie sich **sowas** vorstellen ↑
         could you imagine such a thing ↑
     A: was ↑
         what ↑
     N: <könnten sie sich vorstellen daß sie>   <more loudly>
         could you imagine that you
         in nem + haushalt in nem [privat]
         in a household in a private
(10) A: [ja]
         yes
     N: haushalt
         household
     A: in mein^haus
         in my house
     N: <u>nicht</u> in ihrem haus + in ner andern <u>familie</u>
         <u>*not*</u> *in your house + in another* <u>*family*</u>
     A: ja
         yes
(15) N: <u>kinder</u> betreun ↓
         look after <u>*children*</u> ↓
     A: ah soo
         ah ok
     N: von <u>andern</u>#
         of other people
     A: #vii <u>babysitter</u>
         like a babysitter
     N: so ähnlich ja (. . .)
         more or less yes

Here the anaphoric form 'sowas' (such a thing, line 6) condenses
all the information explicitly stated in the counsellor's preceding,
long and complex turn – which probably also had not been understood by Angelina. Therefore it is impossible for her to interpret
such a shortened reference. As the ensuing sequence shows, her
active interventions (cf. lines 7, 10, 12, 16, 18) get the interviewer to
'package' her question in just the right size of contributions.

Even for relatively advanced learners it is sometimes difficult to infer what pronominal forms refer to, especially when they are used with more abstract or figurative meaning. This might also lead to misunderstanding, as in Abdelmalek's encounter with a lawyer. Abdelmalek has just explained that after a serious accident at work he has been unable to pay his rent and that the landlord has already locked up his room once.

(1) N: oui ↓ et alors **ça** en est **où** pour l'instant ↑
         yes ↓ and so that's where at the moment ↑
(2) A: euh ici à la première arrondissement
         here in the first district
(3) N: non mais la situation elle en est à quel point +
         no but the situation its got to what point
(4)   je veux dire vis-à-vis de + du responsable du + de l'endroit ou
         vous habitez ↑
         i mean as far as the the person responsible for for the place where you live ↑

Here the lawyer's question contains two pronominal forms which need an 'enriched' interpretation by the addressee to be understood in the right way: *ça* and *où*. To interpret *ça* in the way it was meant, Abdelmalek not only would have had to know that it can be used in this anaphoric way, but also infer from knowledge of this kind of interview which of both meanings is more probable at that stage of the conversation. As in most cases, a clarification consists in making explicit again what the pro-form had contracted. The same step is missing in Abdelmalek's understanding of *où*, which is used to describe the (temporal) development of the situation by a spatial metaphor (cf. Lakoff & Johnson 1980) and which he understands in its concrete, spatial sense only.

Another area in which non-native participants are dependent on greater explicitness is the transition to a new topic. Long's (1983a) maxim 'make new topics salient' refers to the importance of this. Even if new topics tend to be announced in very inconspicuous ways – i.e. through prosodic means such as intonation, short pauses, discourse markers (cf. the *oui* of the lawyer in the excerpt above) this signalling is of great importance, since one of the most important sources of contextual information for the hearer is trying to interpret an utterance in the frame of reference given by the actual topic (see *contextualisation* in Chapters 2 and 8). Missing the transition to a new topic means therefore missing support for understanding. The more linguistic means are scarce the more important this contextualisation becomes; and having to deduce the new topic from the content of the utterance can become a cause of non- or misunderstanding. (We will take up this point again in Chapter 7.2 from the perspective of preventative means of managing understanding.)

Content of the utterance

> An aspect of context which is very little discussed, in language teaching or more generally, in terms of how it contributes to the relative ease of participating in the discourse as speaker or hearer, is what is being talked about.
>
> (Brown 1989:98)

The more limited the knowledge from contextual sources such as immediate situation or world knowledge, the greater the dependency on linguistic information is, and thus the greater the degree of difficulty for the participant with a different cultural and language background. This is the reverse of the point just made above about contextualisation and shows the extent to which they are interdependent. It is not mere chance that in encounters where the choice of topic is open (as is the case in conversations) the 'here and now' is nearly always taken as the starting point (cf. also Long 1983b; Esch 1992, Ch. 7). Even if the talk turns to the past or the future, the everyday life and realm of experience of the minority worker remain the preferred frame of reference.

Since research on conceptual difficulty has only begun, our account will be a preliminary one. In the following we shall comment on those two areas where a departure from the 'here and now' frame of reference is a most obvious cause of understanding problems in our data. These are *abstract topics* and *hypothetical issues*.

In an attempt at a provisional definition one could say that abstract topics are distant from the 'here and now' in that they demand specific (often professional) types of knowledge. Asymmetry between interviewer and minority client with respect to preconditions of understanding is strongest here. As we have implied above, abstract topics seldom feature in our data for longer stretches of an encounter. But when they have to be dealt with (for example in counselling interviews) understanding is always 'at risk'. Some instances of this are to be found in accounts of the workings of the building societies with Andrea (from which we have already quoted above) and in the legal explanations furnished in the encounter between Abdelmalek and the lawyer. Here the

latter is explaining the obligations of the employer after an indus-
trial accident.

(1)   N: il doit le faire dans les quarante heures **sinon** il risque une
               sanction penale + il risquait une **amende** de six cent à douze
               cent francs + et à la limite même il risque aussi une **sanction**
               civile en ce sens que les/ la caisse d'assurance maladie du fait
               qu'il l'a pas déclaré dans les quarante-huit heures peut exiger
(5)   remboursement de toutes les sommes qu'elle vous doit

he has to do this within forty eight hours otherwise he risks a penal sanction
he would risk a fine of 600 to 1200 francs + and in the extreme case he
risks also civil proceedings in the sense that the/ the health insurance
companies because he has not declared within the 48 hours can demand
the reimbursement of all the monies it owes you

A: + +

Both examples show the typical close link between this type of
subject matter and difficulties presented by surface linguistic features such as unfamiliar, 'low frequency' vocabulary and
subordination in syntactic constructions. Therefore in most cases it
remains difficult to assess exactly to what extent a lack of specified
world knowledge (e.g. on the functioning of institutions in the
majority society) has an effect on these understanding problems.

In this respect the second group to be described in this section is
more accessible to analysis. The regularity with which *questions*
about possible planned events are misunderstood even by participants
with a quite advanced competence in their second language is both
striking and surprising. They are almost always misunderstood in
the same way, that is, as questions about the real situation, the 'here
and now' which shows how this is foremost in the learner's consciousness as these next examples from encounters with
Abdelmalek and Mohamed demonstrate.

N: hein + c'est bien ça + + bon eh hem +
        hmm + all right then + + good
        et maintenant quel type de + travail vous aimeriez faire là ↑
        and now what kind of job would you like to do there ↑
A: comme le travail ↑
        as a job ↑
N: hem
        mm
A: ah parce que travail pas + le chômage
        ah because don't work + unemployment

> N: là + vous êtes au chômage + mais si vous avez un travail
>   *there + you are unemployed + but if you have a job*
>   quel type de travail vous cherchez/ vous accepteriez ↑
>   *what kind of job you are looking for/would you accept* ↑
>   (. . .)

Obviously the morphological form of the finite verb is not salient enough in these cases to mark the hypothetical mode (against the expectation created by the 'now' at the beginning of the utterance). Even less prominent are the linguistic means used for this marking by the housing officer in the interview with Mohamed:

> N: waar wil je ergens wonen ↑
>   *where [do] you want to live* ↑
> M: ik woon in <xxxx> straat   <name>
>   *i live in . . . street*
> N: ja daar woon je nu (. . .)
>   *yes there you live now*

Apart from the fact that there are again misunderstandings arising from the linguistic surface of the relevant utterances, another level of causes comes into play with hypothetical issues, however, since hypothetical questions in our encounters usually aim at eliciting the personal wishes or plans of the minority participants. So we have reason to believe that many of them simply do not expect to find interest being expressed in their personal wishes in an official situation. We look at understanding problems fostered by differing expectations on the level of discourse in the next section.

3.3 UNDERSTANDING PROBLEMS CAUSED BY INDIRECTNESS AND IMPLICIT DISCOURSE NORMS

The group of problems with understanding that will be discussed briefly in this section centre on the question 'why this now to me?' (Sacks 1971). Understanding speaker meaning (Leech 1983) in institutional settings presupposes that the minority worker as a client will have enough experience of the relevant *implicit* norms and values of such encounters. While the only way to gain this experience is through participation, he or she is nevertheless likely to be assessed according to the way s/he participates. Miscommunication at this level has been termed 'pragmatic failure' (cf. Thomas 1983, who differentiated further between pragmalinguistic failure and socio-pragmatic failure) and rests on a lack of shared schema and frame (as we have discussed in Chapter 2 above). At least in two respects it is different from the range of problems of understanding discussed above. Firstly, where we have talked of the opacity of interview questions before, the implication for most of these cases has been that the professional would have done well to have adjusted their speech to make it less opaque. In the case of pragmatic 'opacity', however, it would nearly always be a nonsense for either side to go 'on record' in order to do away with the inherent intransparency of the utterance.

The second point is that lack of understanding on this level usually results in inappropriate (e.g. impolite) behaviour on the minority worker's part which is held to be of a graver nature than a 'mere' linguistic problem. Misinterpretation on a pragmatic level is often far more face-threatening to both sides and the client's response is attributed to an intentionality which it does not, by design, have. Problems of this type typically surface as *misunderstandings*, since the addressee often is not aware of a possible 'other' interpretation of the question posed to him or her, and it is frequently the response itself which appears wanting, though the cause for this may lie in the minority worker's non-understanding of speaker intentionality. It is seen as a problem of behaviour, not of language (see Goffman 1974, Gumperz 1982a and b).

Pragmatics of openings and closings

A good example of this are the very frequent problems clients have in our data with *formulaics in openings and closings*: greeting and introductory sequences of course presuppose a clear assessment of the degree of formality and the amount and type of relevant information that has to be given in each specific turn. Choosing a greeting form which is too formal (e.g. 'meneer' in the Dutch job interviews often used by Fatima) or over informal (e.g. omitting one's surname in the introduction) is at first sight not seen as a problem of understanding; it is rather felt as a (silent) disturbance of the atmosphere of a conversation. Hesitations to act at all have a very similar effect, like the opening of Ilhami's Job Centre interview shows:

(1)   T: ich bin die frau g. vom arbeitsamt
           i am mrs. g from the job centre
      I: mhm
      T: und <u>sie</u> sind ↑
           and <u>you</u> are ↑
      I: +

(5)   T: wie heißen sie ↑
            what is your name ↑
        I: (xxx) ilhami   (. .)

Recognising pre-closings and responding to them appropriately is also an area where only conversational experience can help to interpret certain indirect utterances in the right way. An example of the uncertainty confronting the participant with a different mother-tongue even when he has acquired a quite good command of the new language is Marcello's counselling interview in the Job Centre:

(1)   M: für mich ist immer besser wenn ich spreche/spreche <u>gut</u> deutsch
            for me its always better if i talk good german
        T: natürlich ↓ für alles ↓
            of course ↓ for everything ↓
        M: manchmal ich höre ↑ aber ↑ + eine worte ich vers/ e versteh ↑
            aber [andere nicht]
            sometimes i hear ↑ but ↑ + one word i und/er understand ↑ but others
            not
        T: [mhm mhm]
(5)   ah ja das is auch übungssache ↓ wenn sie jetzt zu hause n
            bißchen mehr üben
            well that's a question of routine ↓ if you're going to practise a little
            more at home
            <[mit ihrer verlobten] nur noch deutsch sprechen> <laughingly>
            if speak only german with your fiancée
—   M: [ich muß]
            I must
        T: ihr überhaupt keine italienische antwort mehr geben ↑ nur noch
            deutsch
            don't answer her in italian any more ↑ only in german
            < > <laughs>

(19)   M: wir muß vergessen < > <laughs>
            we have to forget
        T: ja ↓ + gut ↓ dann hätten wir die sache für heut ↓
            ok ↓ + good ↓ so we're through for today ↓
            und wenn sie also in zukunft noch fragen haben kommen sie bei
            mir vorbei ja ↑
            and if you have any questions in future you'll look in ok ↑
        M: ja
            yes
        T: <rufen sie an ↑ > ok ↑ <leans back, speaks quietly, looks at door,
            stands up>
            give me a call ↑ ok ↑

M: so und jetzt muß ich gehen ↑
    so and now I must go ↑
(25) T: <ja> [< >]
      M: [< >]   <both laugh>
      T: wiedersehen
          bye
      M: wiedersehen danke
          bye thank you

The final topic of conversation was Marcello's command of German. In lines 6–8 Marcello describes remarkably lucidly his view of problems with understanding at this point in time: of what he hears he understands some words but not others. But the fact that understanding is more than a question of word meaning is shown by the pragmatic problem at the close of the conversation. In lines 18–20 there is a variety of closing signals: the topic has come to a halt, and the counsellor underlines this perception by pre-closing signals spoken with definitely 'closing' intonational contour: 'ja ↓ + gut ↓'. He makes even the internal reason for closing explicit ('we're through for today') before finally giving a résumé and advice for a future meeting – both classical means to indicate a closing. But still Marcello is unsure about interpreting these signs in this way: his 'yes' in (23) can hardly be taken as a corresponding closing signal since he remains seated and looks expectantly at the interviewer. It is not until the interviewer leans back in his chair – in preparation for standing up – that he suddenly realises that they have already started to take leave of each other. His explicit topicalisation in (24) stresses the one-sidedness of the closing and has a near embarrassing effect. This is softened somewhat by the laughter and there is then a 'proper' exchange of closings (see also the discussion of Santo's resistance to a closing in 5.4 below).

As a rule our familiarity with the *aims* of interactions in institutional settings makes it easy for us to infer – on a local level – what is 'behind a question'. In most cases this means that we are used to interpreting a relatively neutral question in a more specific sense. Interviewers can express some things very briefly, because normally we have no problems with tacitly supplementing missing information on the basis of our knowledge about this specific type of discourse activity. Of course this kind of knowledge is culture-specific in more than one way. For a counselling interview at the Job Centre for example, there can be different norms for the general aims and possible topics, the way of proceeding (i.e. sequence of topics, room for initiative on the part of the client etc.) as well as more strictly linguistic norms like the degree of formality of the language chosen (see Gumperz and Roberts 1991).

Lacking familiarity of this kind of contextual background is a frequent source of miscommunication in our data. We shall look at some local effects in the next section.

Assessing the point of an utterance

On a local level the inability of the minority worker to decide *why* a certain question has been asked leads to misunderstandings with a relatively limited scope. From a linguistic point of view it is often again pronominal forms which have to be 'filled up' with contextual knowledge to be interpreted in the right way. A simple, yet very typical example for a misunderstanding of this type is a sequence in which Ravinder makes an appointment at the dentist's.

T: fine ↓ and erm where do you live ↑
R: + walsall
T: whats the address sorry

Since the dentist is in Walsall and people usually go to a dentist in their own home town, the receptionist's question was obviously aimed at eliciting an address, even if the surface form of the utterance allows a more general interpretation. Even if this misunderstanding can be easily cleared up in one turn, the example shows that nevertheless such an 'underspecified' answer sounds clumsy if not un-cooperative.

Ignoring implicit norms sometimes can also have a sort of humorous effect, as in the following extract from Ilhami's Job Centre interview. For a while the topic has been working conditions of Ilhami's previous job in a factory for frozen food, where he had been working during three months.

T: is harte arbeit
      it's hard work
      wieviel ham sie denn da verdient ↑
      how much did you earn there ↑
I: viertausendneunhunderteinundachzig mark
      four thousand nine hundred and eighty-one marks
T: <viertausend ↑ >   <very surprised>
      four thousand ↑
I: [mhm]

T: [nee]
       no
I: e in drei monat^aber (. .)
       er but in three months

It becomes more understandable why Ilhami here 'ignores' the convention of calculating earnings in months, if one knows that he really is very proud of the whole sum that he earned during working for this company, and that they were the first earnings in his life.

Pragmatically inappropriate replies can have more serious effects, however. The following passage occurs when Ilhami applies for an apprenticeship in a garage:

(1)   T: e was arbeit' denn dein <u>vater</u> ↑ was macht der von beruf ↑
             what work does your father do ↑ what is his job ↑
       I: metallberuf [und]
             metal job
       T: [ja] und#
             ok and#
       I: #<wxxx> schnellpresse   <names town of the company>
             stamping press
(5)   T: in der schnellpresse in w.
             in the stamping press in w.
       I: [ja] mhm
             yes
       T   [ja]
             yes
       T: und dort tut er metall/ ↑
             and he does metal there ↑
       I: metall [und]
             metal and
(10)   T: [aha]
       I: + die machen auch/ das macht auch papier
             + they also make/ it makes paper too
       T: mhm ah so ist das ↓
             mhm ah its like that ↓

In one sense (i.e. linguistically) Ilhami understands the garage owner's questions at the beginning of the sequence. There are several signals, however, that his attempts at an answer are never quite on target: the garage owner interrupts again and again to get a more specific reply – but without formulating more explicitly what he wants to know. What he insists on is that *conventionally* the question in (1) is directed at the *social status* rather than at the practical details or type of work. So while there is never any open manifestation of miscommunication, the rather sarcastic tone in which (12) is spoken makes clear that Ilhami's addressee had *not* obtained the information he required.

Work with our data shows that often there are also more 'global' effects of differing conceptualizations of the aims and topics of institutional talk (see also Ch. 8). In some of the encounters a series of miscommunications can be attributed to a kind of underlying misunderstanding with respect to defining features of the communicative activity at hand. Differences at this level of basic schemata and frame – that is a vast difference in the way each perceives their relationship to the other and the types of behaviour expected of them – are likely not only to give rise to recurrent problems of understanding but also to hamper clarification in a serious way.

One instance of a background assumption which can lead to misunderstanding is evidenced in differing judgements about whether something belongs to the private or public sphere of life. This is demonstrated by the fact that Ravinder, Berta, Çevdet, Ilhami and Abdelmalek are all somewhat nonplussed in job interviews when asked about their personal preferences – be it for the type of work, hours of work or training courses. Since mismatch at such a general level can only be discovered by looking at an interaction as a whole, we shall take up this topic again in some of the case studies in Chapter 5.

NOTES

1. 'Le signifiant déformé par la prononciation de l'étranger ou mal perçu par celui-ci lorsque c'est le natif qui parle, fournit aux locuteurs en présence une base floue à partir de laquelle chacun sélectionne une forme compatible avec l'anticipation du sens qu'il projette dans l'échange (contexte et attentes personelles)' (de Hérédia 1986, p. 52).
   (The signifier, distorted by the foreigner's pronunciation or misheard by him when it is the native speaker who speaks, gives both interactants a hazy notion of what is meant from which each one chooses a word compatible with the expectations they have of the exchange (context and individual assumptions) [our translation].)
2. 'They are all errors in which juncture has been misperceived - that is, word boundaries have been added, lost, or shifted. It can easily be seen that, as with slips of the ear in general, metrical structure is preserved - strong syllables are perceived as strong, weak ones as weak. But what is interesting about these slips is the direction of the boundary mislocations. Boundaries tend to be perceived at the onset of strong syllables rather than weak. ' (Cutler 1989, p. 349)

FOUR

Managing understanding from a minority perspective

Marie-Thérèse Vasseur, Peter Broeder and Celia Roberts

4.0 INTRODUCTION

After analysing, in Chapter 3, the multiple and complex sources of understanding problems, we will now turn to the problems themselves. More precisely, we will try to analyse how, in the course of interaction, problems with understanding are perceived and interpreted by the minority participant and how they are indicated to the majority speaker. This does not mean that we are adopting a one-sided perspective, which would be contrary to the notion of understanding as an active, cooperative, joint activity we developed in Chapter 2. But one must admit that, in most interethnic encounters, the efforts are unevenly distributed among the participants (Clark & Schaeffer 1989). Sometimes, it is the majority locutor who feels responsible for establishing understanding, sometimes it is the minority interactants who are expected to work to understand the majority locutor and give indications of the problems they experience in understanding the majority participant's utterances. So, although we do not conceive of interaction in terms of a simple model of action-reaction but rather as a collective construct in which both partners get involved and share responsibility (see Chapter 6), nevertheless we are aware of the very risky position minority participants occupy. Experience shows that they are the ones who are going to suffer more from the consequences of non-understanding. Therefore, the way they handle or are forced to handle the situation is often decisive. That is why the main focus of this chapter will be on the minority participant's point of view and contribution.

Our analysis will be centred on indications of non-understanding because they are traces that lead us to the minority interactants' interpretation of the situation. And also because they represent their contribution to the joint process of solving the difficulty (cf. Chapter 6). The means they use to indicate problems with understanding give (more or less) information about the type of problem, the relative importance it has for them and their preferred way of solving it. The problem may be one of general non-understanding, local non-understanding or misunderstanding.

Of course, the indications given do not automatically make the (non)understanding situation transparent for the participants – or for the analyst – especially when the minority interactant's competence in L2 is still very elementary. The clues given then are frequently vague, unspecific and indirect for different reasons we will develop in this chapter. Clarification is far from being systematic. Because of the tension between the need to understand and the will to cooperate and protect one's face, it often takes the interlocutors a long time to get at a common interpretation of where the understanding difficulty lies. Sometimes the listener's interpretation of the situation and of the speaker's intentions are so divergent that the misunderstanding may extend to important parts of the encounter.

For example, in the encounter which Fatima had with a housing official, she was silent and apparently uncooperative for a long sequence. A subsequent feedback session revealed that, like many other Arabic speakers, she found it insulting to have to provide information about her private life (for example how many of her children sleep in one room) to a public official not known to her. Her subsequent reaction of silence hindered the clarification of several points and slowed down considerably the whole interaction. That is why understanding is, most of the time, very slowly and progressively accomplished (see the case studies in Chapter 5 and the joint negotiation in Chapter 7). For this reason, methodologically speaking, we are wary of isolated immediate turn-by-turn analysis which would not take into consideration whole sequences of non-understanding indications, their background and context, the participants' expectations, intentions and responses and we will be especially cautious in taking account of all those elements in the case studies in the next chapter.

The non-understanding indicators we analyse cannot be just formally and mechanically listed because we consider them as parts of the joint negotiation sequences. However, we need to categorise them in terms of their interactional role (explicit vs. implicit, specific vs. unspecific indications) and their function (global or local non-understanding, misunderstanding) because they are significant determinants in the negotiation of understanding. Also some of those practices demonstrate more consciousness, more will to progress, more developed capacities to handle a situation of non-understanding with some minority workers than others and we are interested in assessing the effectiveness of these different procedures.

This chapter is centred on the different behaviours the minority interactants adopt when facing problems of understanding. The main variable is the degree of explicitness in indicating the problem and, related to this, how specifically the problem is identified. It is organised in the following way: in section 4.0, we make a brief presentation of the different types of problems with understanding the participants in an interethnic encounter are liable to meet, even if they are not aware of them. Section 4.1. develops the different options the participants may take, mainly the option to resolve or not resolve the problem(s). Section 4.2. explores the main procedures through which the minority interactant indicates problems with understanding. Section 4.3. raises the delicate problem of face in the management of understanding during interaction. Finally, in 4.4. we attempt to evaluate these procedures and behaviours and sort out those which lead to better understanding; this, in turn, raises the question of the learning issues, which we address in 4.6.

4.1 THE TYPES OF PROBLEMS WITH UNDERSTANDING

In Chapter 3, we have already presented the variety of problems encountered with understanding but we discussed it from an analytic perspective. In this chapter, we want to present it more in terms of a description of the types of problems before focussing on the minority interactant's behaviour in the different cases.

The problems with understanding faced by the minority participants extend on a continuum from complete lack of understanding to misunderstanding which are never cleared up. They may be unable to make sense of their interlocutor's whole utterance and there is a risk of breaking off. Some indication of this problematic situation is usually evident in the minority worker's behaviour. It is for both participants a problem to be solved. Another situation would be when the exchange runs on with a misunderstanding occurring and without either of the participants having been aware of it. Then the thread of the interaction undergoes no interruption.

For example, when at the cleaner's, Berta enquires about the cleaning of curtains (French *rideaux*) and the shop keeper gives her the price for a bed-cover (she uses the French word *édredon* in her answer). None of the partners becomes aware of the misunderstanding and the conversation runs on.

This extreme case of misunderstanding is interesting because it demonstrates people's inability to perceive and solve problems. But we will not deal with it since it is not an object of focus and work from the point of view of the participants. All other cases will be examined: where there is, in the interaction, a moment of 'trouble' caused by an understanding problem, and as soon as one of the participants becomes more or less conscious of a difficulty and takes steps, whatever they are, to overcome it.

The evidence of understanding difficulties may first appear either in the minority interactants' verbal or non-verbal behaviour, or in both. Since such behaviours are often ambiguous, the analyst also has to refer to the majority locutor's responses. It often is the latter's interpretation of the minority speaker's behaviour which puts us on the track of an understanding problem. More evidence is sometimes also supplied in feedback sessions.

Complete lack of understanding often occurs in the first phases of acquisition when the minority speakers' linguistic resources are very limited. For this very reason it is also very difficult for them to signal their problems and any solution is a long and difficult process.

When the lack of understanding has a local cause, it is generally much easier and faster to repair as long as it has been diagnosed correctly and indicated explicitly. If X is the word or the unit that causes the problem, the question 'what is X?' is the most efficient of the means of clarification. But, generally, a high degree of competence is required to isolate, diagnose and indicate such local lack of understanding. More frequently the cause of the problem is not strictly local, or as we have indicated in Chapter 3, it may be anywhere on a cline between global and local.

When a unit or a group of units has been isolated as causing understanding problems, there are two possibilities: either it is totally meaningless for the minority interactant, or each participant attributes a different meaning to it. It becomes the source of a partial or complete illusion. It is what is called a misunderstanding. A misunderstanding is defined as such when there is a partial or complete illusion, temporary or permanent, of understanding between speakers (de Hérédia 1986).

So, as we have suggested in Chapter 3, it is not easy to make a clear distinction between partial (non)understanding and misunderstanding. The latter may be perceived and immediately indicated by the majority partner. Or it may become obvious after a related question asked in the following turn. This is what happens to Ergün who interprets the verb *expect* (as in *expecting a baby*) as *wait* when speaking about his wife. Of course, the housing officer he is talking to attributes a very precise meaning to *expect*, and Ergün thinks of another. The misunderstanding becomes obvious when Ergün answers the other's question by saying that his wife might have been 'expecting' one or two years. (See Chapter 5).

There is no absolute distinction between non-understanding and misunderstanding. In particular misunderstanding is often the result of a hypothesis formed by the minority interactant as a response to non-understanding (see further 4.2. Hypothesis-forming, tentative responses and comprehension-checks).

4.2 OPTIONS THE MINORITY INTERACTANT CAN TAKE: AVOIDING OR INDICATING THE PROBLEM WITH UNDERSTANDING

Avoiding

Working through understanding problems disrupts any interaction of any type – and not only interethnic encounters. No wonder then that both interlocutors will try to avoid it as far as possible. From the minority interactants' point of view, the choice of avoiding the problem first depends on their personal situation, their attitude and idea of their situation.

The minority interactant's degree of competence

For many minority workers, with little or no experience of the new language or of contacts with the majority community, non-understanding is the rule rather than the exception. In this situation, resolving every single difficulty would make the exchange nearly impossible. Therefore, the most sensible and obvious choice consists of what has been frequently called the 'wait and see' strategy (Voionmaa 1984) in which direct, repeated signalling of non-understanding is postponed and time and developments in the interaction are expected to give further clues to meaning.

Even if not beginners, minority interactants may be in a total state of uncertainty about what they have understood or have not understood. They are unable to make a diagnosis. They are then at a loss about what they should be signalling to the interlocutor, and about what kind of help they could request. So they choose not to signal the problems. This will appear as lack of uptake or minimal response (see further: main procedures, 4.3.)

Whether the same attitude towards difficulties persists into later phases of development when instances of non-understanding decrease and a broader repertoire of more specific indicators has been acquired depends on the individual personality and motivation as well as the difficulty of the task (cf. Brown 1989)

The minority interactant's point of view on the relationship and on the issues

The minority interactants may not want to indicate problems with understanding because they feel that the speaker's goodwill might be affected by interruptions. If they seek clarification in the opening phase of the exchange, it may set the interaction off on the wrong footing. If it comes later in an exchange where cooperation has been difficult to establish, another interruption might endanger an already fragile situation. They have to calculate what effect their decision to negotiate understanding will have on the interaction. At the same time, they may also want to save face. In the doubly asymmetrical position of bureaucratic encounters, the minority interactants are clearly the 'weaker' partners. Even if it has the positive effect of showing the strategic resources of these 'weaker' partners, admitting non-understanding has the consequence of reinforcing the asymmetry and their inferior position. This is a strong argument for them to avoid signalling and so, potentially, resolving understanding problems. Examples of this avoidance behaviour are presented below in 4.3.

One or a number of these reasons explain why the minority interactants choose not to signal their understanding problems. But, whether they choose not to signal at all or to give vague and ambiguous responses, it always means that they leave it to their interlocutor to decide whether it is necessary to initiate a process of negotiation or not and what means are going to be used. It also means that the majority speakers are left to guess at the degree of (non)understanding and at the sources of the problem. This then is a very risky situation for the minority speaker. First of all, the majority speaker might not pay enough attention or give enough time to resolving the problem. Second, their interpretation might prove wrong and then the clarification sequences might not, indeed, clarify, or take a very long time to do so. Only some minority interactants, more competent than the others, seem to be aware of the advantages of facing clarification. This group tend to take the initiative and control the understanding obstacles while using creative and native-like procedures to obtain a legitimate participant status (see further Ergün in 4.3.)

Indicating

Besides personal factors including motivation to learn the new language, some circumstances are such that it is not possible or desirable for the minority interactant to avoid clarification questions or sequences. The type of activity going on is mostly responsible for this, and also the types of problem with understanding.

Activity-type

There is an obvious and very important connection between the type of activity and the frequency or type of way in which the problems are resolved. The goals in an encounter which aim at exchanging concrete and precise information hardly allow for a lack of clarity. For example, in making an appointment at the dentist's, some basic questions about the name, address etc. have to be answered in an appropriately detailed way before other points can be dealt with. Avoidance of clarification in some parts of an exchange like this is hardly possible or else the exchange is a failure. By contrast, if, in an everyday conversation, the minority interactants have difficulties with the lexicon of a particular topic, the partners can easily switch topics, and it is unlikely to have any lasting consequence.

One would also expect fewer 'side sequences' to occur in conversations than in interactions where specific information has to be elicited or exchanged. This is confirmed by the general trend in our data: extended clarificatory side sequences occur frequently in those encounters in which minority participants with very limited command of the new language have to cope with a clearly defined but complex task especially when they are motivated to do this as well as possible. Good examples of this are the Job Centre interviews with Berta and Angelina (see case studies in Chapter 5). If the task becomes too demanding, however, then the minority interactant may resort to other procedures which leave no room for clarification at all (see below).

For this reason, it might be tempting to concentrate only on bureaucratic encounters in identifying how minority participants manage non-understanding. But in some respects it is easier to focus on conversations simply because they are not narrowly task-oriented. So there are more opportunities for clarificatory 'diversions'. For one thing, conversations, which in our data often take place with researchers from the majority group, generally allow more space for such interruptions (Vasseur 1988). They are not usually bound by either time constraints nor those of a particular task. The interlocutors can be unrestrained – at least as far as considerations about conversational strategies are concerned. For another, the increased familiarity between minority and majority participants in the course of data collection means that the admission of not having understood becomes much less face-threatening for the former.

Indeed, in some such conversations the opposite seems to be true in that there is a consensus that they should request and be granted every possible opportunity to learn (cf. Roberts & Simonot, 1987 on pedagogic conversation and Py, 1991 on pedagogical contract). Their participation in initiating clarification (and even metalinguistic side sequences in the narrow sense of the word, for example the explanation of grammatical rules of the second language) is here no longer seen by the majority locutor as a disruption but much more as a positive characteristic (see Andrea in Roberts & Simonot 1987). However, it is always risky to initiate such sequences since the minority interactant will not always admit being taught, as Apfelbaum (1991) has shown. Pedagogical sequences offered by the majority locutor are then resented as imposing too much on the minority interactant's face.

A typical difference in the treatment of understanding problems in 'goal-oriented' interactions as opposed to conversations is that in the former the minority interactants are (nearly) always prompted by the necessity of really needing to know what the word used by the majority locutor meant in this context in order to be able to formulate a reply. But the minority interactants who experience face problems will hardly ever admit to needing this kind of knowledge in a job interview if they can hazard a reasonable guess at the sense of the utterance without this single item. In conversation with a researcher, though, such behaviour is perfectly possible and the minority interactant may ask about word meaning for its own sake.

Type of problem

Besides activity type, the level of the problem is another factor which comes into play in deciding whether or not or how problems with understanding are resolved.

As we have suggested in Chapter 3 problems of understanding which can be located at the linguistic surface, for example an isolated lexical item, are naturally indicated more frequently, more willingly and more explicitly than discursive-pragmatic problems (like indirectness of style) which are more strongly linked to the level of the relationship and more difficult to identify for the minority interactant. For example, it is easier to say, as Ergün does: 'ver? wat is dat?' (*far away? what is that?*) than to explain to the Job Centre adviser that he does not know how to interpret: *what do you do?* (see 4.4 below).

As we mentioned before, the problem for the minority interactants is not only of deciding whether to indicate a problem or not but also how to indicate it. They have to choose which procedures to adopt as the easiest, most practical, most efficient and most adapted to the situation and the aims. Through their choices, the minority interactants have to establish a delicate balance between the maintenance of interaction and the control of understanding. We will study these choices now.

4.3 MAIN PROCEDURES FOR INDICATING NON-UNDERSTANDING

A typical sequence

To illustrate and discuss the different types of indications given by the minority interactant, we will look at a sequence taken from a job application interview in which Ergün, a Turkish minority worker in the Netherlands, has to face important problems of understanding the official's question on his previous jobs:

(1) X: en wat deed je dan ↑
         and what did you do then ↑

     E: wat ↑
         what ↑

     X: wat / wat deed je bij de krant ↑
         what did you do at the newspaper ↑

     E: +
         +

(5) X: wat voor werk ↑
         what kind of work ↑

     E: wat voor ↑ + [die]
         what kind of ↑ + [that]

     X: [wat] voor werk ↑
         [what] kind of work ↑

     E: uh werk [wat]
         er work [what]

     X: [wat]moest je doen ↑
         what did you have to do ↑

(10) E: +
         +

     X: wat doe je ↑
         what do you do ↑

     E: wat doen ↑
         what do ↑

     X: wat doe je ↑
         what do you do ↑

     E: wat doe je ↑
         what do you do ↑

(15) X: bij de krant
         at the newspaper

     E: + ik / ik niet verstaan
         + i / i not understand

[handwritten margin notes: "NS tries to modify his input —"; "No exchange of understanding but at least it's known —"; "SLA would say, 'have a topic shift.'"]

The initial question is a typical one in the ritual of job interviews. But Ergün is unable to diagnose what his problem really is. He is aware that he does not understand but he cannot say what it is exactly that he does not understand. It is a general, hazy non-understanding. Similarly, he also has problems explaining what his difficulty is because of his limited productive competence. But if he wants to proceed, he has to signal his difficulty in one way or another. So, what does he do?

- He responds with a minimal query (what ?) indicating that he has either not perceived or understood and in this case it is received as a request to repeat, which the majority locutor willingly does.
- He keeps silent and blocks up the exchange. His interlocutor then has to interpret silence. Often, like here with Ergün, the majority locutor interprets such lack of uptake as an indication of an understanding problem and takes initiatives like modifying his initial question so that it becomes more 'understandable'.
- He takes up the other's words: the one or two words he has understood
, ('werk wat'?, 'wat doen'?), or the whole utterance. This repetition of the other's words is what we call a reprise, taking up the other's word(s). Here, these reprises are accompanied by a rising interrogative intonation, a sufficient indication that he is requesting his interlocutor to intervene, repeat or explain. This is also an efficient way of reconstructing, piece by piece, the question he has not understood by guiding his interlocutor through those items which are a problem for him.
- He also tries to be more explicit and gives a metalinguistic indication that he has not understood.

As one can see in this extract, the minority interactant has many ways of indicating problems with understanding. Some of them are direct and consciously produced to signal problems with understanding. They may be more or less explicit. They appear on the right side of the chart we present further on. Others, placed at the opposite end of the chart, are indirect and are what we call 'symptoms'. This term refers to behaviours which are not necessarily meant to signal non-understanding but which are interpreted as revealing non-understanding by the majority locutor who responds to them.

Problems of analysis

Most problems of understanding with beginners are conveyed implicitly and it is generally very difficult to decide whether this is done voluntarily or not. In such cases, the majority locutors' interpretation and their response are decisive. The initiation of a negotiation sequence by the majority speaker and the outcome of the encounter will depend on such an interpretation.

Of course, it is quite possible for this implicit behaviour to be wrongly interpreted. Misunderstandings of this type develop even in intra-ethnic exchanges. For instance, reprise of the other's word or minimal feedback such as English *hm*, French *hein*, may indicate astonishment but be interpreted as non-understanding. In inter-ethnic encounters though, the probability is higher of non-under-standing and therefore of an interpretation of non-understanding by the majority speaker.

Besides the conversational sources of evidence of (non)under-standing, the analyst's knowledge of the minority interactant's life and of the type of encounter they were proposed to go through was useful, although not always with total certainty, in judging the minority interactant's degree of understanding (for a more detailed presentation of understanding evidence, see Chapter 2).

Some feedback sessions have also thrown light on the minority interactants' behaviour. These very frequently show that they were aware that they could not understand but preferred not to give a clear indication of their problem.

What eventually matters in the analysis we make of this behav-iour is what develops from it, interactionally speaking. Does the thread of the exchange run on the basis of vague understanding or complete misunderstanding? Does such a behaviour trigger negoti-ation sequences through which both partners will strive to establish common meaning and reach the objectives they aim at? And finally which of the varied procedures are the most effective to reach such aims, considering the competitive issue of imposition and face?

We will now present the different behaviours adopted by the minority interactants which indicate problems with understanding. They run from the most implicit to the most explicit on a contin-uum that is not always as linear as it might seem.

A continuum of procedures

Possible procedures run in a continuum from the most indirect and unspecific (on the left side) to the most direct and specific (on the right side). The placing of the different signalling procedures on the chart is the result of our having, in the analysis, adopted both part-ners' perspectives. We have examined each of the procedures as being a combination of intentionality and of perlocutionary effect – how the utterance is interpreted by the other. And, above all, we have considered how effective they could be in furthering the joint understanding work.

The chart concentrates on the main procedures we have analysed as showing more or less commitment (that is to say being more or less direct, explicit) and focusing (that is to say being more or less specific) from the minority interactant. It shows the minority inter-actant's choice from not indicating to clearly signalling problems of understanding, a choice which is the basis of variable interpretation and clarification work from the majority interactant.

implicit/indirect unspecific	intermediate procedures	explicit/direct specific

◄───►

SYMPTOMS					SIGNALS
	lack of	minimal	hypothesis	reprise of	metalinguistic
over-riding	uptake	feedback	forming	non-understood part	queries & comments

Implicit, indirect procedures

The implicit and indirect type of behaviour, which generally needs more interpretative work from the majority participant, covers a number of varied procedures such as: over-riding, silence, lack of uptake, topic or code-switching, minimal feedback. None of these procedures necessarily indicate problems with understanding but they lead the majority locutor to suspect there are some.

Over-riding is a general term we have borrowed to describe a par-ticular interactional phenomenon in which the minority speakers apparently ignore the others' utterance and carry on with the topic they have already introduced or stay with the schema which they have brought to the encounter. For example, Madan, trying to have the college caretaker open the door for him because he has forgot-ten his purse inside, repeatedly uses the same argument that he needs his money without considering his interlocutor's answers. We call this behaviour 'over-riding' because the locutor appears to ride over his partner's utterances. The minority interactant is thus perceived as flouting the maxim of relevance (Grice 1975, Wilson & Sperber 1981, Leech 1983):

```
        M:  can you go with me please ↑
(10)    T:  well i am waiting for a phone call from a friend who is in the hospital
        M:  yeah
        T:  and + this is most important because i have to pick him up from
            hospital
        M:  yeah
        T:  can you wait five minutes ↑
(15)    M:  + no
        T:  you cant
        M:  excuse me you know no money in the my pocket right ↑
```

Madan gives no indication that he understands what the care-taker means by waiting 'five minutes' but carries on with his own argument. Usually such over-riding is treated as a problem of understanding but not always. In some cases indeed, there remains a doubt whether 'over-riding' occurs because of lack of understanding or because the topic treated appears too important to be side-tracked from or a combination of both. This may be the case with Madan in this example.

Lack of uptake

Silence, non-verbal behaviour, such as shoulder-shrugging, head-shaking, paralinguistic behaviour like laughter, coughing, mumbling or any 'filler': *er, hm, you see* . . . are characterised as **lack-of-uptake.** Verbal lack-of-uptake rarely comes in isolation but is associated with one or several non-verbal or para-linguistic procedures. The combination of verbal and non-verbal features confirms the interpretation of non-understanding. For example, laughter may very well be, when associated with a cohesive answer, a procedure that signals satisfaction, agreement or comprehension. But when it is produced at the end of a series of minimal feedback procedures, it sounds quite different and appears as a symptom of malaise.

Minimal feedback

Another type of indirect procedure is **minimal feedback**. Minimal feedback alone: *yes, hm, yeah* or equivalents, may be very ambiguous. Long sequences in which the minority interactant simply responds with minimal positive feedback over many turns have been called 'linear phases' by Vion (1986) because, by behaving this way, the minority interactant decides not to take any step towards indicating his problems or even the fact of having problems at all and leaves the responsibility and control of the whole sequence with the majority locutor. These 'linear phases' are in contrast to what Vion has termed 'parallel phases' where both partners fully collaborate in the joint production of meaning. In the 'linear phases', the minority interactants adopt a 'wait and see' strategy (Voionmaa 1984) which gives them time to gradually form hypotheses on the majority locutor's intentions.

Adopting linear phases is also a way of keeping the interaction going. But the risk is double: first, such lack of explicitness cannot last for very long especially in the course of goal-driven encounters. Secondly, mutual understanding depends on the inferences and guesses the majority partners have to make and, having to fumble their way through the minority interactant's very vague responses, they will have to interpret them, at the risk of either misunderstanding or continuously checking and interrupting (see below: Face and management of understanding 4.3). Eventually, the majority speaker might become tired (see Chapter 6) or give up on the interaction.

The following example illustrates very well such a situation. Paula, a Chilean woman, has a job interview seven months after her arrival in France. By that time, her repertoire in French is still very limited and she has a lot of understanding problems. Minimal feedback is one of the most frequent procedures she uses to keep the conversation going. The result is a number of linear phases in which the majority locutor is often in doubt about whether Paula understands her questions. As a consequence, she has to check explicitly in order to keep the exchange in control and make new starts each time her doubts are realised (for a detailed analysis of the majority locutor's behaviour see Chapters 6 and 7). Paula has just explained that she has been a dental secretary in Chile:

(1) X: d'accord et vous avez déjà fait des études ↑ pour ça pour être
          secrétaire médicale ↑ vous avez suivi
          *okay and you have had some training ↑ for that to be a medical
          secretary ↑ you have had*

     P: oui
          yes

     X: des études spéciales ↑
          a special training ↑

     P: hm + oui:
          hm + yes

(5) X: vous avez compris ce que je vous ai demandé ↑ est ce que vous
          avez compris la question (rires) non ↑
          *you have understood what i have asked you ↑ have you understood the
          question (laughs) no ↑*

     P: non non non
          no no no

     X: non bon + je vais maintenant voir avec vous au chili
          no well + i will now check with you in chile

     P: hm
          hm

X: ce que vous avez fait comme / à l école comme étude
      what you have done as/ at school what studies have you gone through
(10) P: hm
      hm
X: hein ↑ vous avez compris là ↑ vous / je vais on va voir ensemble/
      je vais vous poser quelques questions
      *eh there you have understood ↑ you / i will we will see together / i will
      ask you a few questions*
P: hm
      hm
X: pour essayer de voir quelle a / quelles ont été + les études
      to try and see what kind of + studies
P: hm
      hm
(15) X: que vous avez suivi au chili ++ vous avez été à l école ↑
      you have had in chile ++ you went to school ↑
P: oui
      yes
X: combien de temps ↑
      for how long ↑
P: eh
      eh
X: jusqu 'à + vous avez fait quelle classe / la dernière classe
      till + what class did you go: the last class
(20) P: classe:de
      class of
X: à l école
      at school
P: eh liceo
      eh secondary school
X: hm hm
      hm hm
P: eh cuarto eh quatre ano liceo
      eh fourth . . . eh fourth year of secondary school

When the majority partner is less cautious and 'methodical' than in this example, there is a risk of non- or mis-understanding as happens in the visit Zahra, a Moroccan woman, pays to a French doctor. The doctor is not aware of Zahra's lack of understanding as she gives minimal feedback, and Zahra herself may not be aware. The researcher who knows that Zahra's father is dead is the only one who can tell she has not understood the question. In the following, Zahra however starts forming hypotheses (*frères?*, *moi?*) which

helps her set up minimal understanding and keeps the majority
locutor alerted (see further 4.2 on the ambiguity of such a behaviour):

(1) I: bon + et vos parents + étaient / étaient en bonne santé ↑ + ils
sont toujours vivants ↑
good + and your parents had a good health ↑ + are they still alive ↑

Z: ++

I: vos parents ↑ + papa et maman ↑
your parents ↑ +daddy and mummy ↑

Z: oui
yes

(5) I: ils vivent toujours ↑   *SLA:*
they are still alive ↑

Z: oui
yes

I: vous avez des frères et soeurs ↑ + oui bien sûr + des frères ↑ +
you have brothers and sisters ↑ + yes of course +brothers ↑ +

Z: euh les frères ↑
eh the brothers ↑   *miscommunication —*

I: frères oui
brothers yes   *SLA: (pragmatic or syntactic*

(10) Z   moi ↑   *transfer — line 15-16)*
me ↑

I   oui
yes

Z: non + [ni des s / y en a euh une euh ma soeur
no + neither s / there is eh one my sister

I: une soeur   *interactions are more than looking*
one sister   *at input.....*

Z   oui
yes

(15) I: elle est en france ou au maroc ↑
she is in france or in morocco ↑

Z: oui
yes

I: elle est en france ↑
she is in france ↑

Z: non le maroc
no in morocco

I: elle est au maroc + vous êtes seule vous n'avez pas de famille
en france ↑
*she is in morocco + you are alone in france you have no family in
france ↑*

(20) Z: euh +c'est pas beaucoup à la france
            eh it is not much at france
      I: pas beaucoup
            not much
      Z: y en a les familles +
            there is some the families
      I: les familles de votre mari
            your husband's families
(24) Z: oui
            yes

Intermediate procedures

Hypothesis-forming

On the implicit-explicit cline, between the avoidance of signalling and explicit metalinguistic comments, there is an intermediate behaviour which is mainly based on hypothesis-forming.

Hypothesis-forming is the basic interpretive process of all understanding. In interactions where understanding is problematic, the minority interactants may choose a high inferencing approach and use their perception, knowledge, experience and linguistic resources to try to solve the problem by themselves instead of requesting help from their interlocutor.

The attempts at hypothesis-forming and the forms it takes at the surface may put the majority locutor on the track of non- or misunderstanding. This is why they can be considered as symptoms of non- or misunderstanding. These procedures are of three types:

- tentative responses to the speaker's question, where the minority-speaker responds to the meaning. There is no uptake of the formal features of the preceding utterances.
- reprise as comprehension check,
- reformulation as hypothesis-checking.

These two last procedures are interactionally more visible and may be more or less explicit and specific.

TENTATIVE RESPONSES

By resorting to this procedure, the minority interactants do not indicate their understanding problem at all. Neither do they keep a passive wait and see attitude. They make a move towards elaboration of understanding by risking a response on the basis of their perception of the situation and the expectations they may have developed from it. If the utterance is cohesive and appropriate, the majority locutors cannot suspect that there has been any problem, the exchange has not been disrupted and the minority interactants' face has not been endangered. Only incohesive utterances are interpreted as symptoms of non- or misunderstanding. In this way, a tentative response may implicitly convey misunderstanding, that is to say an illusion of understanding. The following example shows such misunderstanding very clearly: Berta's answer to the Job Centre clerk who is interviewing her (see Chapter 5: case studies, for the context) is not related to the question at all. The interviewer can therefore deduce that Berta formed a wrong hypothesis:

(1) X: en quatre-vingt un en quatre-vingt-deux vous aviez déjà
         travaillé dans la cuisine ↑
         in eighty-one in eighty-two you already had a cooking job ↑
(2) B: oui ce soir
         yes tonight

REPRISE AS COMPREHENSION-CHECK

Hypothesis-forming may take the form of a reprise of the other's word. 'Reprise' implies a much more expanded and dynamic notion than repetition. It covers a whole range of procedures which consists of taking up the other's words. It runs from simple lexical repetition (with prosodic modifications for instance) to the reformulation of the interlocutor's utterance. Reprise functions minimally as an interactional device by which some consensus can be established on the surface of the discourse. But it may also be used more specifically.

A reprise may identify the only word which has been understood. It thus indirectly signals that the rest of the utterance has not been understood, e.g. the reprise of 'frère' by Zahra in the example above ('euh les frères?' *eh the brothers?*). This, at least, indicates partial understanding of one isolated unit (*frère*). With more advanced speakers, a reprise may also point at the only word that has not been understood. In both cases, the reprise of an isolated form associated with interrogative prosody is a clear comprehension check. Examples of such comprehension checks often follow after minimum feedback when the minority interactant begins participating more actively (see examples from Paula and Zahra above). Reprise of the understood item shows willingness to participate and gives some clue as to what has been understood. The majority locutor may interpret it as a request for help and then develop a clarification sequence. S/he may also only give a short confirmation (see the example of *frère* above) as if there was no other problem. No wonder there often remains some uncertainty about the minority interactant's general understanding.

REFORMULATION AS COMPREHENSION-CHECK

Reformulation is a more sophisticated procedure than reprise. It is a re-elaboration of the other's discourse (or part of it). It is, for the minority participants, a manner of submitting hypothetical meaning to their partner's agreement. When understanding is difficult for all sorts of reasons (complex and abstract topic, complex structures, unfamiliar lexicon, etc, see Chapter 3 on causes), the minority interactants may thus check how far they have understood and take part in the joint clarification work. The following is a good example of the efficiency of this behaviour with an advanced speaker. Berta is in her third year's stay in France and she enquires about taking driving lessons. Both speakers are very active in reformulating each other's utterance to make sure the right information has been conveyed:

(1) X: inutile de prévenir vous venez quand ça vous plaît
          no need to check in advance you come when you like
     B: ah d'accord n'est pas problème *por el*horaire
          ah okay (it) is not problem for the time
     X: comment ↑
          pardon ↑
     B: n'est pas problème
          (it) is not problem
(5) X: non y a pas de problème pour les horaires
          no there is no problem for the time-schedule

Some minority interactants are skilful in associating this hypothesis-forming procedure with minimal feedback and a wait-and-see strategy to prevent any real breakdown in communication and help progress the interaction. For example, Andrea, an Italian, who lived in London, uses this combination of features in the encounter he has with a building society clerk to inquire about how he could get a loan. He first gives minimal feedback over several turns and then offers a hypothesis relating to the clerk's discourse:

(1)   C: we cant/ we cant say how our funds will be available because
              sometimes you have to be saving with us for two years + if you
              approach us at the wrong sort of time
       A: ya
       C: at the moment youd have to be saving with us for six months
              but/ + you know I cant say what its going to be like in six
              months time it might have changed again
       A: yes
(5)   A: and/ and depend of how much money I need for the borrow ↑
       C: + ya well no it/ really it depends + on how long you have been
              saving and how much funds we have available whether we are
              helping people that have been/ + that havent got accounts with
              us so whether its/ you have to be saving with us for a year or +
              two years
       A: yes
       A: hm
       C: two years is the worst it can [be]
(10)   A: [ya]
       A: + is the minimum ↑
       C: (+++) two years is the worst / there is not any / +++you know it
              can be anything from / up to two years +++ [so youd] get a lot
              of help from us then I can give you some leaflets about
              mortgages as well + if you are interested if you are a home
              buyer (xx) and that just gives you an idea of the repayments

Although still sometimes ambiguous, these procedures based on
hypothesis-forming are helpful for both participants. They give
more direct indications on the minority interactant's problems with
understanding and contribute to setting the clarification work in
motion. The minority participants, show a high level of inferencing,
an active engagement in negotiating understanding and, of course,
a certain level of productive competence.

The final set of procedures we will discuss are the most explicit
and they do not usually indicate this high level of inferencing
although they may be associated with these active forms of
behaviour.

Direct and explicit procedures

Some procedures used by the minority interactant help the majority
speaker to form a better idea of what the understanding problem is.
They are more direct, more explicit and sometimes more specific.
Through them the minority interactants either request clarification
from the other, or comment on their problems

The main procedures to request clarification are:

– reprise of beginning of non-understood utterance
– minimal query
– metalinguistic questions and comments which may be general or very specific

Reprise of part of non-understood utterance

Besides being an ambiguous signal of (non-)understanding (see 4.2 above), reprise can be an active means of confronting non-understanding. It consists of repeating the beginning of an utterance which has not been understood. It may also be used to repeat that part of the utterance beyond which the speaker has failed to understand. It is interpreted by the majority speaker as conveying general non-understanding and requesting repetition or clarification. It tends to lead to long negotiation sequences.

Marcello, who was very successful in acquiring German, is one of those minority interactants, like Ergün, who has a preference for reprise as a systematic procedure to cope with non-understanding, even global non-understanding. Very early in his interactions, he abandons lack of uptake and inappropriate minimal feedback to choose an organised strategy of reprise whose main function is the deconstruction/reconstruction of his interlocutor's utterances as in the following excerpt from a Job Centre interview:

(1)   X: wieviel ham sie in italien verdient ↑
             how much did you earn in italy ↑
       M: wieviel ↑
             how much ↑
       X: in italien wieviel ham sie verdient ↑
             in italy how much did you earn ↑
       M: hams ↑
             did you ↑
(5)   X: wieviel haben sie in italien verdient ↑
             how much did you earn in italy ↑
       M: verdient ↑
             earn ↑
       X: wie hoch war der lohn ↑
             how much was the pay ↑
(8)   M: wie hoch *e alto*
             how much is high

By successively taking up words or unidentified fragments of his interlocutor's question, Marcello plays a very active part in the construction of meaning. He has an effective way of guiding his interlocutor, through a progressive scanning of the elements of the utterance he has not understood, towards a discovery of the source of trouble (and the choice of a procedure of reformulation) which is far more efficient than the simple repetitions he resorted to at first.

His active participation in the exchange is sometimes based on the multifunctional reprise of a limited item. In the following sequence in which he talks about his past job in an ice-cream parlour, he uses the same unit *keine* to show agreement (7), to request, in a standard way in German, repetition of non-understood part (9), to take his conversation turn and give feedback and also elaborate a new utterance of his own (11). By doing this, Marcello takes his full part in the construction of the exchange:

(1)   M: und der chef dann mir gesagt äh äh für diese monat ↑
             and the boss then said to me er er for this month ↑
        N: hm
             hm
        M: äh mach du pause
             er you make a break
        N: hm [also sie ham]
             hm [well you have]
(5)   M: [und däs is/]
             [and that is]
        N: im moment gar [keine arbeit]
             at the moment [no job]
        M: [ja keine] arbeit
             [yes no] job
        N: und auch kein einkommen dann ↑
             and no income then ↑
        M: und keine ↑
             and no ↑
10   N: kein einkommen ↓ kein verdienst ↓
             no income no ↓ earnings ↓
        M: ja keine < und ( ) auch keine geld >
             yes no < and also no money >
        N: hm
             hm

Later, when the problems are more clearly identified, Marcello associates this systematic technique with metalinguistic questions, 'was ist x?' (*what is x?*) and with more native-like, less obtrusive expressions like 'bitte' (*excuse me*). And so he finds a good balance between indicating problems with understanding and jointly conducting the interaction with his partner.

Metalinguistic queries and comments

Indications of non-understanding may become even more direct and explicit with metalinguistic queries and comments on the source of trouble.

A minimal query is unspecific: *sorry?*, *what?* It may also be a simple general comment: like Ergün's (above) *I don't understand* or Gilda's *no comprendo* (see below 4.4 for comments in the first language in relation with face work).

These procedures usually point to a general misunderstanding while a more specific metalinguistic question specifies the precise object (linguistic unit or block of units) that is not understood. When reprise relates to a non-understood unit it becomes more specific and it tends to be more explicit with the use of metalinguistic forms. For example, the way Ergün rapidly makes explicit what it is he has not understood in the majority partner's utterrance:

(1)   X: is dat ver ↑
              is that far away ↑
(2)   E: ver ↑ wat is dat ↑
              far away ↑ *what is that* ↑

Considering the specificity of the question, the clarification sequences which follow are very short and hardly disturb the interaction.

In contrast to the option of not indicating problems and relying on implicit procedures (lack of uptake or simple feedback) in order to maintain apparent understanding, the use of metalinguistic indicators always results in better understanding, because it clearly, precisely and cooperatively triggers working sequences.

These procedures rarely come in isolation. They can appear as the final phase of a series of context-sensitive efforts to work on the understanding problem. The minority workers may start indirectly with minimal feedback to progress through a difficult interaction. Then they may turn to tentative responses or reprises (cf. Andrea, Ergün & Marcello above). And finally, the metalinguistic comment often comes at last as the best procedure to face up to the problem explicitly. They end up going 'on record', allowing the majority locutor to gain time and focus with the minority speaker on a solution to the problem.

An adapted use of the different procedures

As we have seen in the different extracts, combining different procedures is a frequent strategy for both sides. But a wide repertoire of direct procedures is not in itself an indication of effective means of managing non-understanding. It is the adapted use of these procedures which is significant. By adapted, we mean the most flexible, adaptive and effective use of the signalling procedures in the emerging context. Such use is effective because, first, it leads to a better management of understanding and, secondly, because, through the monitoring activity it pre-supposes, it helps the minority interactants to develop their ability to understand. Through an adapted use of direct and indirect means the best 'understanders' find a balance between continuing the interaction and frequently halting it for clarification. With the development of understanding, comprehension checks and clarification requests become more integrated into the discourse, more native-like. The following example is taken from Ergün's last encounters during the project. It shows how well the minority interactant can integrate the understanding indicators into the exchange:

(1)   X: 't is/u krijgt 't minimumloon
           it is / you get the minimum salary
      E: welk ↑
           which ↑
      X: u krijgt 't minimumloon
           you get the minimum salary
      E: minimumloon
           minimum salary
(5)   X: minimum
           minimum
      E: ja loon weet ik
           yes salary I know
      X: loon + en 't is veertienhonderd gulden
           salary + and it is fourteen hundred guilders

Presumably, this adapted use of procedures is a sign of increased confidence in inter-cultural communication and can act as a face-saving frame for the whole interaction. This face-saving activity is very important for minority interactants and it takes a lot of their energy. We will turn now to this activity.

4.4 FACE AND MANAGEMENT OF UNDERSTANDING

As we have said, in intercultural exchanges and especially in institutional settings in which most majority-minority interactions take place, the power position of the gate-keeper makes the unequal relationship doubly unequal. In this situation, what does intercultural communication mean for the minority interactant? It often means verifying, confirming and reinforcing one's inferior position. And this mostly works through difficulties of understanding.

Because of the difference in linguistic competence, problems with understanding inevitably happen and regularly endanger the face of the less powerful speaker. The face loss these problems cause and the consequences it brings with it, combined with unresolved misunderstandings may well damage the minority worker's prospect of getting access to scarce resources. Small interactional problems may have large material outcomes.

Non-understanding, face-loss and consequences

Not only is non-understanding an obstacle to achieving goals, it is also a source of intense frustration for the minority interactant.

For example, Berta who goes to a specialised shop to have shelves cut to measure for her is thoroughly discomforted by the wood-trader's technical question which she does not understand. Unwilling to publicly confess her non-understanding, she tries to save her face and not keep silent, and replies with a general declaration that she wants to have the shelves fixed on the wall. Obviously, her answer is not cohesive and embarrassment is perceptible in her pauses and hesitations. But after this embarrassing experience, she fears being exposed to another of those shameful non-understandings. So she does not feel like asking her question or any other question again. Hearing her awkward hesitations and silence, and pressed by the presence of other customers, the shop-keeper does not make any move towards repair nor does he give her room to return to her topic, as we see some majority speakers do (cf. Chapter 6), and he finally abandons her to take care of other customers:

(1) N: ouais on peut vous découper les planches avec / vous venez
         avec les mesures on vous découpe euh les planches
         yes we can cut up the boards for you with/ you come with the
         measurements we cut up the boards for you

     B   bon c'estde + un mètre
         well it is + one meter

     N: ++ un mètre sur quelle euh ↑
         one meter by what eh ↑

     B: ah *y yo no se *+ je crois qué c'est + vingt comme çà
         ah i i do not know + i think it is + twenty about

(5) N: ouais on peut vous les découper + que les planches simplement
         yes we can cut them up for you + only the boards

     B: ouais y combien coûte le ↑
         yes and how much the ↑

     N: ça dépend en quoi vous le prenez en soit du contreplaqué ou du
         latté
         it depends what type of wood you want either plywood or slat

     B: no c'est + por mettre :le / sur :le mur
         no it is + to put the / on the wall

     N: sur ↑
         on ↑

(10) B: sur le mur
         on the wall

     N: avec des équerres ↑
         with braces ↑

     B: ouais

     N: oui ↑

     B: ouais ↑ + *y* quoi ↑ / y +++
         yes ↑ + and what ↑

(15) N: excusez-moi
         excuse me

Berta then leaves the shop with a sense of failure that she
expresses once she is in the street: *'no me fué muy bien'* (*it did not go
very well*), but does not analyse. Primarily, she knows that she did
not get the information she was looking for (she wanted to know
the price it would cost her) and was conscious of having been
passed over by her interlocutor. This is never a very pleasant
experience.

In the long run, such an experience and the feeling that accompa-
nies it may cause the minority worker to retreat permanently and
avoid any contact with the majority ethnic group. A happier example than this one, in a similar situation of information gathering, is
Berta's visit to the driving school. The main reason why it ends up

happily is that both participants use a succession of explicit preventative procedures (reformulations of their own and of the other's
utterances) (see Chapter 6 for the majority locutor's preventative
strategies) all the way through the exchange so that no understanding problem occurs and Berta who, by contributing fully to the
exchange, has offered a positive constructive public image leaves
the shop satisfied:

(1)   B: *y* c'est intensivo ↑
              and it is intensive ↑
       N: non non pas spécialement
              no no not especially
       B: non ↑
              no ↑
       N: quand vous voulez non
              whenever you want no
(5)   B: ah d'accord *y* les jours *y* de/ c'est
              ah ok and the days and / it is
       N: lundi mercredi vendredi vous venez quand vous voulez
              monday wednesday friday you come when you want
       B: ah d'accord alors
              ah ok then
       N: voilà les jours pour les/ vous venez faire ce test quand vous
              voulez aussi
              here are the days for the/ you come for this test when you want too
       B: d'accord
              okay
(10)   N: inutile de prévenir vous venez quand ça vous plaît
              no need to give notice you come when it pleases you
       B: ah d'accord n'est pas problème *por el* horaire
              ah okay is no problem for the time schedule
       N: comment ↑
              sorry ↑
       B: n'est pas problème
              is no problem
       N: non ya pas de problème pour les horaires
              no there is no problem for the time schedule
15   B: bon voilà merci + au-revoir
              well that's it thank you + good bye
       N: au-revoir
              good bye

Certainly here, the context and the complexity of the task are different from the first encounter, but it is the attitude and discourse
behaviour which often makes the difference. The participants' soli-

darity, based on common points of view and aims has concretized and been reinforced by positive understanding procedures. Non-understanding and loss of face for the minority interactant have been prevented. A positive dynamic may develop for future inter-actions.

Metamessage

As is shown through the previous examples, much of the behaviour the minority speaker adopts depends on the majority speaker's own behaviour. The interactions are, we reiterate, jointly con-structed. Through their behaviours and reactions towards (non-) understanding, voluntarily or not the partners convey their view on the relationship they are willing or refusing to have. Whatever one says, one always says more than just what is said, which Bateson (1972, 1979) reformulated through his distinction between the mes-sage and the metamessage.

[handwritten margin note: not a thing we can do about this as teachers]

An example of this double level of communication is the power discourse of some of the majority group. A negative metamessage is sometimes all too obvious to the minority workers, and strongly resisted. But, most of the time they lack the communicative means to fight back. The sense of anger and frustration they experience is particularly evident in cases of emergency. For example, Berta reported her interaction with the surgeon who had operated on her daughter after an accident at school. When she ran to the hospital, it was late and past visiting time. The surgeon took a very bureau-cratic line. The only message he had for her was to tell her that she should not be in the hospital so late and that she should leave at once. He never for a moment moved out of his administrative 'frame' to tell her something about her daughter's health. The metamessage that she interpreted was that he refused to consider Berta as a legitimate speaker and above all as the mother of the injured child he had just taken care of. Berta, who received the dou-ble-message ordering her both to leave the premises and refusing to sanction her as a speaker experienced a double frustration. Later on, she told the story with renewed emotion and anger as she re-lived her frustration and embarrassment:

(1)   B: ouh lala + *y* je le dis c'est pas c'est pas ça pasqué vous /jé /jé / vous / voulez que vous m'expliquiez la situation + non non non il me dit+ *por otro* jour

    ouhlala + and i told him it is not it is not that because you i i w/ want
    that you explain the situation to me + no no he told me + another day

N: oh lala

B: il me dit que je sorte tout de suite de/*del hospital* pasque bon
    je crois que c'est l'heure pasque + c'est la / la neuf + vingt ↑ /
    vingt et un ↑ vingt et un heure je crois que c'est possible *por* ça
    he told me that i leave at once from/ from the hospital because well i
    think it is the time because + it is nine + twenty ↑ twenty-one ↑ twenty-
    one i think it is possible that's why

N: oui mais c'est quand même pas normal
    yes but it is not really normally like that

(5) B: oui c'est ça *lo que* jé dis pasque je suis très fâchée avec lui je le
    dis bon je n'/ *yo / yo* voudrais que vous m'expliquiez qu'est-
    ce qui passe non non non il me dit
    yes it is what i said because i was very angry with him i told him well i
    don't/ i
    i wish you would explain to me what happens no no no he told me

N: qu'est-ce que tu as fait alors ↑
    what did you do then ↑

B: bon je suis fâchée avel/ avec lui *y* je le dis beaucoup de choses
    avec m/ + :et + je m'énervé beaucoup
    well i got angry with h/ with him and i told him a lot of things with m/
    and + i got very worked up

N: ah oui + je comprends ça oui + et tu es partie ↑
    yes + i understand it yes + and did you go ↑

B: alors oui il est parti pasque je n'avais le / avais le + que je suis
    fâchée je ou / je oubliais les mots en français *por por* dire + je
    ne / je ne trouvais + rien de mots *por* dire les choses que/ que
    je le dis à lui *por* pasque n'est pas bon la manière qu'il me dit
    au revoir
    then yes he went because i did not have the / have the + that i was
    angry i for / i forget the words in french to to say + i did not / did not
    find + nothing of words to say the things which / which i tell him
    because it is not good the manner he said goodbye to me

Berta's main frustration did not come from linguistic non-understanding. It had its source in the meta-message the surgeon sent her
on his conception of their relationship and in the total lack of care
for her face. As we may expect, the consequences of such an experience are that Berta is unable to find her words in French to protest
and argue (9) (je oubliais le mots en français *por* dire + je ne trou-
vais rien des mots *por* dire les choses *i forgot the words in French to
say + i could not find no words to say the things*).

This everyday discrimination, real or perceived, is a very frequent type of experience for minority workers. Indirect messages
of discrimination surround them and they progressively learn to
interpret verbal and also non-verbal signals produced by the
majority group as discriminatory whether there are overt racist
intentions or not, to the extent that they may tend to generalise
their interpretation and feel discriminated sometimes more than
they are. Paula reports on one of the visits to a hi-fi shop during
one of her project outings and right from the beginning she men-
tions her malaise and feeling of being discriminated, explaining
how her interpretation was based on the shop-keeper's facial
expression and his type of question (on this question of discrimination see also Chapter 8).

-je suis très nerveuse pasque madame je l'ai vu la face (mimique)
i feel very nervous because, madame, i saw his face (. . .)
et il me dit ah madame quelle nationalité?
and he says to me eh madam what nationality?

Surely these are not ideal conditions to construct good understanding. It is not therefore surprising to find with a lot of minority
workers a preference for avoidance as a general strategy: avoidance
of contact, avoidance of interaction, avoidance of signalling and
misunderstandings based on a negative expectation of the majority
speakers' discourse.

Accommodation, over-accommodation

In contrast to the doctor's attitude with Berta, some majority speakers, researcher-interviewers on the project and some of the
professionals in the simulated gatekeeping interviews, adopt
encouraging behaviour and keep protecting their interlocutor's
face. The following sequence in which Paula explains the possibility
offered to her or her husband of entering a French course is a typical example of a majority speaker (who is a researcher)
exaggerating approval and sympathy to emphasize what Scollon
and Scollon present as 'solidarity politeness' (1983):

(1)   H: oui mais il veut aller lui ou il veut que toi tu ailles ↑
             yes but he wants to go himself or he wants you to go ↑
       P: eh + si eh + si travailler ↑ travailler ↑ + comment *se dice* ↑
             eh + si eh + si work ↑ *work* ↑ *how do you say*

H: vas-y vas-y vas-y
go ahead go ahead go ahead

P: *ante ante ante de* eh après *de diciembre*
before before before eh after december

(5) H: hm
hm

P: *diciembre* ↑
december ↑

H: hm d'accord
hm okay

P: eh il *me da* + la possibilité à moi
eh he gives me the possibility to me

H: d'accord très bien
okay very well

(10) P: *para el* stage
for the course

H: oui oui je te comprends très bien
yes yes i understand you very well

P: sinon si n'est pas de travailler de travailler
if not if not work not work

H: hm
hm

P: eh *yo no* estage il *si*
eh i not the course he yes

(15) H: d'accord oui oui j'ai compris ce que tu voulais dire
okay i have understood what you wanted to say

[handwritten margin note: 1) No interaction negotiation — but 2) Encourages production —]

Rampton (1990) has signalled the risk of such an 'over-accommodating' attitude. It will not necessarily encourage initiative and progress and might, in the long run, beside the risk of being patronising and reinforcing power difference, be demotivating. A very typical feature of this over-accommodating discourse is when the majority speaker interrupts the minority's laborious utterance with a conclusive *I see what you mean*. At least, what can be said is that, when it is used with a general attention to the minority interactant's understanding, it conveys a positive and encouraging message which may be temporarily helpful if the minority speaker is under stress.

With this type of discourse, no initiative concerning understanding and clarification work is taken by the majority speaker. As Dausendschön-Gay and Krafft (1989) have noted, there seems to be, in some types of interaction, a contradiction between face-work and clarification or more generally 'pedagogical work'. A balance between these two types of work, a strategic recourse to management of face and indications of problems (cf. 4) seems however necessary if one wants to develop one's competence in understanding.

Resistance

Clarke et al.(1976) use the term 'resistance' to describe a type of communication strategy 'designed to overcome potentially threatening social and linguistic differences'. We use 'resistance' to designate procedures which, cumulatively, express opposition to the interactional relationships they have to endure (see also Rampton 1987).

To resist face threats, the minority interactants can choose between two types of interactional practice: maintain a low status or claim equality or, reworded into Brown and Levinson's terms, take care of their negative face or of their positive face (Brown and Levinson 1987, Scollon & Scollon 1983). The positive face of individuals corresponds to their will to be considered as legitimate, contributing members of the community. Their negative face is centred on their wish to preserve their own territory, not to be impeded on. The minority interactants protect their negative face when they do not want to be imposed upon by the others or expose themselves to their judgement. They then resist collaboration and maintain their low status. Through an exaggerated insistence on their problems as minority interactants, they insist on their different identity as foreigners.

Resistance through negative face

On the lowest scale of the resistance continuum is pure and simple avoidance. Paula refuses to go on outings (project or personal outings) because of the stress it puts on her in what is a difficult moment in her life. She would rather let her husband meet the administrative and school authorities.

On the next scale up is maintaining low status by insistently signalling non-understanding in a blocking manner. An example of this is Gilda's way of entering into interaction with one of the French researchers. Admittedly start ups are always delicate and understanding uneasy, above all when it is a start from zero with an unknown speaker. But it is not the case here. Gilda already knows the researcher she is talking with and she is used to making conversation with her. But, by the time this interaction took place she seemed to have had enough of those arranged encounters. Through the accumulation of non-understanding markers (and the blocking up of the interaction), Gilda conveys a metamessage of resistance to involvement. It then takes all the native's energy to get the conversation going. Majority speakers who are not researchers may very well show less patience and insistence and break off the conversation. Let us have a look at the whole introduction sequence:

(1)   N: alors on a un peu parlé dans la rue mais ça fait longtemps qu'on
              s'est pas vu hein ça fait combien de temps ↑
              *we have talked a little in the street then but it is a long time that we
              have not met isn't it how long is it ↑*
       G: *qué es lo qué* vous me dites ↑
              what is it you tell me ↑
       N: ça fait combien de temps qu'on s'est pas vu? tu te rappelles
              quand je suis venue chez toi ↑
              *how long is it since we have met ↑ do you remember when i came to
              your place ↑*
(4)   G: *no la comprendo*
              i do not understand you

Answering and signalling problems with understanding in her L1 is an interactional practice Gilda goes on using more and longer than the other informants. When she says 'no la comprendo' (*i do not understand you* in Spanish), the tone of her voice is harsh and irrevocable. The tension is extreme between the two interlocutors. The majority locutor, held in check, has to try hard to get Gilda interested in recalling their last meeting in time. She adds more context to prompt Gilda's memory:

(5)   N: tu tu te souviens j'étais avec nicole
              do you remember when i was with nicole
       G: hm hm
              hm hm
       N: et je suis venue chez toi
              and i came to your place
       G: hm hm
              hm hm
       N: oui ↑
              yes ↑

(10) G: hm hm
          hm hm
      N: hm
          hm
      G: *cuanto tiempo hace que me vio* ↑
          how much time it is since you saw me ↑

Does Gilda then guess the meaning of the initial question or is the fact of mentioning that they met at Gilda's place a sufficient indication? Nonetheless, she maintains the use of L1 in her comprehension check. She thus keeps on her territory before accepting to introduce a few items in French and discuss the topic any further.

The majority locutor then asks another routine question about the informant's life since then (qu'est-ce qui s'est passé depuis? [*what's happened since?*]). Gilda's tries to establish a specific referent for this question and the response leads to a misunderstanding based on the word *moment* heard *maman* [momã/mãmã]. It is only then, after the native has reformulated her question that Gilda starts collaborating

      N: alors et qu'est-ce qui s'est passé depuis ↑
          and what's happened since ↑
          . . .
      N: qu'est-ce que tu fais en ce moment ↑
          what do you do now ↑
      G: eh +++
(30) N: hein ↑
      G: (XX) ++ *a/ a/ en la ultima grabacion con* nicole ↑
          (XX)++ a/ a/ in the last recording with nicole ↑
      N: non non non là en ce moment, là ↑
          no no no here now right now ↑
      G: *con mi mama* ↑
          with my mother ↑ .
      N: non maintenant qu'est-ce que tu fais la journée qu'est-ce que tu
          fais là ↑
          aujourd'hui par exemple
          no to-day what do you do in the day time what do you do now to-day
          for instance ↑
(35) G: aujourd'hui ah oui aujourd'hui par exemple que (je) n'ai pas le
          travail
          to-day ah yes to-day for instance that (i)have not work

Such difficulties or expression of difficulties with understanding raise new problems. Since right from the beginning she blocks up the exchange, saying she does not understand, she is perceived as uncooperative and unwilling and the majority locutor must make great efforts in long clarification sequences to obtain collaboration. But the minority worker may also cease resisting and abandon the attempt to interact at all (cf. Berta and the bookshelves above).

A researcher will not give up and this raises many questions about the right to interview someone and how far to press them. But some majority speakers have no reason, no time and no interest, in some circumstances, to strive to maintain the interaction. They break off, and it is then the minority interactants' responsibility, if the issues are important to them, to set the conversation going again or, at least, to catch their interlocutor's attention and encourage their good will. The energy it takes may progressively discourage minority interactants and lead them to give up.

In these sequences of 'resistance', the minority worker's sentences in L1 *yo no comprendo/ no le entiendo* (I don't understand) or *yo no se como se [di]* (I don't know how to say) when repeated again and again, are more than a simple indication of non-understanding. They may indicate a claim for equal rights to stand on one's own linguistic territory and/or a choice of low status and identity in the face of pressure from the majority speaker.

Positive face

An alternative for countering face threats is for minority speakers to offer a positive face. In order to be thought of as legitimate interlocutors and contributing members of the community they adopt native-like behaviour. They indicate explicitly that they have understood as does Ergün (cf. ex in 4.2) or use excuse formulas when they have to interrupt. Thus, through 'solidarity politeness strategies' (Scollon and Scollon 1983), they hope to prevent the native's negative reaction and overcome their tendency to distrust the other's capacity to understand.

Very occasionally, the minority interactants compensate for the imposition they feel by threatening the majority partner's face. Berta, for instance, in the job interview, queries the social worker's apparent lack of understanding. Ignoring the point (which was an inquiry about her husband's qualification) or, undoubtedly, unaware of it, she takes advantage of the situation to recover a little power balance in the interaction:

(1)   N: et votre mari qu'est-ce qu'il fait comme travail en ce moment ↑
              and your husband what does he do as a job right now ↑

       B: eh imprimerie   *explicit* vs *implicit*
              eh printing

       N   eh c'est-à-dire ↑
              eh that is to say ↑

       B: imprimerie ↑ + no connais pas imprimerie ↑
              printing ↑ *you don't know printing* ↑

(5)   N: mais pas tout / ça dépend qu'est-ce qu'il fait comme travail
              dans l'imprimerie ↑
              but not all/ it depends what kind of work does he do in printing ↑

From the two choices made by the non-native speakers: maintain
a low status through repeated signals of non-understanding as
Gilda does or progress towards equality in the interaction through
adopting a near-native attitude as Ergün or Berta and others do, the
first one might in the short term gain the native's attention. But it is
the second one which helps the minority speaker to gain the other's
acceptance and makes for a workable interaction.

4.5 POTENTIAL FOR LEARNING:

It is beyond the scope of this book to discuss in detail language-
learning strategies or to attempt to account for understanding
competence from a cognitive and developmental perspective. Given
that language learning is indisputably a social activity and that the
perspective of this study is an interactional one, the understanding
process can only be traced as part of a holistic interpretation of each
interaction. Developmental trends and cognitive processes that can
only be identified by flattening out the variability of interactions
ignore the contextual reality which is the minority workers' experience with the majority group. Any statements about learning to
understand must therefore be approached with caution.

There is an ever increasing body of literature on cognitive
processes in language development and, particularly, on the role of
consciousness. Schmidt (1994) has developed a useful heuristic,
drawing on the literature over the last twenty years, for considering
different types of consciousness: intentionality, attention, awareness and control. But this perspective ignores the interactional, the
social which, along with Vygotsky, Volosinov, Bruner and Wells,
we would argue, is the essential environment for learning.

The studies of language strategies and of the good language learner (Rubin 1975, Stern 1983, Naiman et al. 1978, Wenden 1991 and Kellerman 1991) acknowledge the interactional dimension as do some studies of tutored and untutored learning environments (see Day 1986, Py 1987, Bange 1987). These studies refer to some of the notions of consciousness, attention, noticing, control, and so on. They show the back and forth moves the participants make from form to content. But these studies either look cross-sectionally at a group of learners at one time in order to draw out generalised procedures or at particular features of productive competence in isolation, for example, in SPA, 'séquences potentiellement acquisitionnelles,' as De Pietro, Matthey & Py (1989) call the learning-teaching sequences which develop in the interaction.

Our perspective has been more holistic and concerned with the interactants' behaviours in constructing understanding. Given this holistic approach we can identify certain procedures which, at least partly, contribute to potential for learning, but these strategies, both singly or in combination, are not necessarily stable. They are as much constructed out of each interaction as they are more global developmental trends.

What we want to do now is discuss the minority workers' ability to manage their problems with understanding, the variable ways they have to react to them and to elaborate on them with the aim of bettering their understanding capacity and potential for learning.

In this chapter, we have been analysing the different ways minority interactants work, jointly with their majority interlocutors, on understanding and more particularly on non- understanding. Difficulties are enormous but they tend to more or less diminish with time. A lot depends on how the minority interactants react to their problems of understanding and of the types of procedures, they choose to manage them. We have also noted that some procedures or rather some combinations of procedures are more efficient than others. The remarks which follow are only tentative preliminary hypotheses and a basis for further research. We would be very cautious in aiming for highly generalisable conclusions.

First, certain patterns are emerging, for example the strategic use of direct and indirect means of conveying non-understanding. On the whole, signalling explicitly is better than being implicit. This covers the following procedures (see 4.3 above):

reprise of beginning of non-understood utterance
minimal query
metalinguistic questions and comments which may be general or very
specific

Signalling the source of the problem is even better when one has
been able to diagnose it. This usually becomes possible at a more
advanced stage. This is what Ergün does in the example quoted
above 'Wat is "ver"?'.

As soon as their linguistic resources permit it, good understanders tend to use a wide range of indicators in a more
collaborative and integrated way. From the first stages, the active
minority interactants also base their effort in joint understanding
upon a high inference strategy as a complement to the explicit signalling of non-understanding (and see Rost and Ross 1991). So, a
pattern emerges in which signalling and asking for help in the most
precise way possible is combined with more detailed analysis and
context sensitive inferencing. These two approaches are both
needed to give understanding a real chance, especially in the early
stages of learning to communicate in the foreign language. In addition, as we have suggested, there needs to be an awareness and a
subtle management of face issues. Thus, learners who understand
and acquire the fastest are those who combine negotiating on non-
understanding with sensitivity to issues of face and an eye on the
conversational climate.

But understanding cannot be looked upon in isolation from production for either of the participants. One does not understand first
and then produce. Understanding is developed out of learner fragments and hypotheses responded to sensitively by the majority
participant. Therefore we have the continuing problem of circularity: do learners become better speakers because they notice and
signal non-understanding or are they better managers of non-
understanding because they are better speakers?

As their situations and aims may vary a lot, all minority interactants do not necessarily choose the most efficient procedures or
manage to combine them. Above all, they do not all even choose to
attempt to control and organise their capacity to understand the
majority speaker. In other words, they do not focus on learning. If
we define learning as the decision the minority interactants take to
organise and develop their capacity to understand in the new language and therefore to select the means to do it, it should be clear

that learning is not natural or spontaneous in most intercultural situations. This is all the more true for minority workers. As a matter of fact, the socio-economic situation of those minorities and the psychological factors which often go with them leave them with a very fine margin of freedom to make the decision. However, such a 'decision' can be fundamental for their future and that of their family in the new country. This decision again means refusing to satisfy oneself with a minimal understanding competence which, as a result, often contributes to keeping minority workers uneducated, unemployed and marginalised.

But, as we have suggested above, what looks like a choice is rarely a choice for ethnic minority workers, and it is surely not by chance that so many of the women informants take the option of not indicating their problems with understanding and therefore progress less. Some minimum conditions are necessary to become aware of the possibility and necessity of learning and to involve oneself in it. The wish to learn will have little impact without repeated opportunities to communicate interculturally and, in most cases, a pressing need to do so and speakers' willingness to adjust cooperative principles (Grice 1975) to an intercultural setting. Most of the time, such interactions other than institutional ones are infrequent and limited and it takes a lot of energy on the part of the minority speakers to undertake and maintain conversational involvement. So, the will to learn is not necessarily constant and stable. It can change when the conditions of life change. For example, if minority workers are ghettoised in a so-called 'ethnic work unit', opportunities and motivation to learn will be strictly limited as compared with periods of enforced contact with the majority during, for instance, a long stay in hospital. It can also vary with more local factors such as the task, the interlocutor and the issues at stake (see Chapter 2.5, Issues of variability)

When the rare favourable conditions are present, what is it then that characterises someone who has made the choice to be a learner and not just an interactant? Given the complexity and variability of factors, we must admit that the distinction between the two types of status, interactant and learner, is often unclear. In any case, it is not possible to speak in terms of presence/absence of typical traits but in terms of degree and balance. It is more like a constellation of procedures and approaches which, appearing in the interactional behaviour of a minority speaker, seem to be linked with an attention to understanding and general linguistic competence. This subtle and variable 'mix' leads to understanding improvement (whether it be the source or the consequence of the learning we are unable to say).

The different 'mixes' result in different profiles. For example, the Moroccan informant Mohamed, despite his high level of competence in Dutch, keeps being a poor communicator while another Moroccan, Abdelmalek who is rather a good communicator maintains his linguistic competence in French at a very elementary level till the end of the project.

The data we have analysed show that the discourse of minority interactants who seem to be conscious of the learning issues and of the necessity to work on their ability to understand (and be understood by) their majority partners involves:

- the use of metalinguistic comments on understanding and non-understanding and attention to the linguistic items,
- initiative rather than dependency in their relationship to the majority partner in the interaction,
- a sensitive management of issues of face,
- an awareness of the issues in general.

Attention to the system is associated with a preference for an active role in the interaction. Taking the initiative of signalling non-understanding, of forming hypotheses on the units' meaning and so orientating the majority interactant's choice of procedures to help solving non-understanding is a guarantee the minority interactants take against too much lack of understanding. It makes them better able to control the interaction and build their capacity to understand.

The management of face, their own and their partner's, is also part of the candidate-learner's profile. Non-understanding is a constant menace to the minority interactant's face. Interrupting to signal non-understanding is face-damaging for both the minority and the majority speakers although to a much lesser extent for the latter. One option is avoidance (see 4.3), but it is not bearable for long if one wants to keep the encounter going at all. A more efficient solution is to evaluate the source and the importance of the non-understanding, so that taking the initiative to interrupt and ask for clarification can be limited to central problems, briefly executed and well embedded in the discourse (see 4.4). More advanced speakers of the new language tend to use more native-like procedures and include polite forms when signalling non-understanding. Ergün and Marcello, who have the opportunity to interact daily and intensively with members of the majority group, offer two good examples of this type of behaviour. Ergün uses a direct standard indication 'hoezo?' (how is that?) instead of the simple 'welk?' (which?) which empowers him rather than making him feel in a dependent role. Another informant, Mohamed directly interrupts his partner but finds ways of mitigating these face threatening moments by introducing formulaic conversational 'stoppers' into his discourse such as *effe kijken* (let me see) and *even wachten* (wait a little). In the later stages, Berta uses very common native-like reformulations as comprehension checks (such as the example at the driving-school, 4.3), Marcello and Ergün also check understanding but they postpone it to after the encounter and they search for explanations from friends and family whom they use as a substantial help in their linguistic difficulties.

This set of characteristics is sometimes completed by explicit comments from minority workers on their will and decision to learn. Some of them like Tino or Madan mention the regular meetings they are having with project researchers as language lessons. Others, such as Berta, explain how they have become aware of the necessity for them to make a step forward and meet people for a start:

> je me (suis) dis c'est pas possible rester toute la journée ici il y a de sortir d'ici sinon (rires) après j'ai commencé à sortir toute seule
> *i told myself it is not possible to stay all day here (=home) it is necessary to go out of here (laughs) and then i started to go out by myself*

And then, like Berta they can come to see the value of learning and guided training in the second language, becoming more involved in the majority society and finding a job:

> c'est très bien pasque c'est pasque la pratique del/ de *las* personnes c'est c'est mieux pasque *por* ça que je parle un ptit peu plus le le français sino je ne parle
> *it is very well it is because the practice/training of/ of the people it it is better because of this that i speak a little more french, otherwise i do not speak.*

After a while those who have become aware of their understanding competence may be able to assess the progress they have made:

> B: mais mainnant n'est pas comme avant hein comme avant ah la la pasque la personne parla parla * y y * si je ne comprends pas ah la la je je ne sais que faire pour * por * eh je dis

but now is not like before isn't it like before ah la la because the person
speak speak and and if i don't understand i i do not know what to do
for for i i say

Controlling, assessing and planning are basic activities for minority speakers who have made the choice of being learners and who talk about it. Berta spontaneously explains how they, in the family, have organised their learning, choosing a day a week when the majority language is spoken at home to train with the children who learn faster at school.

On the other hand, those who show less propensity to improve their understanding ability are satisfied with using general feedback (for example Paula or Zahra in 4.2 above) or general queries. This reliance on indirect means of conveying non-understanding frequently leads to long linear sequences and a climate of uncertainty and unease. This trouble is often expressed and mitigated by non-verbal manifestations like laughter, particularly for female informants (e.g. Fatima). As a result of such a behaviour, the minority interactants who prefer not to indicate non-understanding, let the majority speaker go on record with problems of understanding and rarely notice and repeat units proposed by their interlocutor when checking or ratifying their own understanding. Letting the majority interactant check, diagnose and repair non-understanding, as Zahra or Gilda do, reflects a low propensity for learning and is not favourable to development. But, as we said, the 'decision' to learn is not 'natural' and, often for obvious reasons, the conditions for making that decision are rather unequally distributed.

4.6 CONCLUSION

Minority workers have diverse ways of reacting to non-understanding. Although bureaucratic interactions tend to reinforce interpretations of discrimination and create a negative understanding cycle, some of the minority group break the cycle by daring to interrupt and signal their problems explicitly. By doing this, these 'efficient interactants' gain time and energy. They also show a capacity to diagnose the source of their problem, which, as well as drawing on their pragmatic competence, requires them to focus on the linguistic forms. This positive and collaborative approach is reinforced at every opportunity they have to interact and construct understanding. Providing certain conditions are present, they can make the most of their exchanges with the majority interactants and progress in their understanding capacity. This capacity to adapt to situations where they have understanding problems, which of course varies among informants, is what we want to illustrate now through the presentation of extended interactions for four of the informants.

FIVE

Case studies: the making of understanding in extended interactions

Katharina Bremer, Peter Broeder, Margaret Simonot and
Marie-Thérèse Vasseur

5.0 INTRODUCTION

In the previous chapter we focused on the minority interactant's
behaviour when faced with problems of understanding. We have
shown how varied it could be according to the different contexts,
interactions and individuals. We have also demonstrated that efficiency in understanding was linked with a strategic use of different
types of procedures. Above all, we have insisted on the positive or
negative dynamics understanding or non-understanding could create in the joint enterprise of an intercultural interaction which is the
responsibility of both partners.

But, of course, this is only one point of view on the joint work of
constructing understanding. Chapters 6 and 7 will adopt the other
partner's point of view. They will analyse the majority speaker's
behaviour and how this interacts with the minority speaker's. As
for this central chapter, we want it to be a meeting point in which
the reader will see the joint making of understanding at work. So it
will not only be a sum of illustrations of the different behaviours
we have been analysing in the previous chapter. It will be a presentation of four gatekeeping encounters from both points of view: the
minority and the majority interlocutors'.

Analysing problems from a 'systematic' perspective necessarily
entails a certain neglect of the context; data excerpts have to be chosen to illustrate a specific point, thereby abstracting them from
what a particular non-understanding may have meant for the participants in that encounter, how it was brought about and its
impact on subsequent turns and the interaction as a whole.

For each encounter, therefore, in this chapter, we focus on the
whole or a very substantial part of the interaction, presenting it in
its context, i.e. underlining the interrelations between the biograph-

ical situation and the communicative aims in the encounter, the constraints of the institutional setting, the asymmetry of roles and the discursive devices. The four informants are the following:

> Berta, a Spanish-speaker who has emigrated from Chile
> Tino, an Italian who came to Germany
> Ergün, a Turk who lives in the Netherlands
> Santo who moved from Italy to London

(see brief biographies in Appendix A)

As a thorough analysis of the complete four encounters would take too long we will concentrate on certain key sequences which will be examined from the point of view of:

—the causes of the problems with understanding as they have been studied in Chapter 3
—the diagnosis of the cause: how it is done and by whom
—the whole set of procedures used by both partners whether for preventing, signalling or repairing non-understanding
—the issue of the main sequences examined within the interaction as a whole.

All useful data, biographical, non-verbal and especially feedback data, will be used in this presentation to illustrate and support the analysis of the minority interactant's difficulties, both partners' reactions, the joint discursive work they undertake and the analyst's view on the interactional accomplishment of understanding.

5.1 BERTA (SPANISH-FRENCH): JOB-CENTRE INTERVIEW

> + difficile eh né pas de comprender *por por* français à + à travail de de cuisine
> (+ *difficult eh not understand for for french at at work of kitchen*)

Berta came to France from Chile to follow her husband, a Chilean too, who had already been in the country as a political refugee for a year or so. Of course, she did not choose to emigrate to France. She is in her thirties and has had eight years of primary and secondary education in Chile. Without any professional training, she arrived a month before the project started and had no knowledge of French. She has three children, then aged seven to fourteen, who started to receive French schooling on arrival. For the first six months, the family lived in a refugee centre then they moved to a flat of their own in the Paris suburbs.

While still living in the centre, Berta seized the opportunity offered to her of working there as a replacement kitchen helper. But this was not a secure job and she was keen to better her social status. Her children were adapting rather well to French school life, and her friends and family, settled close to her (her mother had joined them in Paris for a while, her husband's sister had married a French man), provided a helpful environment. So she was getting ready to fight her way through the French world of work. This was her state of mind when she met the Job Centre counsellor. She was looking for an apartment and for a job and she knew she would have to fight. These interviews she had at that time, and the support of the people she met, reinforced her will to acquire some linguistic and professional competence, which she did later on.

However, at the time of the interview, Berta's competence in French was very limited since she had only been in France for seven months. But her life was changing. She had left the refugee centre and from then on she has had to take charge of everything: housing, living, job. The main interest she expressed in the interview (which took place at the unemployment office) was that she hoped very simply to find a regular job of whatever kind. The woman counsellor spoke very slowly but with long and complex utterances. She was very professional in the way that she strictly followed the standard script for a first interview, her questions aimed at the construction of a personal document of Berta. A strategy she used, very typical of these gatekeeping encounters, was to approach the different topics through indirect questions, which did not facilitate Berta's understanding.

Although, as a beginner, she had very few linguistic resources in French at her disposal, Berta was very willing to contribute to solving the understanding problems. This explains the high degree of commitment she kept maintaining during project interviews. She was also very much aware of problems of face and of the necessity to keep the interaction going smoothly. This combination resulted in a reduced use of direct signalling except for key misunderstandings (like the sequence on formation/information, see below). When she did not understand, she would rather signal her non-understanding by a minimal general query ('quoi?' *what* ?). She even refrained from interrupting and would rather produce short minimal feedback utterances (hm) and let her partner continue or explicitly check on her comprehension.

At the same time, she tried to use her inferencing capacity and worked on forming hypotheses. Her limited linguistic means still prevented Berta from diagnosing her problem of understanding. So, the majority speaker made every possible effort to take this part of the joint work on herself. This explains the length of the diagnosis phase in some sequences.

The first third of the interview started with Berta's wishes and was centred on exploring the working conditions she was ready to accept: time, location, type of work. Then the counsellor turned to Berta's working and education experience (the second third of the interview) before testing her reaction regarding language and professional training and concluding on the necessity for Berta to be actively looking for a job herself (last third).

Wishing to present the partners' joint work in instances when understanding is difficult, we will analyse the main clarification sequences from different points of view:

the causes of the problem
the minority interactant's procedures in facing the problem
the majority locutor's complementary procedures and the type of collaboration.

The different sequences selected here focus on:

1   a general failure in understanding,
2   a problem in understanding solved by joint effort,
3   a lengthy misunderstanding and its costly clarification.

The first excerpt that will be presented here is a good illustration of the limitations of the possible exchanges when the minority interactant's resources are very restricted and of the difficulties that are to be expected in such an interaction, considering the topics, the diverging expectations and the discourse style usually developed. The situation is as follows: after considering different possible time schedules, the counsellor is trying to suggest to Berta that she might have to travel far away from her home on the outskirts of Paris. Then she wants to go into more detail, in particular she wants to check how far Berta is ready to travel. The problem is that she approaches the matter through an indirect and rather complex question which starts a rather frustrating sequence of non-understanding:

N: d'accord + combien d'heures de transport vous pouvez faire par jour ↑
ok + how many hours of travelling can you do every day ↑

B: quoi ↑
what ↑

(120) N: combien d'heures + dans les transports en commun dans le métro ou dans le bus ↑
how many hours + on the public transport in the underground or on the bus ↑

B: *por* metro ↑
by underground ↑

N: oui combien d'heures | vous pouvez faire ↑ ++ vous comprenez la question ↑
yes how many hours can you do ↑ you understand the question ↑

B: (je) ne compris pas
i do not understand

N: d'accord + alors dans paris je note hein dans paris
ok + then in paris i write down ok in paris

(125) B: hm

N: ou proche de votre domicile
or close to where you live

B: hm
hm

N: près de chez vous + si c'est possible
close to your home+ if possible

B: euh *seis* + rue + *seis seis* + eh ↑ la *direccion* de moi ↑
eh six + street + six six + eh? ↑ the address of me ↑

(130) N: non
no

B: non ↑
no ↑

N: vous accepteriez de travailler
you would accept to work

B: hm
hm

N: euh près de chez vous
er close to your home

(135) B: hm
hm

N: près de font/à fontenay
close to font/in fontenay

B: hm
hm

N: ou alors + dans paris + mais pas à l'extérieur de paris
or then + in paris + but not outside paris

    B: ah non *en el esterior de* paris non (rires)
          ah no in the outside of Paris no (laughs)

(140) N: d'accord ++ alors + bon maintenant vous allez m'expliquer ce
          que vous cherchez comme travail
          ok ++ then + well now you will explain to me what sort of work you
          want

This is a typical example of a failure in understanding, frustrating for both partners. Berta does not make any sense of the counsellor's question about transport (118) and is unable to link it with the problem of distance between workplace and home. The counsellor cannot go any further into her exploration of Berta's wishes and, finally, only makes a distinction between Paris and outside Paris and switches to the next topic.

One must not forget that, compared to many other informants, Berta is a real beginner. This is why she accumulates difficulties in what is most of the time for her a global problem of understanding. Her linguistic repertoire is limited and the surface as well as the content of the counsellor's utterances are problematic, notwithstanding the pragmatic meaning. The only understanding approach available is for her to search for recognisable words. She herself explains, in the subsequent feedback interview, that she identified only two words from the counsellor's first utterance: combien *(how many)* and jour *(day)*. And the difficulty is increased, as we would expect, by the indirectness of the question. Berta's minimal query: quoi? (what) indicates that she is at a complete loss concerning the surface topic of the new question presented to her. And, even more so, the covert topic (the distance from her home she is ready to travel for a job).

It is not the first time in the interview that the partners experience non-understanding. It has already happened twice when the counsellor has proposed some hypothetical situations as a means to get more precise indications on Berta's wishes and possibilities:

    -et si on vous propose un travail plus tôt que huit heures ↑ vous
        accepteriez de le prendre ↑
    and if you were offered a work earlier than eight o'clock ↑ would you accept it ↑
    and
    -et + vous accepteriez d'aller en banlieue ↑
    and would you accept to go to the suburbs ↑

Hypothetical topics are a common source of non-understanding for minority interactants. Confronted with that type of question, they simply do not understand or take those questions for questions about the real situation (cf. Chapter 3 on causes of non-understanding). In such a situation, Berta cannot even imagine that her preferences could be taken into consideration.

In the case we are analysing here, the counsellor, who tries to be helpful but does not diagnose the cause of Berta's non-understanding, reformulates in a way that is more explicit and more concrete. She offers specifications (public transportation) and common examples of Parisian means of transport in Paris (metro, bus)(120). But this is not enough for Berta to get the point. She manages to pick up one more word in the counsellor's reformulation (121: *por metro*?). Her reprise of the only word she has understood indicates that she needs more explicitation and help to figure out the counsellor's topic: acceptable distance for her to travel to work. This is why, considering that one more reformulation has got her nowhere, the counsellor decides to surface the problem and go on record (vous comprenez la question? *you understand the question?*). Berta answers clearly and explicitly, taking up her partner's words: no compris pas *I don't understand* (123).

Ratifying Berta's acknowledgement of non-understanding, the counsellor turns to her usual procedure of making a fresh start, summing up step by step what they have agreed on till then. Berta who feels very awkward not being able to understand after the question has been formulated several times chooses not to be explicit about her degree of understanding and sticks to minimal feedback. But, as the reformulation progresses, she feels she has to make a move towards elaborating meaning. Unfortunately, the new words used in the place of the proper names proposed first by the counsellor bring up another understanding problem. Berta who does her best to make inferences catches the word *domicile* ('home' in an official context), and turns to hypothesis forming. She starts an answer based on the plausible hypothesis that the counsellor is asking for her address. But, probably warned by the non-verbal symptoms produced by the majority speaker, she shies back and checks her hypothesis. She was right to be uncertain: the counsellor confirms that her hypothesis was wrong.

Partly aware of the cause of misunderstanding, the counsellor reformulates again keeping the hypothetical form (a conditional) which Berta is unable to grasp but also using proper names: Fontenay and Paris. And this gets them back to the more general agreement they had reached earlier. But the counsellor does not pursue any further. Considering the difficulty caused by this step backwards and willing to save both their energies for the rest of the interview after this partial failure, the counsellor ratifies and proceeds to the next topic.

The following excerpt bears on Berta's actual working experience. This time, Berta is so involved and she engages so much in the joint effort that she succeeds in overcoming another understanding problem. For this, she again has to draw inferences from the counsellor's very general question on what she does :

(180) N: ah ah d'accord et là qu'est-ce que vous faites alors ↑
          ah ah ok and there what do you do then ↑
      B: qu'est-ce que tu / eh la personne *del* chef* que el* m'explique
          + *el* m'explique eh que je prepare de manger
          what do you / eh the person of the head who he explains to me + he explains to me eh what i prepare to eat
      N: eh c'est / vous faites le menu avec elle ↑ ou
          eh it is / you do the menu with her ↑ or
      B: elle me dit *el* manger que *yo* préparé
          he/she tell to me the meal that i prepare
      N: hm et donc vous euh vous faites quoi dans la cuisine ↑ vous
          faites les achats aussi ↑ non
          hm and then you eh you do what in the kitchen ↑ you do the buying too ↑ no
(185) B: oui
      N: vous allez acheter ↑
          you go buying ↑
      B: oui + eh *por* trois mois solament
          yes + eh for three months only
      N: vous achetez pour trois mois ↑
          you shop/buy for three months ↑
      B: oui hm aujour/eh aujourd'hui + de septem/septembre à à
          décembre je trav(aille)
          yes hm to/eh to-day + from septem/september to december i wor(k)
190   N: ah ↑ vous travaillez d'accord pour trois mois
          ah ↑ you work ok for three months
      B: oui *por* trois mois
          yes for three months

This time again Berta is confronted with one of the counsellor's indirect questions and she has to infer her interlocutor's intention. The counsellor wants to know about her qualifications and the degree of responsibility Berta has in her cooking job. But Berta does

not understand her point and first responds to the surface meaning
of the question, describing very concretely what she does at her
working place. And then, thinking her answer is satisfactory, she
shifts topics and, as she holds the floor, she makes sure that the
counsellor has understood that she really needs another job
reminding her that this one is temporary (187: *por* trois mois sola-
ment). The counsellor has not followed her line and, still expecting
her to give details on her qualification as a cook, she misinterprets,
before rapidly rejecting such an irrelevant interpretation, Berta's
remark (188: vous achetez pour trois mois?), helped in this by
Berta's explanations (189: de septembre à decembre je travaille).
And, as she does not give up, which she had to do last time, she
attempts to specify her question, although without telling her
exactly what she is aiming at:

(192) N: quelle partie de/ enfin quel euh + la chef de la cuisine vous dit
          ce qu'il faut faire mais vous faites quoi ↑ les plats ↑
          *what part of/ i mean what euh + the chef tells you what to do but you
          do what ↑ the main dishes ↑*

      B: no no no elle seulement me dit eh moi moi prépare el + manger
          eh je suis eh el chef de la cosi/ de la cuisine
          *no no no he/she only tells me eh me me prepare the + meal eh i am eh
          the chef*

      N: ah d'accord vous êtes le chef de la cuisine
          ah ok you are the chef

(195) B: oui
          yes

      N: je croyais qu'il y en avait/ qu'y avait une personne [qui vous]
          i thought that there was one/ that there was a person [who]

      B: [non non non]
          [no no no]

      N: [vous indiquait ce qu'il fallait]
          [told you what you had to do]

      B: seulement la personne me dit à *mi* + que moi pré/ eh manger
          elle me dit à *mi* + que moi préparer *el* manger que elle me dit
          *only the person tells to me + that me pre/ to eat he/she tells to me +
          that me prepare the meal that she tells me*

(200) N: le menu
          the menu

      B: oui oui + [*el*menu]
          yes yes + [the menu]

      N: [pour faire] le menu mais vous vous faites toute la ↑ préparation
          [to make] the menu but you you do all the preparation

```
         B:   oui oui
         N:   des ↑ plats
              of the ↑ dishes
(205)    B:   oui oui oui
         N:   et la la préparation
              and the the preparation
         B:   oui oui
```

In (193), Berta suddenly guesses what the real question is. Her very clear reaction indicates her understanding of the counsellor's intention. The counsellor then initiates a long series of check-backs to ascertain their mutual understanding and make sure that she has received the right information. Only then can she continue her exploration of Berta's working experience before arriving in France.

It will take another sequence of non-understanding and successive reformulations for the counsellor to obtain the information from Berta (who just cannot figure out what *avant*, the adverb expressing anteriority means). As she signals her non-understanding right from the beginning, all the counsellor has to do is to find the adequate reformulation, guided in her successive tries by Berta's reactions.

Then the interview continues with a smooth elicitation of Berta's qualification's and diplomas and then we reach the part when the counsellor wants to suggest the necessity of some adult training. The problem then is one of misunderstanding and it takes both partners' joint efforts to overcome it:

```
(342)    N:   d'accord ++ bon + et ya pas d'autre / bon si vous aviez la
              possibilité de faire une formation ↑ qu'est-ce que vous choisiriez
              comme formation ↑
              ok ++ well + and there is no other / well if you had the possibility to
              receive a training ↑ what training would you choose ↑
         B:   information, que que dit moi information?
              information, what what say to me information ↑
         N:   quelle formation vous aimeriez faire ↑
              what training would you like to receive ↑
(345)    B:   à l'ANPE ↑ que moi :eh ++le travail + eh + com / j'aime qui le dit
              moi ↑ eh une information pour chercher de travail ↑
              at the agency ↑ what i :er ++ the job + how / i like what say to me ↑ eh
              an information to look for a job?
         N:   non
              no
         B:   non ↑
              no ↑
```

N: non + euh bon là j'ai noté bon les deux pistes possibles pour
vous de travail
*no + eh well here i have written down well the two possible pathways
for you for work*

B: hm
hm

(350) N: qui sont sur la cuisine
which are cooking

B: oui
yes

N: euh qu'on appelle la cuisine de collectivité ou alors dans une
famille hein, cuisine de collectivité c'est dans une petite
entreprise + ou euh une pet/ comme à la maison de france +
mais d'autres organisées comme ça hein et puis le nettoyage +
bon mais je vous demande + ↑ maintenant
*er that we call catering or else in a family ok? catering is in a small
organisation + or eh a sm/ like at the (name of the refugee centre) + but
others organised like it ok? and then cleaning + well but i ask you + ↑ now*

B: hm
hm

N: vous aimeriez euh suivre une formation ↑ + ya la possibilité par
l'ANPE
*you would like to follow a training course ↑ + there is a possibility
through the agency*

(355) B: hm
hm

N: dans certaines conditions
in certain conditions

B: ya
yes

N: de suivre une formation professionnelle ou une formation en
français vous avez déjà suivi une formation en français ↑ vous
avez déjà appris ↑
*to follow a professional training or a training in french you have
already had a training in french ↑ you have learnt already ↑*

B: oui (soupir)
yes (sigh)

(360) N: est-ce-que vous avez déjà fait des stages ↑
have you already attended courses ↑

B: *si*
oui

N: vous avez fait des stages ↑ en français ↑
you have attended courses ↑ in french ↑

B: es/ oui
es /yes

       N: vous avez + ah d'accord ++ oui ↑
            you have + ah ok ++ yes ↑

(365) B: oui ↑
            yes ↑

       N: qu'est-ce que vous avez fait comme /
            what did you have as |

       B: eh ↑ *del* stage de moi eh + de de français ↑
            eh ↑ of the course of me eh + of of french ↑

       N: hm
            hm

       B: *en* à l'école ↑
            in at school ↑

370   N: oui

       B: *solament* trois mois
            only three months

       N: trois mois
            three months

       B: oui
            yes

       N: hm
            hm

375   B: *y + y *n'est pas beaucoup de à / à la classe
            and + and not much to/ to class

       N: d'accord vous n'avez pas beaucoup suivi les cours
            ok you have not attended the classes very much

       B: oui
            yes

       N: hm et si on vous proposait une autre formation euh ↑ vous
            préféreriez quelle formation ↑ vous comprenez ce que je vous
            demande ↑
            hm and if one offered you another training eh ↑ what training would
            you prefer ↑ you understand what i am asking you ↑

       B: eh ↑ information ↑
            eh? ↑ information ↑

(380) N: une formation un stage
            a training, a course

       B: *si si *
            yes yes

       N: si vous pouviez suivre un stage
            if you could follow a course

       B: hm
            hm

       N: quel stage vous [aimeriez suivre] ↑
            what course would [you like to attend] ↑

(385) B: [stage eh] de français
           [course eh] of french
       N: un stage de français [d'abord]
           a course of french [first]
       B: [oui oui oui] oui
           [yes yes yes] yes
       N: vous aimeriez | bien
           you would like it | well
       B: oui
(390) N: re-suivre un stage de français d'accord + et si on pouvait vous
           trouver + une formation + euh dans la cuisine euh vous
           accepteriez de faire une formation dans la cuisine ↑
           attend a course of french again ok + and if one could find you + a
           training + er in cooking er would you accept to have a training in
           cooking ↑
       B: oui ↑
           yes ↑
       N: vous comprenez la question que je vous pose ↑
           do you understand the question i am asking you ↑
       B: *a ver cua* /eh ++ del information *por* #
           let us see wh/ eh ++ information for #
       N: une form/ un stage de cuisine
           a trai/ a course in cooking
(395) B: ah
       N: pour apprendre
           to learn
       B: oui oui
           yes yes
       N: oui ↑
           yes
       B: oui oui ↑
           yes yes

Here, the misunderstanding is a surface confusion between two
phonetically close units in French: *une formation*, meaning training
and *information*, meaning information, the first syllable of which
sounds very much the same as the feminine article for Spanish
speaking people who do not produce the nasal vowel [ɛ̃] for 'ĩn'
and do not make any distinction between phoneme /y/ and
phoneme /i/.

Berta first takes up the word which is the source of her understanding problem (343). Her own pronunciation [informasjon]
might cover both expressions *une formation* and *information* and,
therefore, it does not put the counsellor on alert. And as this latter

does not clearly diagnose the misunderstanding, she reformulates her question using the same word again (344). Berta becomes more explicit and develops her interpretation about the counsellor's utterance (345). She immediately rejects Berta's hypothesis with a definite *non* which makes the situation very tense and very painful for Berta.

The counsellor then uses six turns to make a fresh start, first summing up Berta's preference for a type of work and then explaining to her that she is entitled to some training, professional or language. And, trying to be more concrete, she evokes her recent experience in learning French, first reformulating *suivre une formation* as *appris* and then as *faire des stages*, the most common expression. Berta sticks to minimum feedback and, as she showed in the feedback sessions, the misunderstanding is still there when she explains that she was offered a French course which she rarely attended (367-375). She thinks the counsellor is asking for more information as to why she had not regularly attended the French classes offered at the refugee-centre. This interpretation is not surprising in such a situation. Her immigrant experience encourages self-depreciation and a sense of guilt. Then, twice again after her long reassuring sequence, the counsellor goes back to her initial question with the ambiguous word *formation*, twice again she goes on record with a general metalinguistic question (377: vous comprenez ce que je vous demande? *you understand what i ask you?*, 391: vous comprenez la question que je vous pose? *you understand the question i'm asking you?*). In this most embarrassing situation, Berta keeps signalling her version of the unit that is causing the problem (379, 393). This is how she makes the counsellor progressively discover that it is the word *formation* which is the source of the problem. In a kind of reversed 'scaffolding' (Bruner 1986, Scollon 1976), the majority interactant is progressively made aware of the necessity to replace the word *formation* and substitute the word *stage* (*training*) for it (380, 382, 384, 386, 390, 394). Berta's spontaneous and insistent answers: *si si* or *oui oui* confirm and reinforce her guidance of the counsellor's efforts. At last, they reach a measure of understanding. This the counsellor checks a little later after a few comments on the necessity to start with a course in French.

Then she uses the time that is left for the interview to try to persuade Berta that she has to be actively looking for herself. Berta is too exhausted to furnish more than a very minimal feedback and they finally part with a new date for another visit to the agency.

On the whole, despite knowing very little French, Berta proves to be an active and willing partner. Her contribution to the construction of understanding is strategic. When her non-understanding is too general and she cannot diagnose the cause she chooses unspecific but direct comments like *quoi?, no compris pas.* Whenever possible, she uses reprise of the problematic item to signal difficulty, combined with hypothesis-forming. And this is a good omen for the future. In the following encounters, she will become a good problem solver, a very good interactant and a real learner. During her second year in France, she attended several courses, French and vocational, hoping to make the best of her training. In an analytic sequence in one of the third year interviews she demonstrates her awareness of the learning issues and the choice she has made to learn and to become involved in French society.

(1) V: et après ça (le stage que berta suit) va t'amener des possibilités de travail ↑
and afterwards, this (the training course berta is on) will give you some job opportunities ↑

B: oui je crois pasqué déjà je commence à entrer dans le *mundo frances* (rires) * por * parler * por * comp/ * por * comprende le * frances y *je crois que je s/ je suis/ eh je suis capable * por * faire * por *de travail avec l/ + hm avec la / le* mundo * de la france (rires)
yes i think because already i begin entering the french world (laughs) to speak to understand french i think i am able to make to work with the world of france (laughs)

V: +++ comment est-ce que tu vois que ton français est maintenant meilleur tu vois une différence qu'est ce que tu as l'impression (d'avoir appris) ↑
how do you feel your french is now better you see a difference what do you see you (have learnt) ↑

B: bon pasque *como* je t/ comme je te dis il y a de des des moments que je ne/ je ne parle bien le français mais eh je com/ je comprenne beaucoup * y * c'est ça c'est / c'est ça + on avance beaucoup mieux pasque si la pe/ si la personne me dit quelque chose je ne peux parler bien mais je / je fais la là chose qu'(elle) me / que me dit pasque je le comprends bien
well as i told/told you there are moments when i don't speak french well but i understand a lot and this is it because one improves much better because if the person tells me something i cannot speak well but i do the thing s/he tells me because i understand her well.

5.2 TINO (ITALIAN-GERMAN)

Even if I speak better German – which job is there?
Auch wenn ich spreche besser deutsch – welches beruf gibt es?

Tino was born in Southern Italy. By the time of the job centre interview, he was 21 and had been living in Germany for one and a half years. He had eight years of schooling (and two of military service) but he had no professional training and had earned his living in Italy by several different unskilled and badly paid jobs. Having no prospect of good employment there, two events favoured his decision to emigrate: he had met a German girlfriend when she spent her holidays in Italy, and a friend could offer him his first job in a pizzeria.

But soon this kind of work turned out to be frustrating in many ways, since in five different jobs (as a kitchen hand or a waiter in Italian restaurants or ice-cream parlours) working conditions were very similar: extremely long working hours (ten to twelve hours a day, often work till late into the night), no holidays during summer, no work if the employer closed for seasonal reasons (ice-cream), and a payment that forced him to share his small room with a co-worker.

In order to improve his working conditions, therefore, he was desperately looking for a change. This was not the whole story of his life in Germany, however. In one respect, Tino liked this kind of work because it meant being in touch with many different people – Italian or German, customers, work-mates and friends. In the little leisure time he had, Tino enjoyed going out with lots of friends (mostly Italians but also Germans and people from other countries). On the whole, he would not think of his time in Germany as being only hard work. Apart from this, he was aware of the difficulty of starting a different career.

Some comments he made in a conversation with one of the researchers gave an impression of how he himself looked at his situation – critically, but at the same time with an effort to see things positively. He had just found a new job in an Italian restaurant, where meals during work were included in payment and he had at least one day off.

T: ich nehme wenig geld ↓ + ich kann e mein/ meine zimmer zahlen +
       i get few money i can pay my room
       und dann wenn ich arbeite nicht ↑ ich muss <u>auch</u> essen ↓
       and the time i don't work i also have to eat

N: mhm mhm
T: vielleicht ich verdienen acht e hundert mark am monat <u>vielleicht</u>
      maybe i earn eight er hundred marks per month <u>maybe</u>
N: ja
      yes
T: ich glaub + <ah ich hoffe> <laughingly> oder siebenhundert mark
      i think i hope or seven hundred marks
N: mhm
T: aber ich kann leben ↓ + wenig ↑ aber ich kann leben ↓
      but i can live + ↓ not much ↑ but i can live ↓

The Job Centre interview we are going to explore below took place about one month after this conversation. Tino had in mind to ask for information about finding a better job in a rather practical sense: keeping what he liked about working in restaurants, but earning better and having shorter working hours. The counsellor – a women in her early thirties – saw her task differently, however. Beginning with rather detailed questions about his past (this part covers more than the first third of the whole interview) her approach at finding alternatives is more 'top-down', starting from the qualifications one would need to find a better job.

In the following this interview will be looked at from two different angles. First, two longer excerpts will be analyzed with respect to the *ways Tino responds* to different difficulties he confronts during the encounter and how they contribute to a clarification of the problem. In a second step this will be complemented by *Tino´s own comments* on the session. (For a case study of this session with emphasis on the analysis of the counsellor´s interview style see Bremer [forthcoming].)

The first excerpt is from the beginning of the interview, right after the opening sequence. The counsellor has just started to inquire about background information.

(1)   N: wieviel jahre waren/ wieviel jahre war denn die schule
            how many years were/ how many years was the school
            die <u>grund</u>schule in italien ↑
            <u>elementary</u> school in italy ↑
      T: wieviel jahren ich habe gemacht ↑
            how many years i have done ↑
      N: mhm
(5)   T: acht jahren ↓
            eight years ↓
      N: <u>acht</u> jahre
            eight years

T: ja
  yes

N: mhm

N: däs isch dann mit dem abschluß gewesen + hauptschulabschluß +
  that has been with gcse[1] + gcse

(10) in der schule da ↓
  in the school there ↓

T: abschluß _ ↓ tut mir leid ich, versteh nich
  gcse ↓ I'm sorry I don't understand

N: so mit einem zeugnis + am schluss der schulzeit
  well with a certificate + at the end of school
  ham sie mit eim zeugnis abgeschlossen ↓
  did you finish with a certificate ↓

T: <mh> <sighs>

(15) N: oder ham sie abge#brochen
  or did you break off

T: #<u>*ah ja*</u> <suddenly loud, lively>
  oh yeah

N: verstehn sie ↑
  you understand

T: ich habe die <u>ganze</u> schule gemacht ↑
  I did the <u>whole</u> school ↑

N: mhm

(20) T ja ja
  yes yes

N: bis zu ende gemacht
  finished until the end

T: ja ja zu ende ↓
  yes yes till end ↓

N: <u>nicht</u> abgebrochen als sie zum militär gegangen sind
  <u>not</u> broken off when you joined the army

T: <mm> <negates question>

(25) N: ah ja
  ok

Getting to understand one another seems to be hard in this encounter, for both partners and throughout the whole interview. For example, in this sequence – which is quite typical in this respect – it can only be achieved by a continuous series of clarifications. So many difficulties with handling even relatively straightforward topics is not what one would expect, since Tino is no longer a beginner in the new language at that time, and in other contexts managed quite well to understand and express himself in German.

What kind of 'special' difficulties is Tino facing here? One important factor – to which other problems are added – is that during the whole interview conditions for the 'perceptibility´ of the questions posed to him are problematic. The counsellor, Mrs. M., speaks fast, her questions often are formulated in long utterances with no clear chunking through pauses or other prosodic cues. Her frequent use of self-interruptions and repetitions makes it difficult for the hearer to assess the beginning and ending of an utterance. In this way her question right at the start of the sequence (1/2) is interrupted two times – with a new start in (1) and a self-correction in (2) where she specifies the type of school she has in mind.

During most of the encounters, Tino's general attitude towards problems of understanding has been one of active engagement. Whenever possible, he attempts to formulate a hypothesis on what he *has* understood. Or, as a second option he tries at least to narrow down the causes as far as he is able to.

This is what he does in this encounter, too – at least at the start. With the 'best guess´ (3) he uses to indicate a problem with understanding he expresses *what* he has understood. It makes clear that he was not far off the mark, since his formulation involves only one minor simplification compared to the counsellor´s original question (i.e. Tino reports on his attending school in general, whereas she had wanted to ask for elementary school separately). Thus a simple confirmation from the interviewer´s part is enough to settle the problem and go on. This is one of the ways in which Tino successfully contributes to minimizing the effort of clarification during the interview. But at the same time he is not unaware of the awkwardness that frequent explicit signals of non-understanding mean for a conversation, as will become clear in the subsequent turns.

Mrs M.'s next question poses a *lexical problem* for Tino: he does not yet know the word 'Abschluß' (roughly corresponding to GCSE in English). Again he faces up to it and tries to make explicit what his problem is. The means used here are a *reprise* of the problematic item and a *metalinguistic comment* in two parts: first he apologizes for interrupting again ('I´m sorry'), then adds an explication of what the problem with 'Abschluß' is, namely that he does not understand the meaning of this word. But in spite of so much 'preparation' for the clarification already done by him, Mrs. M. has difficulties in finding a simple way of explaining this meaning. In her reformulation she relies mainly on one synonym for 'Abschluß', namely 'Zeugnis' (certificate), which is again a new, unknown word for Tino. This time, however, he chooses not to be explicit about his problem. Instead he uses a *minimal feedback* (spoken with a prosodic contour that signals 'helplessness'), which is meant to let Mrs. M. *infer* that he still has not understood. This departure from his general approach of being explicit with respect to his understanding is typical for 'second tries' in clarificatory sequences. Expressing one's non-understanding again is much more face-threatening than doing it for the first time, because it implies (among other things) that the interviewer's attempt at clarification has failed. Having to state that an already extensive and interrupting activity was not successful is of course more difficult than taking on the fault by oneself. A possible way to tone down this message and make it more polite is by leaving the decision of whether to continue the negotiation of meaning or not to one's addressee.

The counsellor is still bent on explaining the meaning of 'Abschluß'. For a new start she uses a negation of the opposite concept (i.e. 'break off'). Tino now understands and is so eager to demonstrate this that his confirmation check in (16) even comes as an interruption of her turn. An extended series of check backs ensues, until finally Mrs. M. is sure to have an answer reliable enough for the aims of the encounter.

But beyond the counsellor's problem in making her utterances 'transparent' from a linguistic point of view (see also Chapter 6 below), there is a second level of difficulty Tino has with the type of questions posed to him here. As the second excerpt will underline, what is meant here is a particular way his addressee has of *not* drawing inferences one would draw in an informal conversation. For example, when Tino stated earlier that he attended 'the normal school' he had meant this to include the information that he finished it. In a casual conversation the *Maxim of Relevance* would ensure that until stated otherwise, the 'normal case' should be understood. It is therefore a characteristic of the institutional setting that especially crucial information has not only to be expressed explicitly, but in many cases a ratification of mutual understanding seems to be necessary.

It is not only Tino who has a problem with this, of course. In the context of this interview difficulties on the linguistic level are multiplied on both sides by differing background assumptions on the *relevance* of certain questions. Clarification is hardly possible because most of the questions are established in a one-sided way by the interviewer and (at least initially) not shared by the migrant as a client (see also Becker and Perdue 1984; Roberts and Simonot 1987). This kind of misunderstanding on discourse level tends to have serious consequences for the further development of an encounter, because not being explicit about certain facts can easily be misunderstood as trying to hide something or refusing co-operation.

After this sequence the interview continues in a similar mode, riddled with non- and misunderstandings that have to be clarified. For her next topics Mrs M. tries to elicit information about Tino's working experience in Italy and Germany and, later on, his current situation. She gives up a first attempt at questioning him about starting a professional training course because of language problems. When it is broached for a second time, Tino finally understands the question, but says – somewhat vaguely, however – that he does not think of taking a course (see also the excerpt in Chapter 4.3). The counsellor now asks him explicitly what the alternatives are, in his opinion. Tino´s answer to this makes it quite clear that there is a contradiction between their lines of thought. He says: 'what i would like to do? . . . also work as a waiter but less hours a day' ('was ich möchte machen ↑ . . . ja auch kellner aber mit wenige stunden arbeite am tag ↓'). In response, Mrs. M. argues that this is not an alternative, since waiters always have this kind of working hours. She then starts a resumée by looking back on the jobs he has done as an unskilled worker – because such a job would at least guarantee a 'normal' work schedule. At this point of the interview, Tino himself brings in an alternative. A job he had really enjoyed doing had been door-to-door selling of books in Italy. But unfortunately he has so many problems linguistically in describing adequately what kind of job this was in detail, that Mrs. M. is not sure she has understood him correctly. The second excerpt below starts with her attempt to obtain again a ratification for those facts which are relevant from her perspective as a counsellor.

N: un dann ham sie <u>geklingelt</u> ↑ und ham gefragt ob das buch
    abgekauft werden möchte
    and then you rang the doorbell ↑ and asked whether they want to buy
    the book
    oder oder dann ham sie geklingelt un ham die bücher gezeigt ↑
    or or then you rang the bell and showed the books ↑
    un ham er/ auch er/ ham die auch/ ham sie auch erklären müssen
    and did he/ also he/ did they also/ had you also to explain
    was in so m buch drinsteht ↑
    what is written in such a book ↑

(5)   T: <mm – tut mir leid>   <laughingly>
            <mm – i am sorry>

       N: zu schnell ↑
            too fast ↑

       T: zu schnell ja ↑
            too fast yes ↑

       N: ja äh ich mein o.k. das ist auch ne berufliche m – sache in/
            yeah er i mean o.k. that was   a kind of job in/
            aber in italien halt gewesen ↓ äh +
            but in italy er +

(10)   ich mein ich/ mich würds immer noch interessieren warum sie
            nicht mehr/
            i mean i/ i still would like to know   why you no longer/
            heute
            today

       T: heute
            today

       N: jetzt in deutschland + warum sie keine aus/ warum sie nicht
            mehr lernen wollen +
            now in germany + why you don't / why you no longer want to learn

       T: äh weil äh ich will nicht lernen ↑
            er <because> i dont't want to learn ↑   <= why>

(15)   N: ja ↑
            yes

       T: äh < > + + weil äh +   <sighs>
            er + + because er +
            aber lernen auch deutsch ↑ oder eine *professione*↓
            but also learn german ↑ or a job ↓

       N: ja [ein/ ein beruf]
            yes [a/ a job]

       T: [*professione*↓]

(20)   N: ja
            yes

       T: ein beruf ↓ < >   <takes breath>
            a job
            weil äh äh ich spreche au ↑ kein deutsche ↓ für mich is schwer ↓
            because er er I speak no german ↓   for me its difficult ↓

       N: sie sprechen recht **gut** deutsch
            you speak fairly _well_ german

       T: mm <nein> + +   <laughingly>
            mm <no>

There are several indications in this sequence that the burden
caused by continuous extra efforts at understanding during the

encounter has by now increased uncertainties about the right way of expressing oneself on both sides.

So in her turn (1-4) Mrs. M. obviously does try hard to make answering easy for Tino – she gives several alternative formulations and what is wanted is only a ratification. The way she does this, however, creates a series of utterances so complex and lacking transparency (and spoken without clear 'punctuation') that Tino is at a loss. This constellation of non-understanding problems (cf. Chapter 3.3 above) typically makes it difficult to spot a specific problem and ask about it. It seems that Tino has no alternative to the unspecific indication of non-understanding he gives in (5) 'I'm sorry'). How deeply uncertain he feels about the exchange by now can be seen in the way in which he tones down his indication of non-understanding in three ways. Firstly it is an apology, an implicit means of conveying a problem with understanding. Secondly, he uses ellipsis 'Im sorry' rather than the full metalinguistic comment ('I'm sorry – I haven't understood') and thirdly on a paralinguistic level his laughter functions to mitigate the signal. In the subsequent turns (6-8) a consensus about the cause of Tino's non-understanding is worked out – but does not lead to any attempt at clarification: Mrs. M. does not modify her original question by reformulation, but gives up and switches to another topic – she turns again to the 'key question' of the interview ('. . . why you don't want to learn something'). At the same time she *devalues* Tino's contribution as being not really relevant to the search for alternatives, since it was a job 'in Italy'.

Before Tino finally starts to answer the central question on training (and this time get down to what he really thinks) he again initiates two further checks on his understanding (14 and, after having already started with his explanation, 17). It may again be an indication of the uncertainty accumulated by now, or it may be a slight hesitation before 'talking straight'.

There are, however, again examples of a joint attempt at understanding. Unlike in previous sequences, where the word 'Ausbildung' was explained and repeated several times, Tino now takes up the word 'Beruf' for 'professione' and uses it throughout in his responses (21, cf. also the excerpt below). And however bothering Mrs. M.'s insisting on the difficult question of 'training' might have been – it shows that at least she is willing to take him seriously with respect to his future life, where many counsellors choose to avoid further trouble by switching to some small-talk.

Before we turn to Tino´s own comments on the experience of this interview below, we will give some more room for what he says when he finally took the floor on the question of starting a training course or not.

(continuing from end of second excerpt above)

N: glauben sie daß sie das in/ daß das/ daß das <u>schwierig</u> ist ↑
    you believe that you / that this/ that this is <u>difficult</u> ↑

T: ich weiß es [<u>nicht</u>] wie mache
    i do [<u>not</u>] know how to do it

N: [ja]   mhm
    [yes]   mhm

T: äh wenn/ äh auch äh wenn ich spreche <u>besser</u> deutsch ↓ welches beruf gibt es ↑
    er if/ er even er if i speak german <u>better</u> ↓ what job is there ↑
    in deutschland äh es gibt äh <u>zwei millione</u> < >   <takes breath>
    in germany   there are <u>two million</u>
    äh zwei pers/ zwei millione persone ohne <u>arbeiten</u>
    er two peo/ two million people without <u>work</u>

N: mhm
    mhm

T: <u>oder</u> ↑
    or ↑

N: mja [stimmt]
    yeah [right]

T: [ohne arbeit ↓]
    without work ↓

N: ja ja
    right

T: stimmt ↑
    right ↑

N: ja das stimmt# [schon]
    yes that is right

T: # [ich bin] auch ausländer ↓ stimmt ↑ < > <short laugh>
    i am a foreigner ↓ right ↑

N: <ja>   <irritated>
    yes

T: wie ich muß machen ↓
    how i should do ↓

N: es gibt zwei millionen leute ohne arbeit aber auf der anderen seite is es/
    there are two million people without work but on the other hand it is/
    sind immer <u>die</u> leute vor arbeitslosigkeit <u>besser</u> geschützt die/
    always <u>those</u> people are protected <u>better</u> against unemployment who/

die einen <u>beruf gelernt</u> haben ↓
who got <u>professional training</u> ↓

T: mhm ↑
      mh ↑

N: die/ viele leute die jetzt arbeitslos sind die ham <u>keinen</u> beruf gelernt ↓
      the/ many people who are unemployed now they haven't had <u>any</u> training ↓

T: mhm
      mhm

N: wissen sie ↓
      you know ↓

T: ja ja
      yes yes

When we asked Tino one month later about his impressions of this interview, he remembered well that starting a training course had been one of the central questions. Interestingly, in the reflection elicited by the Italian researcher, he mentioned an argument against taking a course which was never discussed during the interview itself:

T: + cioè qua dero/ devo vivere per forza capisci non ho sol/
      well i have to live here in any case   i have no money
      cioè chissà quali soldi per poter fare questo corso +
      well who knows how much it would cost to make this course
      o anche tanta volontà non è che ce ne abbia tanta capisci
      and also so much a wish – i don't want it so much you know
      e poi magari – però devi avere anche risorse da parte per poter –
      capisci
      and then maybe – but you also must have resources to be able to – you know
      il che non mi è possibile per niente cioè sta tutto qui comunque
      and that is absolutely not possible for me well that's the problem

What we understand now is that with respect to the financing of a potential training Tino started from a totally different set of presuppositions from the counsellor. For him it was clear that training cost money and that he would have to pay it by himself – and there was no chance of this in his situation. From the point of view of the counsellor, however, the decision of wanting or not to gain further qualifications has priority above practical questions like costs and so on. And besides there are many possibilities of getting funding for a training, which she takes as a matter of course and does not feel a need to explain to Tino. So again in this case differing background assumptions led to a kind of hidden misunderstanding which could not be clarified and blocked understanding during important stretches of the interaction – a misunderstanding which could be responsible for missing an important chance to change his life.

In our analysis above we have tried to show that a good deal of Tino´s problems with understanding can be attributed to Mrs. M.'s way of speaking (and of organizing the interview as a whole). In Tino´s own view, however, it´s mainly him who is to blame for the communicative difficulties. This judgement becomes quite clear when the researcher asks for the impression he had in retrospect of the counsellor and himself:

N: che impressione ti ha fatto l´impiegata ↑
what impression did you have of the employer ↑
T: + cioè cordiale ma + proprio persona d´ufficio capisci ↑ abbastanza
seria +
well friendly but a really official person you know ↑ *rather serious*
seria no ↑ ma anche diciamo cordiale cioè senza segni di – non so
serious ↑ *but also let´s say friendly well without signs of – don't know*
+ senza (lei) (che) (si) spazientesse perché io n/n/ non ho capito o
non so
*without that she would have lost temper because i hadn´t understood or
what*
cercava di sforzarsi anche no ↑
she also tried to make some effort do her best ↑

And some turns later:

N: + e che impressione hai avuto di te stesso ↑ come ti sei visto ↑
what impression did you have of yourself ↑ *how did you see yourself* ↑
T: male + cioè perchè ancora non riesco a fare il discorso come si deve
bad well because i´m not yet able to lead a conversation like one should
neanche facile capisci neanche lo riesco a fare
it´s not easy you know i´m never able to do it
N: + che/ che impressione pensi di aver fatto ↑
what impression you think you have made ↑
T: ( ) come il solito straniero cioè lei avra (xx) capito
like the usual foreigner i mean she will have understood
che io n/ non so neanche cosa voglio
that i don´t even know what i want

A specific asymmetry is remarkable here: when Tino judges the counsellor´s presentation, he clearly acknowledges the difficult situation they both faced – she 'did her best', she really has struggled, and if she has failed somehow this is a relative failure. For himself, however, he only notices a general, absolute failure to behave as one (and he himself) would expect. Possibly his assessment is

biased by situational demands for politeness. But there is also a sus-
picion – that the counsellor´s way of interviewing not only makes
understanding difficult but, on a discourse level, also makes it hard
for the minority participant to realize and appreciate his own contribution to the making of understanding.

5.3 ERGÜN (TURKISH-DUTCH)

After five years of primary school Ergün started working as a
mechanic in Turkey. At the age of seventeen he left Turkey and
joined his parents, who had been living in Tilburg in the
Netherlands for some years. Soon after his arrival he attended a
Dutch language course for two hours a week for a period of five
months. His attendance was rather irregular and at the beginning
of the data collection period his command of Dutch was judged to
be very limited. After five months he found a job as a factory
worker on a temporary basis. Subsequently he went through periods of employment and unemployment. At the time of the first
session in the ESF project, Ergün had been living in the Netherlands
for about eleven months. He was still very much a teenager at this
stage. His contacts with native speakers resembled Mohamed's, one
of the Moroccan learners of Dutch. Being a youngster and living
with his family, he enjoyed life very much: visiting friends, going to
discotheques, playing football in a mixed Turkish/Dutch team, and
meeting Turkish and Dutch friends. After two years, because of
many parental rows, he moved to Groningen, a city in the northern
part of the Netherlands. He started working there as a car-wrecker
at a breaker's yard. Given the fact that there are not many minority
workers living in Groningen, Ergün's contacts with native speakers
of Dutch increased.

Ergün, over time, developed the capacity to communicate well.
Even with limited Dutch syntax/lexicon he was willing to make
explicit his understanding problems (see Broeder 1991). In this
way, he created learning opportunities for himself. He negotiated
more varied input and more precise specification of meaning with
the majority speaker. His basic orientation was to try and say
something, even if it was not entirely appropriate or accurate
rather than give no reaction. Ergün was very aware of his own
level of proficiency when asked by the Turkish researcher to comment on his knowledge of Dutch:

N: telaffuzun üzerine, cümle kurman üzerine nasıl bir fikrin var ↑
      what do you think about your pronunciation and syntax ↑

E: geleli bir buçuk sene oldu, halen bir şey bilmiyoruz. bir burada ve bir
      de kızlarla falan hollandaca konuşuyoruz, yoksa hiç hollandaca
      konuşmuyoruz.
      i talk already one and a half year with you and still only i know nothing. i
      only talk dutch here and with dutch girls or so. for the rest i never speak
      dutch.

N: hollandaca telaffuzunu nasıl buluyorsun ↑
      what do you think about your pronunciation ↑

E: sallanıyor
      very bad

N: cümle kurman nasıl ↑
      what do you think about your syntax ↑

E: bildiğim kelimeler oldu muydu, onları biliyorum, evet. yalnız
      konuşurken, cevap verirken, onu kelime kelime kurması var. o
      zaman aralarındaki kelimeleri tam anlamıyla bulam ıyoruz.
      if i know some words or sentences, then i use them. however to talk and to
      give answers requires that one should be able to construct a correct
      sentence. and that is what i can not do

N: nasıl yani, ↑ bir türkçe misal ver ↑
      how do you mean, ↑ could you give an example in turkish ↑

E: mesela: ben eve gidiyorum, ik ga weg 'ga' yı duymadığımdan veya
      bilmediğimden konşurken 'ga'yı atıyorum ve 'ik weg' diyorum.
      cümle kuramıyorum. bu tabii ki kitaplardan öğrenilebilir.
      for example 'i go away', because i do not know what 'go' means, i drop 'go'
      and say 'i away'. you see, i can not construct sentences. this is what one can
      only learn from books. i have no time for that

But these comments also indicate that Ergün underestimates his
ability to communicate and his strategic competence (cf. Canale and
Swain 1980) in managing problems of understanding (see below).

The interaction that we shall focus on is an interview with an official associated with the municipal department of the housing office
chiefly visited by ethnic minorities. The interview took place two
years after Ergün's arrival in the Netherlands when Ergün was still
living in his parents' home and was having serious conflicts with
his father. In the interview, Ergün tries to convince the official that
the present living conditions are desperate because of continual
parental quarrels and an intended marriage within three months.
Something has to be done. The housing official fills in an application form. He discusses with Ergün the topics relevant to filling in
this form such as present living conditions, special circumstances

and urgent needs. A feedback session took place one month later. The Turkish researcher and Ergün jointly go through the video recording of the interview. They discuss in Turkish those passages which are unclear or where there are contradictions and overt or suspected understanding problems.

In the housing interview Ergün prefers to be on record rather than leaving understanding difficulties implicit. He uses a variety of procedures to indicate understanding problems, ranging from less explicit minimal responses to general metalinguistic requests. One of the most remarkable aspects of his behaviour are face-saving features (that is, face-saving for Ergün). As we have shown in Chapter 4, he 're-uses' the utterances of the native interlocutor. The reconstruction consists of (mostly partial) reprises that leave the structure and the prosodic features of the interlocutor's utterance intact. The reconstructions clearly help Ergün to process the information and help the majority speaker to negotiate understanding. Re-using is also done through well-considered repetitions and reformulations. Ergün seems to check whether his understanding is complete. He highlights the keywords of the preceding interlocutor's utterance. It is a response-preparing strategy which provides him with a stronger guarantee of an appropriate answer.

Ergün seems to compensate for the face-threatening explicit marking of non-understanding by also stating that he understands the housing official and implying that he does not need further clarification. For example he uses the general metalinguistic comments *ja snap ik wel* ('yes I understand'), and *ja dat begrijp ik wel* ('yes I understand that'). However, Ergün's inclination to indicate understanding problems also affects the degree the housing official adapts. He relies on Ergün's ways of indicating when there are non-understandings and consequently misunderstandings occur when Ergün's behaviour implies that he has understood.

We will now discuss some sequences from the housing interview. The first sequence starts at a point where the official is explaining the complicated rules for the assignment of housing accommodation. Ergün needs to understand the detail of this. The housing official accommodates his speech, speaking remarkably slowly, emphasizing keywords, specifying and reformulating. He also uses several turns in his explanation, each time evaluating Ergün's response to a particular piece of information.

N: ja ja en hier moeten we nog ook even invullen wat u graag zou willen
yes yes and here we have to fill in what you would like to have

E: ja
yes

N: als u gaat/ gaat trouwen/ gaat samenwonen
if you are going/ going to marry/ going to live together

E: ja
yes

N: hier mag u `n voorkeur uitspreken wat `t mag zijn + wat u graag zou
willen
here you can specify your preference + what you would like to have

E: ja
yes

N: weet u wat ↑
do you know what ↑

E: weet ik niet
i don't know

N: nee ↑ wat u graag zou willen 'n/ 'n kamer of 'n flatje of 'n huis
no ↑ what you would like to have a/ a room or an apartment or a house

E: oh ja ja ik heb/ ik wil thuis hebben
oh yes yes i have/ i want to have a home

N: ja
yes

E: maar die stad of flat ah dat/ dat maakt niks uit
but that city or apartment ah that/ that does not matter

N: hmhm nou je wordt gevraagd wat je graag zou willen
ehem well you are being asked what you would like to have

E: ja
yes

N: maar er zijn ook de toewijzingsnormen he + d'r zijn wat spelregeltjes
die zeggen wie wat mag hebben + jullie zijn straks met z'n tweetjes ja
man en vrouw
*but there are also the assignment norms eh + there are some rules of the game
that regulate who can have what + you soon will a couple yes man and wife*

E: ja
yes

N: en dan kun je in aanmerking komen voor een flat [ja]
and then you can be considered for an apartment [yes]

N: flat kan + een bejaardenwoning dat hoeft nog niet he
apartment is possible + a house for the elderly that is not necessary eh

E: nee
no

N: is voor oude mensen straks als je ouder wordt
is for old people later if you are getting old

E: <laughs>

On the surface there seem to be few understanding problems. However, the feed-back session provides us with a view, below the surface, of exactly what Ergün did not understand and what his interpretation was:

N: spelregeltjes'in ne olduğunu biliyor musun ↑
    what does rules of the game mean ↑
E: spel oyun demektir, regeltjes'in ne olduğunu bilmiyorum
    game means game i don't know what rules means
N: bejaardenwoning nedir ↑
    what does home for the elderly mean ↑
E: bilmiyorum
    i don't know
N: peki, sen neden 'nee' dedin ↑
    but why did you say 'no' ↑
E: anlamadığımdan öyle dedim
    i said it because i didn't understand
N: bejaardenwoning'i sen nasıl bir anlama alabilirsin ↑
    what do you think house for the elderly means ↑
E: temelli bir yerde kalma evi. hayır dedim, hani kimbilir sonradan
    bana para yetmez de çıkmak isterim
    *a house where you can live for ever. i said no because in the future I might
    have not enough money and then i may want to move*

It is possible that the meaning Ergün assigns to the word *bejaardenwoning* ('house for the elderly') is because of the association of the lexeme *jaar* ('year').

In any event, either Ergün was completely at a loss as to the meaning of 'house for the elderly' or he forms a wrong hypothesis about its meaning. However, interactionally, his response in the negative and then his laughter *appears* both cohesive and relevant.

In this short extract there are two sets of tensions which interact together to produce an interesting dynamic of comfortable moments and understanding problems. The first tension is the classic bureaucratic one between personal choice or preference, on the one hand, and qualifying regulations on the other. Ergün is asked to specify what he wants but is also told there are some 'assignment norms'. This tension is made explicit as a result of the housing officer's accommodation strategies. He reformulates 'specify preferences' as 'what you would like to have' and makes a comment on the bureaucratic procedures as 'rules of the game'. This process of shifting down to a less formal register not only illuminates the tension but it may also send a misleading message to

Ergün: that there is real choice and any tiresome restrictions are only a game.

The other tension is an illustration of the issue discussed in Chapter 4, between seeking clarification and managing both face and interaction. Ergün's capacity to sustain the interview is surprisingly native-like given his limited knowledge of the linguistic code in Dutch. He even manages appropriate responses when the housing officer introduces his joke about a home for the elderly although, subsequently, it is clear that he did not understand. At this stage in the interaction, therefore, despite misunderstandings, conversational involvement is maintained and there seems little or no loss of face.

The second sequence (a few minutes later) from the housing interview shows a misunderstanding which lasted for several turns. Ergün misunderstands the offical's question *vrouw niet in verwachting he* ('wife is not expecting eh'). He confuses the Dutch word *verwachting* ('expecting') with *wachten* ('wait') and this is further compounded by the ambiguity illustrated in the preceding sequence over whether Ergün is yet married.

N: er is nog geen kind op komst denk ik ↑ nog geen baby ↑
      there is no baby coming i think ↑ not yet baby ↑

N: he ↑
      eh ↑

E: nee nog niet
      no not yet

N: komt ook nog niet he ↑ vrouw niet in verwachting he ↑
      is also not coming yet eh ↑ wife is not expecting eh ↑

E: ja
      yes

N: vrouw wel in verwachting ↑
      woman is expecting ↑

E: jawel
      yes

N: wel in verwachting ↑
      is expecting ↑

E: ja wacht
      yes wait

N: wanneer komt de baby ↑
      when does the baby come ↑

E: weet ik niet
      i don't know

N: niet ↑
      not ↑

E: nee
    no

N: hoe lang is ze in verwachting dan ↑
    how long has she been expecting then ↑

E: oo misschien een jaar twee jaar [ik]
    oh maybe one year two year [i]

N: [oh]
    [oh]

E: weet ik ook niet
    i don't know – me either <laughs>

N: dat lijkt me wat onwaarschijnlijk + nee [kijk]
    that seems unlikely to me + no [look]

N: ik denk dat je me verkeerd begrijpt + ik vraag of je vrouw in
    verwachting is + of ze 'n baby krijgt je vrouw + of je aanstaande + er
    is geen baby op komst
    *i don't think that you understand me correctly + i ask whether your wife is
    expecting + whether she will get a baby + or your fianceé + there is no baby
    coming ↑*

E: ik begrijp niks
    i understand nothing

N: nee ↑
    no ↑

E: nee
    no

N: weet je wat 'n baby is ↑
    do you know what a baby is ↑

E: ja dat weet ik/ weet ik wel
    yes i know that/ i know that indeed

N: ja <laughing>
    yes

E: ja
    yes

N: ja maar die/ d'r is geen baby in 't spel + vrouw is niet in verwachting
    \[vrouw]
    yes but that/ there is no baby + woman is not expecting \[woman]

E: \[niet] wachten ↑
    \[not] wait ↑

N: vrouw krijgt geen baby ↑
    woman gets no baby ↑

E: oh
    oh

N: of wel ↑
    or does she ↑

E: + \[(xx)]

N: \[krijgt] vrouw baby ↑ nu ↑
      \[gets] woman baby ↑ now ↑

E: nee nou niet
      no not now

N: nu ↑ geen baby he ↑
      now ↑ no baby eh ↑

E: nee
      no

N: nee nee dat gaat geen jaren duren he
      no no that does not take years eh

E: ja
      yes

N: 't gaat geen jaren duren als `n vrouw in verwachting is + d`r staat
      negen maanden voor
      it does not take years if a woman is pregnant + that will take nine months

Er: ja
      yes

N: bij olifanten duurt `t negen jaar geloof ik + dat is wat anders. en zijn
      er omstandigheden op medische gebied + waarop urgentiepunten te
      krijgen zijn he ↑ bent u of uw aanstaande vrouw ziek ↑
      with elephants it will take nine years i think + that is something else. and
      are there other medical circumstances + for which you can get urgency
      points eh ↑ + are you or your fianceé ill ↑

E: ja
      yes

Ergün misunderstands the official's question about whether his
wife is expecting a baby. The source of this misunderstanding is the
confusion between *verwachting* ('expecting') and *wachten* ('wait')
which Ergün confirms in the feedback session. But this simple lexi-
cal confusion is underpinned by a deeper misunderstanding. Ergün
is surprised by the question of the housing official. How could his
wife be pregnant if he is not married? He makes this clear in the
feedback session afterwards:

(1)   N: vrouw in verwachting nedir ↑
            what does woman is expecting mean ↑
      E: kadın bekliyor mu ↑ ben de he dedim ++ bak, bunu sorması hata.
            Galiba evdeki kalabalığı kastediyor. yani ben evlenirsem evde
            kalabalık olacak diyor. onun için bunu soruyor
            he asks whether the woman is waiting for me. i said yes.
            look he asks me an irrelevant question. maybe he means the problem of
            overcrowding in the house. in other words, it will be very crowded at
            home, if i would marry. that's why he is asking this.

N: niye hataymış ↑
why irrelevant ↑
E: ben daha evlenmedim ki ↑ nasıl çocuğum olsun ↑
i am not yet married ↑ how can i get a child ↑
(5) N: in verwachting means hamilelik
expecting means pregnant
E: öyle mi, yahu ↑ bunlarda bir kelime çok çeşit manaya geliyor.
kafamı karıştıran budur
really ↑ with the dutch people a word has different meanings. this is
also a problem for me.

Again, as in the previous sequence discussed above, Ergün's mis-understanding is masked by his strategic and interactional competence. Ergün's first response *nee nog niet* ('no not yet') confirms the housing officer's assumptions. This stage of the interview could have been completed at this point. However, the latter chooses to make some further confirming checks by reformulating and so triggers a lengthy misunderstanding with the word *verwachting* ('expecting'). Over the next six turns the misunderstanding is sustained despite Ergün's hypothesis-forming reprise at line 9 *ja wacht* ('yes wait') which the official does not respond to. Despite his apparent surprise that Ergün does not know when the baby is due, it takes another five turns before he shifts the interaction into a 'side sequence' marked by overt metacommunication and a progressive deconstruction of the concept of 'expecting a baby'. The response is a form of 'hyper-explanation' (Erickson 1982) in which an assumed lack of understanding leads to lengthy explanations at increasingly lower levels of abstraction.

In Erickson's context, that of the white bureaucrat, 'the man', talking to black American clients, 'hyperexplanations' are clearly perceived as a put-down. Ergün's response at line 25 *ja dat weet ik* ('yes I know that') suggests that he interprets such procedure in the same way and compensates for the potential face threat by explicitly indicating his understanding.

Again, at line 29 Ergün uses the same hypothesis – forming reprise *niet wachten* ('not wait ↑)' because the native speaker reintroduces the source of the confusion *verwachting* ('expecting'). But since the latter is now thoroughly involved with his own clarification sequence, he again ignores Ergün's attempt at clarification. His pidginised reformulation at line 30 *vrouw krijgt geen baby* ('woman gets no baby') triggers what we might call a watershed marker for Ergün, 'oo' which is then followed up by the crucial time-marker *nu* ('now') at line 34 from the housing officer and in Ergün's next turn, there is evidence, at last, that he has understood the question. The 'woman gets no baby' proposition, excluding any reference to waiting/expecting starts the final and successful attempt at clarification in which over the next four turns, the understanding problem is progressively resolved.

It is not clear whether Ergün then understands the housing officer's back reference to Ergün's earlier response that his fianceé has been 'expecting' for one or two years. But again, the native speaker turns the misunderstanding into a joke which may also be interpreted as a compensation for the potential face threat. The subsequent phases of the interview combine a similar mix of accommodation, misunderstandings, compensations for face-threats, smooth interactional sequences and, finally, an explicit statement about goal accomplishment from the housing officer:

N: om 't gezin te herenigen + ja ↑ dus dat is ook niet + dit ook niet + dat ook niet + nou dan is 't formulier in ieder geval zo ver goed ingevuld
      to bring the family together + yes ↑ that it is not + that also not + that also not + well now the form is filled in properly so far
E: ja
      yes

However, although there is a sense of an ending, the form has not been filled out accurately because of further misunderstandings. In particular, Ergün has not been able to indicate that there are family problems at home and that is one of the main reasons why he is applying for housing accommodation.

This interaction illustrates the mix of strategies Ergün used throughout the research period. He deployed a wide range of strategies to indicate understanding problems, maintain a relatively smooth interactional environment and save face. He often preferred to be on record in explicitly indicating difficulties but also wished to keep the interaction going and, with his native-like responses, often, but not necessarily consciously, deluding the majority speaker that all was well. The response-preparing behaviour (see Broeder 1992), although not evident in the two illustrative examples here, is another example of his active participation in the encounter.

5.4 SANTO (ITALIAN-ENGLISH)

Santo was in his early twenties when he moved to London to join his English-speaking Italian girlfriend ten months before the start of the project. He had been to 'scuola media' in Italy, making a total of eight years of education, and after that he had worked in the catering trade in his home city, Naples, and on ships. He came from a large family of eleven children of which he was the fifth.

On arrival in England Santo found himself accommodation in a bedsitting room in suburbia near to where his girlfriend's family lived. He found employment in the centre of London. The job he held for the duration of the project was as a chef's assistant in a restaurant in the City. The other workers in the restaurant came from other countries in Europe and South America. No one was a native speaker of English. However, Santo's contact with English was not as limited as some other workers in similar situations. He spoke some English with his girlfriend, talked to the other tenants in the house he lived in and went out to pubs and the cinema. Because of these contacts he did not give the impression of being isolated in any way. Although he was someone who evidently enjoyed communicating, and who enjoyed the data collection sessions of the project, occasionally even going out voluntarily to record conversations and day-to-day interactions, he did not attend any language classes. This was not for lack of motivation to learn the language but, as for so many others in his position, there was little real opportunity given the nature of his work and the long hours spent in the restaurant. Unlike some other informants, he did not have children, and so there was no added incentive to learn in order to increase his career prospects or provide a better chance for the next generation. If anything, his girlfriend, with whom he finally returned to Italy, was more interested in encouraging their joint return rather than remaining in London. Of his own volition, Santo returned to Naples whenever possible, that is at Christmas and in the summer holidays, to visit his parents and siblings whom he was helping to support financially through his employment in London.

From the outset, Santo was one of the most outgoing and lively of the Italian informants. He appeared to be very confident and frequently initiated conversations with the researchers as well as taking the lead in guided tours. He frequently chose to keep to the conversational goals he had set himself and combined this with good interpersonal skills. Even in gatekeeping situations, he would attempt to create an atmosphere of joviality which sometimes misfired but which was generally taken as good humour. As the project data has shown, learners who themselves set the agenda as far as subject matter is concerned display fewer difficulties with understanding. Santo was certainly quite masterful in controlling conversations. By nature he appeared to be a *raconteur* and thus often wrested control of the topic away from his interlocutors.It is on this assertiveness that we focus.

In his initial interview, Santo was able to give evidence of the fact that he had understood in a very concise way, by correcting a statement made by the researcher:

N: when are you going away ↑ twentieth of aug/ no +
      that's right ↑
S: september

Santo was so much at ease that on seeing the neck mike that he would need to wear for the recording he asked, in Italian, to put it on with no more ado:

(1)   S: *microfono + microfono*
             -< = microphone microphone>
       N: that's right. do you want to put it on ↑
       S: one two three four + come in + +
       N: you can put it on your shirt
(5)   S: aah + + (xx) you now *hai* television ↑
             - < = have>
       N: there's no television
       S: ah no
       N: it's only recording
       S: *ma* this *microfono* only for me ↑
             - <= but> -<= microphone>
(10)   N: yeah but it/ it takes/ it carries the sound very well + it records
             our voices too
       S: alright

Santo's confidence went hand in hand with a tendency to set the conversational agenda. In the first encounter he was quick to indicate that he had not understood, and asked the researcher for help:

(1)   N: and can you read and write english too ↑
       S: + + repeat
       N: can you read and write english ↑
       S: + +

```
N:   can you read books in english ↑
S:   + + no no no no + eh or any thing
N:   nothing
S:   nothing yeah
```

Later in the same episode, this statement was shown to be misleading. Santo could read English since he read out loud several
words from a picture in a book. One assumes that what he meant
was that he could not read and understand continuous prose,
whereas he evidently could cope with words and short phrases.

Despite this apparent confidence, Santo was also very conscious
of the need to expand his English vocabulary. In the second meeting with the research team, he asked the Italian speaking researcher
for vocabulary.

```
(1)   S:   this er round + you know the name of this around?
            *cos e* ↑
            - <= what is ↑ >
      N:   finsbury park
      S:   finsbury ↑
(5)   N:   mhm?
      S:   a very + er + *come si dice trascurata? + in inglesi vedi queste
            frase mi mancano perche son complicate*
            <= how do you say run down? in English, you see, I lack these
            phrases because they are complicated>
      N:   *trascurato ↑ *
            <= run down>
      S:   eh
      N:   it/its not looked after is ver
      N:   run down yeah
      N:   run down ya
      N:   run down
      S:   run down ↑
```

Partly as a result of his desire to talk rather than remain silent,
Santo's problems with understanding were easier to identify than
those of the learner who does not respond or gives only a minimal
response when confronted by an item they do not understand as in
Fatima's case.

In this way one can see that because Santo volunteers information, lack of understanding is relatively easy for the majority
speakers to detect. The way in which they respond varies greatly.
The next excerpt shows that the majority speaker does not always

make a sympathetic response to difficulties with understanding. Santo had gone into a travel agent's to ask the price of the coach from London to Birmingham.

(1) S: excuse me only for information how much one ticket the *corriera*
         - <=coach>
     S: *da londra a* birmingham
         <=from London to>
     N: from london to birmingham ↑
(5) S: yeah
     N: yeah what ↑
     S: er how much the price ↑
     N: what do you want to go by ↑
     S: next week
(10) N: + on what ↑ + on what ↑ bus ↑ train ↑ what ↑
     S: birmingham
     N: yeah but what do you want to travel on + donkey ↑
     S: anyone
     N: any < go by>
         <laughs>
(15) S: yeah
     N: is it coach ↑ + coach or bus ↑
     S: coach [coach]
     N: [one way] / coach
     S: yeah
(20) N: one way ↑
     S: yeah ++ one way
     N: <laughs>
     S: *me la devi spiegare questa*
         <you must explain that one to me>
     S: (xxxx) you eh ↑
(25) N: what you want to go on ↑ horse back ↑ and you say any one ↑
     S: anyone no problem
     N: <laughs>
     S: anyone the same for me
     N: <laughs>
(30) S: you know what I mean ↑
     N: yeah yeah <oh I like that>
         <laughs>
     S: very funny
     N: <london birmingham>
         <laughs>
     S: one person
(35) N: mhm <++++++>
         <very long pause whilst consulting information sheets>

```
     N:  london birmingham one way ↑
     S:  yeah
     N:  four fifty
     S:  four/ four [pound and fifty]
(40) N:  [four pounds and] fifty pence four pounds and fifty pence
         alright
     S:  thank you very much indeed
     N:  all right
     S:  goodbye
```

In this interaction Santo shows great tenacity in adhering to his original goal. He first misunderstands at (8) and mishears 'what' for 'when' in the travel agent's question. He then fails to pick up on the agent's next question at (10) which has been reformulated so as to include specific lexical items ('bus', 'train') as well as omitting non-salient items, thereby simplifying the load. Santo does still not process this correctly and hazards another guess, having deduced that the time was not being asked for, that the question has to do with his destination. It seems that Santo has still not understood the agent's next reformulation in which he starts to show at (11) signs of frustration, and it is not until (16) where alternative meanings are explicitly offered that Santo is able to answer the question. Santo's perseverance in narrowing meaning down until he is certain that he has understood means that his difficulties with understanding are usually readily recognisable and recognised by the majority speaker who is then able to help resolve them. There are of course moments of awkwardness which are good examples of how costly it can be to resolve non-understanding, but Santo's own good humour overrides the potential loss of face. He glosses over the possibility that the majority speaker is being sarcastic – and he gets the information he requires.

In the subsequent session in which he is asked to comment on this interaction, he describes his own perception of what happened in the following way:

```
(1)  N:  did you like making the recording outside ↑
     S:  ++ <in>
         <very hesitant>
     S:  er in - what ↑ \
     N:  in the street in the [travel agent]
(5)  S:  [uh is] very very + very funny
     N:  yes ↑
     S:  i like [ya]
     N:  [ya] you enjoyed it ↑
```

When pressed by the researcher to evaluate which of the encounters on the guided tour he had enjoyed the most, Santo responds

S: for me ↑ is very fun/ <for>
      <prolonged>
S: travel agent
N: mhm
S: because very <funny>
      <laughs>

It would appear, though, that at this stage Santo refers to the travel agent simply because the researcher has mentioned this particular encounter. It is at points such as these that the value of 'debriefing' in Italian becomes evident as these next comments show:

(1)   N: mm + *dov dov e che ti sei sentito meglio con il tuo inglese dove hai avuto successo con il tuo inglese ↑
             <= where did you feel best with your english? where were you successful with your english?>
       S: uh when I ask <the> boys in the road
             <prolonged>
       N: uh uh
(5)   S: <for> the one di/ one shop I ask information + [for]
       N: [mhm]
       S: my/ the one people
       N: mhm
       S: try the road i ask /is very perfect information
(10)   S: +++*invece*
             <=whereas>
       S: the people in a /agency
       N: ya
       S: for information <the>
             <prolonged>
       N: mhm
(15)   S: the ticket + is quickly nervous yes what you want ↑ what ↑ <>
             < imitates someone talking very fast>
       N: yeah yeah
       S: because me before when going for [in] formation don't understand don't understand nothing you know what i mean ↑ understand/
       N: [mm]

We see from these comments that Santo was, all along, aware of the tension between achieving understanding and losing face, and that the humour he engaged with in fact masked an unease that was not at all apparent.

Santo's assertiveness comes into play at several points in the encounter we have chosen to examine in detail which took place in an estate agent's office. During the actual recording, the estate agent was not aware of being recorded as she talked. Santo was accompanied by the Italian-speaking researcher on the project and occasionally addressed remarks to her in Italian, thus giving the impression that she was a friend accompanying him.

Although Santo was not seriously considering house purchase at the time of the recording, he had mentioned it as a possible option were he to stay in England. The encounter at the estate agent's is different from many other situations in which the minority speaker usually interacts because the power imbalance is not so heavily weighted towards the majority speaker. This is because the client goes to an estate agent voluntarily and, as a potential buyer, has to be courted. The client of course needs somewhere to live but there is a degree of customer control that would be unthinkable in the case of an applicant for council housing or for privately rented accommodation. The estate agent's aims are to provide a service. She wishes to match the client's interest and means as closely as possible to the property she has available and to provide the client with details of any property that might be considered suitable.

Santo opens the interview by stating his wishes and then waiting for the agent to respond with further questions or information, a strategy that, as Gumperz and Roberts (1991) point out, is common to many interethnic encounters.

(1)　S:　i want to buy + the house
　　　A:　yes
　　　S:　maybe three bedroom
　　　A:　three bedrooms
(5)　S:　yeah
　　　A:　erm what/ roughly what price were you thinking of
　　　　　paying for the house
　　　S:　forty thousand ↑
　　　A:　forty ↑
(10)　S:　max yeah
　　　A:　yeah erm i haven't got any houses around forty thousand for
　　　　　sale i don't think erm. i'll give you our list
　　　S:　yeah what you think ↑
(15)　A:　that goes up to fifty i think (xxx) in the area that we cover erm
　　　　　for forty thousand you/ it'd probably be a flat.
　　　S:　not a house ↑
　　　A:　yeah you want a house though, do you ↑

	S:	yeah a house
(20)	A:	yeah i haven't got any houses around forty erm + you see, around \<here> it's quite expensive
		\<indicating on the map>
	S:	\<islington>
		\<reading>
	A:	yeah whoops \<low aside>
	S:	too small this one
	A:	yeah erm you see, we're here
(25)	S:	in islington is possible three bedrooms for forty thousand ↑
	A:	two bedrooms ↑
	S:	three
	A:	well you might get a /perhaps a flat a large, but not round here for forty thousand erm you've got to go further north.
(30)	S:	oh
	A:	perhaps say towards \<tottenham or somewhere up there>
		\<points to map>
	A:	you'd get i think you'd get a house there for about thirty five forty thousand but that's
	S:	too long
(35)	A:	yeah i mean there is a tube station out there if you want to get into london central london quite easily
	S:	\<seven sisters>
		\<reading the name of the tube station on the map>
	A:	yeah but erm i think you'll find it very difficult to get at you/to get a three-bedroomed house for forty thousand we just haven't got anything like that
(40)	S:	(xx) how much you think it cost for three bedroom ↑
	A:	three bedroom ↑
	S:	fifty ↑
	A:	er + erm depends where= if it's around here then [it would probably be] about seventy between seventy
(45)	S:	[in this area]
	A:	and seventy five if you go out say to stoke newington around \<here>
		\<indicates on map>
	S:	mm
(50)	A:	then you might get one for about fifty + sixty + or say forty eight sixty something like that
	S:	very expensive area any way
	A:	well this this is expensive this is less expensive

By (52) Santo demonstrates agreement with the agent's assessment of the situation. This agreement has been an extended process and demonstrates Santo's ability as a learner to pursue his own goals, even though the majority speaker he is interacting with may not share his aims and has, in this case, already signalled very firmly that she does not believe that they have any property on her books that would meet Santo's requirements. The implied message behind 'I'll give you our list' (12) is, then, an indication that Santo should go away and use the detailed information on the list to realise that it is impossible to find a house at the price he wants in the area he wants.It is a pre-closing statement and it could, and probably would, be perceived by a majority speaker as an invitation to leave. Santo, however, does not (choose to) hear this and engages the estate agent with his next question which constitutes the start of a long process of familiarising himself with the variables of buying property in this part of London.

What is established next, then, at (15) is that for £40,000 one might find a flat but not a house in that part of London. Santo then checks back quite explicitly at (16) with 'not a house ↑' which prompts the agent in turn to confirm that Santo is indeed looking for a house. There is then a re-run of the same information until (28) where the agent makes her earlier statement 'not . . . around here' more particular by specifying 'you've got to go further north . . . perhaps, say towards tottenham'. This information, combined with the following utterance, 'i think you'd get a house there for about thirty five forty thousand', makes it clear to Santo where the boundaries of expensive and less expensive property lie in this part of London. What has now been established for him is

i)   he can't buy a house, only a flat, for the price he wishes to pay in the Finsbury Park area
ii) he might find a house for that price, but it would be further north, around Tottenham.

The statements by the agent at (16), (29) and (31) all indicate that really Santo is looking for property in the wrong location. On none of these occasions does Santo acknowledge the possible closing force of these utterances and instead pursues his own goals of refining his knowledge of the property market. The topic moves on to Santo's need for ease of access to public transport into the centre of London:

     S: too long
(35) A: yeah i mean there is a tube station out there if you want to go into london central london quite easily
     S: seven sister

A: yeah but erm i think you'll find it very difficult to get at/ you /to get a three bedroomed house for forty thousand we just haven't got anything like that.

(40) S: how much you think it cost for three bedroom ↑

A: three bedroom ↑

S: fifty

A: er + erm + depends where + if it's around here then [it would probably be] about seventy between seventy

(45) S: [in this area] a: and seventy five if you go out to say stoke newington around <here>
<indicates on map>

S: mm

(50) A: then you might get one for about fifty + sixty + or say forty eight sixty something like that

S: very expensive area anyway

This shift is very typical of the way in which Santo frequently conducts conversations, and in this interaction, it is a method of maintaining involvement even when the agent evidently feels that she cannot meet Santo's demands.

Although he appears to understand what the estate agent is telling him by concurring remarks such as, 'very expensive area anyway', (52) the agent's reply amends his perspective and she follows this up by a reiteration of her opinion at (56)

(56) A: if you go further north you know it tends to be a bit cheaper + but i don't/ i think you'll find it difficult. the only place i can think of around here would be somewhere like tottenham where you might get that / one for that price

Again, Santo ignores the implied message that the interview is at an end and, instead, he proceeds to give an explanation of why he needs a two bedroomed house and why this particular area would suit him.

(60) S: it's important for me two bedroom because i have the + the brother and the sister [uh]

A: [yeah i see] yeah

S: is very important for me and er work in central london i work in the city + in holborn

(65) A: i see

S: city

A: yes

S: i think for every morning in the underground you know half hour forty minute

In other words, he repeats the point he made earlier at (34) about travelling time and which the estate agent has already responded to in (35).Nonetheless the agent takes up the topic as to whether a house in this area would be conveniently situated and it is Santo who then returns to the issue of price at (79).

	S:	any way for er forty thousand very complication [ ]
(80)	A:	[yeah you've got er] very difficult + erm even two bedroomed flats is not too easy now
	S:	no
	A:	erm + but I think if you want a house and if you want three bedrooms you'd have to go and call at the agents out this way more
(85)	S:	seven sister
	A:	round tottenham seven sisters yeah
	S:	i no like this area for me (laughing)
	A:	you might even if you go a bit further north you might get something out here with three bedrooms i've got a house
(90)	S:	in this area ↑
	A:	for forty seven thousand that's in hermitage road this road here.
	S:	yeah
	A:	three bedrooms but erm
	S:	but/
(95)	A:	but i don't/i think you'd find it difficult
	S:	for this price ↑
	A:	yes yeah especially three bedrooms + + you can take the list and have a look [but]
	S:	[yeah yeah]
	A:	i can't think of any thing [really]
(100)	S:	[tonight ↑ yeah]
	A:	that would be suitable
	S:	yeah i know is not easy for found
	A:	no no
	S:	okay
(105)	A:	might be agents in haringey they might have something
	S:	yeah
	A:	maybe going that way a bit but its not very good for the tube there you see + you could get a train couldn't you + to finsbury park ↑ from haringey
(110)	S:	+ do you have er in this road or one house ↑
	A:	well for forty seven thousand
	S:	forty seven
	A:	yeah forty seven
	S:	is house isnt it ↑
(115)	A:	a house yes yeah its in the bit there

```
         S:   okay well [i think]
         A:   [okay but i] think you'd have to try agents more [out that way]
         S:   [yeah] for that price
         A:   yeah its difficult very difficult round here
(120)    S:   for me plenty difficult (laughs)
         A:   yeah
         S:   okay
         A:   sorry i cant help you any more but er you know
         S:   i think maybe more five six months i possible spend this price
              for three bedrooms
(125)    A:   mm
         S:   yeah because i / coming the people no ↑ from italy
         A:   + yes
```

It is remarkable that despite the agent's attempts at closure (at 84, 105 and 117), Santo continues to set his own agenda. At (86) he explains why he does not want to consider Tottenham as a possible area to live in and from (97) to (100) there is evidence that he is so intent on finding a property he wants that he misunderstands what the agent is saying. She is suggesting looking at the list of property available but Santo believes her to be offering to take him to see a house - hence his question at (100), 'tonight?'

The agent has made several attempts to persuade Santo to look elsewhere for accommodation. It is only at (120) that Santo indicates both that he has understood and that his opinion converges with that of the estate agent and finally, at this juncture, he takes up the pre-closures. Through the next exchanges the interaction moves into a new phase in which there is tacit agreement that Santo will not find a house that conforms to his wishes unless he is able to pay more.

Santo's refusal in this encounter to let the agent set the agenda is interesting from two perspectives. The first is concerned with why Santo chose to resist the agent's attempts at closure. We can only surmise that it could be one or a combination of many factors that include the wish to please the researchers by getting more data, or real lack of understanding on Santo's part that the agent was trying to close the encounter, or his wish to establish what the parameters to house purchase really were.The second is concerned with the behaviour of the majority speaker: what was it that prevented the estate agent from showing exasperation or impatience towards Santo openly? One possibility is that politeness constraints prevented the agent from being any more explicit than she was, although the cumulative force of her comments would be sufficient for any majority speaker to terminate the interaction at a much earlier stage. Another explanation lies in a feature of Santo's interactional skills which he brings to bear in this encounter and which he consistently displays in many others, namely, his ability to maintain conversational involvement.

There are two ways in which Santo manages to keep the conversation going. The first is to ask questions that will elicit expert advice at points at which it looks as if the interaction is about to grind to a halt. There are examples of this at (14), (40) and (110) and each time the estate agent is persuaded into proffering more advice.

The second feature of Santo's interactional style that appears to work in his favour is that he volunteers comments that induce further suggestions and advice from the agent. Two examples of this occur during the discussion about travelling time and transport at (79) and again at (87).

	A:	take you twenty five minutes i suppose twenty minutes twenty five minutes
	S:	anyway for er forty thousand very complication yeah youve got er
(80)	A:	very difficult + erm even two bedroomed flats is not too easy now
	S:	no
	A:	erm + i think if you want a house and you want three bedrooms you have to go and call at the agents' out this way more/
	S:	seven sisters
	A:	round tottenham, seven sisters yes <i no like this area for me> <laughing>
	A:	you might errm if you go s bit further north you might get something out here with three bedroom i've got a house
(90)	S:	in this area ↑

Such a feature contributes to the ease of his conversational style since it takes account of the unspoken needs of a conversation partner to remain engaged in the topic and has the advantage of triggering new information from the agent.

Throughout the project, Santo used his interactional skills in order to obtain the information he needed. At times, it is not clear whether he had understood or not. Most majority speakers chose to assume that he had, and not to embark on a clarification process with its accompanying risks. For such a learner who appeared to have good interactional skills, it is puzzling that by the end of the project Santo had not acquired more English than he did.

There are several possible reasons for this. It may be that Santo lacked the very strong motivation necessary to improve his English; his personal circumstances did not demand acquisition. He also lacked the physical opportunity to learn because of his long working hours. Another possibility, and one for which there is some evidence, is that he was so intent on achieving his own particular conversational goals that he sometimes appeared to disregard the contributions that his conversational partner made or certainly did not use them as part of an active learning process (see 4.5 above). Repeated behaviour of this kind could be interpreted as evidence of being a poor listener and could thus have a negative effect on the majority speaker's willingness to participate as well as Santo's own readiness to engage.

Nonetheless, through Santo's interactions we have evidence of a learner who uses his assertiveness to redress the imbalance of power between minority and majority speaker and yet who manages to do so in most situations in such a way that neither he nor his conversational partner loses face in the process.

NOTE

1. GCSE (General Certificate of Secondary Education) is the British equivalent of 'abschluß' and is used here, in the English translation, to indicate that Tino is having to grapple with a relatively technical term in the education domain.

SIX

Preventing problems of understanding

Katharina Bremer with Margaret Simonot

6.0 INTRODUCTION

While in Chapter 4 we focused on the options minority participants have to respond to problems of understanding, in this and the following chapter we are going to explore the means speakers use to pre-empt non-understandings they anticipate (this chapter) and to handle problems already manifest (Chapter 7). In a way, this will involve a shift in perspective to the 'native speaker'. Since they have greater resources with respect to language competence and structuring power, as a rule they also have a bigger share in the negotiation of understanding. Where both interlocutors have to try to reach a maximum of comprehensibility for the other, the minority speaker's limited language abilities are not only the source of understanding problems but at the same time make it difficult for them to contribute to their clarification.

There is a rich body of literature on adjustments native speakers use. In the earlier phases these were mainly described for second language learning environments (e.g. Hatch 1983); then gradually research aims opened out from 'modified input' to 'modified interaction', thereby partly shifting perspective from success of learning to communicative success (cf. Faerch & Kasper (1986) for a summary of this development; see also Long (1983a and b), Gass and Varonis (1985) for overviews of earlier work). Recently many additional aspects have been added to the conceptualization of such interactions, but still casual conversation is seen as the basic (or most 'natural') type of discourse in much recent work (e.g. Gass & Varonis 1991).

Our analyses show, however, that data from other types of interactional tasks can add to the general picture – not only because the participants here use different means to make each other understood, but because these data demand a different research perspective if one wants to arrive at a useful description. Taking up on earlier comments on our approach in Chapter 2, this might be clarified in three points.

When describing tough interview sessions, the analytical perspective must be 'functional' in the sense that we are always concerned with the joint resolution of a 'genuine' communicative problem: each of the two speakers wants to understand what the other wishes to say in order to solve a common task. This may appear trivial but it has not always been taken for granted in other studies.[1]

Thus our question is not 'How does input become comprehensible?' but, 'How do both speakers jointly solve a task by getting their message across?' In this, the term 'task' means a shift in perspective in comparison with conversational data in the sense that there is a list of open questions (to establish basic biographical facts of the interviewee, her or his plans and wishes for the future job and so on) the interlocutors have to tackle. Therefore a general strategy such as 'treat topics briefly' (Long 1983:133) in order to facilitate understanding is precluded in a job interview.

On similar grounds, we intend to take a perspective related to causes; that is, we try to include what we have learnt from the earlier chapter on causes in the description. The way in which an understanding problem is solved or pre-empted naturally depends on what its origins were. In so doing we start from the assumption that speakers, in principle, have a competent estimate of what it was in any one case that could have caused a problem with understanding and how – in the given situation with all its intertwined set of circumstances – it can best be dealt with. The accuracy of this knowledge and the speaker's degree of awareness of it will depend on experience and skill but it plays its part in every resolution.

In conversations between native speakers the speaker is assisted in identifying the causes of problems by the fact that he can turn to a conventionalised system of the ways in which problems can surface. Here, there is a definite relationship between the way in which non-understanding is signalled and the particular problem it refers to. Indeed, in many cases the form of the indicator itself already categorises the type of problem (cf. Selting (1987), Schegloff (1987)). However, since the minority worker does not yet have this system at his or her disposal – or at best has only a part of it – and therefore frequently uses only very indefinite indicators of non-understanding (see Chapter 4) the interlocutors in our encounters rely more heavily on other sources of information through which they can assess problems with understanding. One important source consists of previous experience in similar intercultural encounters.

As a consequence of these points, in our view, the analysis of encounters, where getting the facts clear is really urgent to the participants, makes it necessary to address not only the question of immediate 'effectiveness', but also the consequences that different styles of negotiating understanding may have in the long run (see also Chapter 7). In other words we are forced to try to go one step beyond a purely descriptive approach – by instead tackling the question of what it is that certain procedures contribute in reaching a 'good' resolution of the problem. In a way, then, this perspective has an *evaluative* element.

The chapter is organized around two central (pairs of) distinctions: (i) *preventative versus post-hoc procedures*, and adjustments with reference to (ii) *knowledge versus utterance* information. The first distinction is well established – as Long (1983b:131) has put it: 'native speakers appear to modify interaction to two main ends: 1) to avoid conversational trouble and 2) to repair the discourse when trouble occurs.'

Even though it is inherent in the nature of problems with understanding that some of the linguistic means of resolution (for example reformulations) are suited both to preventing difficulty before the event as well as to being used afterwards in the process of resolution, we shall be retaining this distinction, which seems to be widely accepted now. Section 6.1 deals with preventative procedures along these lines. Section 6.2 consists of an exploration of the question whether or not a problem which has been registered by one of the participants is taken up or not.

The second distinction underlying the description has already been introduced in our analyses so far (see Chapter 3 on causes and the case studies in Chapter 5). It will come as no surprise that in their effort to create 'optimal' conditions for understanding participants consider *both* threads of information (i.e. knowledge and utterance information) for their addressees: comprehensibility of the *utterance itself* (that is 'bottom-up' creation of understanding) and its 'connectability' to previous or actually focused *knowledge* ('top-down' components of the process). In many of the interactions understanding is only possible if both resources are maximally exploited. (For empirical work on the role of contextual information in understanding in general see Brown (1989) and Fritz (1991); for its role in second language understanding see e.g. Wolff 1985, 1986; Kleifgen 1989).

6.1 SOME OPTIONS TO PREVENT NON-UNDERSTANDING

Whereas post-hoc procedures to facilitate understanding can be more or less easily identified by comparing the way an utterance is formulated before and after an indication of non-understanding, this is more difficult for prevention. What a speaker may have meant to be an 'adjustment' to anticipated difficulties is much more open to interpretation. And often it is a matter of degree rather than using a distinct 'procedure'. Comparing the encounters analyzed nevertheless reveals some typical patterns which are recurrent in the data, and whose ability to support understanding seems plausible in that they show many similarities to the means used in managing non-understanding.

Fostering chances for participation

As has been shown again in our case studies, it is of course not only specific procedures at a local level that decide on preconditions for understanding. Their use and effect also relate closely to the general way in which an interview is structured, for example with respect to topic management, tempo and rhythm, the personal involvement established on both sides and so on. Given the structural asymmetries of the encounters analyzed, conversational organization at this level is mainly the responsibility of the interviewer. The expected, 'usual' role of his or her client is a very passive one – underlying power structures and manifest dominance are running parallel here. (For some basic results on the interrelations between social power, manifest dominance patterns, symmetry and mutual responsiveness see Linell, Gustavsson and Juvonen 1988.) Every attempt to enlarge the minority interviewee's participation therefore means to actively and consciously downplay the gatekeepers' own dominant role.[2] This can involve different levels, some of which we will discuss in the following sections.

Topic management

In our data particularly those interviewers with some experience in intercultural encounters attempt to encourage some contribution to the selection of topics by their client – even if they have to fulfil a relatively fixed agenda. Participation in topic control improves the chances of more successful understanding in three ways.

Firstly, self-initiated topics involve a high degree of control and 'expectability' for the minority participant (cf. also p. 167 below). Secondly, such sharing of responsibilities feeds into the development of a cooperative relationship and thereby also contributes to a *metamessage* (Bateson 1972, 1979) where the interviewer indicates that reaching understanding is an important aim for her or him. And, thirdly, this is of course the only way to ensure that the client's goals will be considered in the discussion. The example discussed in 7.4 below, where Angelina is encouraged to start to ask questions herself after a phase of repeatedly answering the interviewer's questions, may illustrate these points. Evidently participation at discourse level has to be realized and complemented by a number of more local conversational moves to which we will turn now.

Giving 'room' to speak

This point may appear trivial but in many of the encounters analysed it can by no means be taken for granted, that the *underlying* condition for active participation of the 'weaker' partner in an encounter is that room is made for him or her to speak (on the function of tempo shifts in crosscultural gatekeeping encounters see also Fiksdal 1989). This can mean *tolerating longer pauses* as the minority participant plans what s/he wishes to say (which implies self-restraint from the majority speaker whilst the minority participant is formulating their utterance), or *turns may be offered* to the learner explicitly or implicitly. The following extract from Marcello's Job Centre interview demonstrates how the attempt to hand over the initiative leads indeed to quite a lengthy exposition of Marcello's concerns.

(1)   T: nehmen sie bitte platz ↓
             please sit down ↓
             so herr m sie haben ein bestimmtes anliegen
             well mr. m you've got a particular matter to discuss

          sie haben sicher ein paar fragen an mich
          you must have a few questions for me
     M: ja aber ich äh ich spreche nicht so viel deutsch
          yes but er i er i don't speak very much german
(5)   T: ja das macht nichts wir können uns sicher verständigen
          yes that doesn't matter i'm sure we'll understand each other
     M: gut ↓ so ich bin schon zwei jahre hier in deutschland
          good ↓ well i've been here in germany for two years now
     T: mhm mhm
     M: in italien ich eh eh mein arbeit ist eh drehen und fräsen
          in italy i er er my work is er turning and milling

Such an opening contributes to a more relaxed atmosphere. Marcello now feels free to mention his big problem right at the beginning and the fact of 'lacking language' is openly acknowledged by his addressee. This makes it less embarrassing if non-understanding should occur later, because the double task of tackling thematic subjects and language understanding at the same time has been established between the participants by now. And in fact this cooperative beginning paves the way for successful understanding in the following encounter.

An example of the implicit type of strategy occurs in the following example in a conversation between Andrea and the researcher where the latter allows unusually long pauses almost flouting conversational rules.

(1) A: to check the wiring
     T: + + +   yes
     A: and er to repair + + and er +++ *<ma>*   <but>
          well now i don't remember very well
(5) T: + +   mm mm

Given that most of our data consists of question-answer sequences, another very important factor affecting the 'space' the interviewee is allowed is the *type of question asked* to her/him. A delicate balance has to be considered here. On the one hand, formulating relatively narrow questions is a means to make a contribution quite easy for the addressee (as with yes/no or 'choice'-questions) and this may be necessary or helpful in some situations. Noyau describes the effect as following:

> La forme la plus simple de ces stratégies de mise à la disposition de moyens linguistiques est de substituer à une question ouverte nécessitant une réponse construite une question fermée en fournissant des alternatives qui permettent à l'étranger de répondre par oui ou non. (Noyau 1984:29)

The simplest of these strategies to put linguistic means at the other's disposal is to substitute an open question requiring an answer to be formulated with a closed question offering alternatives which allow the foreigner to reply yes or no. (our translation)

If, however, this kind of 'narrow' question dominates the structure of an interview over longer stretches, this cuts off the possibility of genuine contributions from the interviewee in a dangerous way. Relevant examples in point are for example the interviews between the Turkish youths and a German garage owner. Here regularly the potential of serious understanding problems increases through a type of question that already carries the whole answer in it and only needs to be confirmed (a case study on this effect is given in Bremer (forthcoming); for the relation between different types of questions and potential participation of interviewees see also Evans (1986).)

Taking up and Restructuring of fragments or incomplete contributions

Our analyses show that slowing down the rhythm of turns or encouraging the minority participant to talk become all the more important for understanding when the minority participant is experiencing major difficulties with the new language. But it is precisely here that the strategy of making space for the development of early productive skills is quickly brought up short quite simply because he or she cannot yet make use of this space. There must, therefore, be another side to 'giving room to speak', that of giving support when the non-native partner finds it difficult to formulate his or her contribution in the new language.

Noyau describes one of these types of formulation supports – in contrast to the 'question forms' described above – in this way:

La forme la plus caractéristique est cependant un peu plus élaborée: il s'agit de reformuler l'énoncé minimal de l'informatrice (consistant en un mot, une réponse oui/non) en un énoncé développé, ce qui permet la vérification de la bonne compréhension de part et d'autre, et simultanément fournit à l'étranger de bonnes données pour apprendre, puisque correspondant directement à un besoin d'expression.

(Noyau 1984:29)

The most characteristic form, however, is a little more elaborate: it consists of reformulating a minimal utterance (made up of a single word, or a yes/no answer) in a developed form thereby permitting the other to check that s/he has

*understood properly and at the same time providing the foreigner with good
learning data whilst corresponding directly with the learner's need to express
him/herself.* (our translation)

An isolated example (at line 7 below) of restructuring occurs in
the following extract from a conversation between Ravinder and
the researcher. One function it fulfils is to validate the minority
speaker's own contribution in the previous turn (line 6):

(1)   T: good + and erm what about christmas
              what + what are you going to do then ↑
              are you going to have some holiday ↑
       R: no
(5)   T: no holiday ↑ + no ↑
       R: no this still can working + wife
       T: yeah oh she s working all over christmas is she ↑
       R: yeah

There are other encounters, however, where the native speaker
repeatedly comes to the assistance of the minority participant both
by adjusting their own language and by more frequent restructuring of their addressee's fragments. One such encounter is the
counselling interview between Zahra, a Moroccan Arabic speaker
acquiring French and a social worker. In the following extract, the
interviewer builds quite extensively on Zahra's fragmented contributions in a way which enables her to participate more fully in the
conversation. Thus, this particular majority speaker not only proac-
tively facilitates understanding for Zahra, but is a fund of a lot of
new linguistic information for her.

(1)   Z: parce que euh une est passé + et ma fille a huit ans +
              l'est parti à la colonie
              *because er one happened + and my daughter is eight years +
              went to the camp*
       T: oui
              yes
       Z: et qu'une moi l'est regardé à la télé
              and one i saw on the telly
       T: oui
              yes
(5)   Z: (x) l'est trompé et moi j'ai j'ai peur
              (x) was wrong and me i'm i'm afraid
       T: ah vous avez peur de les envoyer
              ah you're afraid to send them
       Z: ouais
              yeah

T: en colonie de vacances à cause de tout ce que vous avez vu à la
télé
to a holiday camp because of all that you've seen on the tv

Z: oui
yes

However, both ways of accommodating to understanding difficulties through majority speaker formulations – either by
anticipating or even prescribing replies within the question itself
and by restructuring – also run the risk of missing what the other
wanted to say altogether or at least of only partially understanding
them. Or to put it differently, by 'taking the words out of his or her
mouth' one can once again reinforce the asymmetry of the
encounter. Careful comprehension checks after each step will
finally determine whether or not prescription has been avoided and
true co-operation achieved. We shall take up this point in the next
chapter again.

Raising the right expectations

We have consistently attempted, especially in the chapter on causes,
to demonstrate how little understanding for the minority participant
has to do with perception and comprehension of a given utterance
alone and how instead the emphasis falls on the expectations which
guide their interpretation. Whether consciously or not, interlocutors
take this into consideration when they attempt to prevent problems
of understanding. Again this can occur at the level of discourse,
topic or more locally.

Raising expectability for the entire interaction

A procedure used by the professionals can be described as a *cluster
of metadiscursive comments* on what is about to take place. In the
inter-cultural encounters studied here, this use of 'advance organiz-
ers' gains a particular status. The aim here is to reduce one element
of the communicative load for the minority participant by making
explicit information which s/he would otherwise have to deduce
from contextualisation cues. Typically this information includes:

– identifying the type of interaction
– establishing the degree of the other's previous knowledge
– identifying the kinds of speech acts to be expected.

The interviewers in our data give advance orientations of this kind when the task necessitates an interaction of complex structure. One such example is the counselling interview but it also occurs in other lengthy 'structured' interviews as in the examples given below. In the following opening extract from Berta's Job Centre interview, one can see that the counsellor first establishes what knowledge is shared (l.2) and then goes on to identify what type of interaction and what type of speech acts they will be engaged in (ll.4 and 10). Of course this type of metadiscursive comment is also common in intra-cultural communication but in the latter case it is likely to be less protracted and less explicit.

(Social worker speaks very slowly throughout)

(1)   T: bon alors je suis/ on est ici à l'anpe et vous avez reçu une
           convocation
           well so i am/ we're here at the anpe and you have received an invitation
      B: mhm
           mhm
      T: pour qu'on discute ensemble des problèmes de travail
           de ce que vous souhaitez euh en ce moment faire +
(5)   alors comme je ne vous connais pas et que j'ai votre dossier sous
           les yeux mais que je n'ai pas eu le temps de le feuilleter
           je vais vous poser quelques petites questions
           pour savoir un peu mieux qui vous êtes ↑ hein ↑
           so that we can discuss the work problems
           and what you hope to be able to do at the moment +
           so since i don't know you and i have your file in front of me
           but i haven't had time to look through it
           i'll be asking you some questions
           so as to know a bit better who you are ↑ okay ↑
      B: hmhm
(10) T: bon alors vous êtes de nationalité ↑ (. . .)
           well so ↑ your nationality is ↑ (. . .)

Another such passage which displays strikingly similar features is that from the opening of an interview with Marcello about what kind of media he uses.

(1)   M: guten tag
           hello
      T: guten tag nehmen sie platz bitte
           hello   please sit down
      M: danke schön
           thank you

T: hat frau p. schon erzählt äh worum es in dem interview geht ↑
    has mrs.p. already told you what er we are going to do in the
    interview ↑
(5) M: aber < > ich glaub ni/es nicht ich spreche nicht viel noch nicht
                                  <laughs>
    but < > i think its not i don't speak much not yet < >
    T: ach so ja das macht nichts + so äh gut wie das geht
        und so wie's spass macht eben
        also das ist ein interview für ne radio und fernsehgesellschaft
        und äh
        wir möchten gerne wissen was sie so in ihrer freizeit machen
(10)   und ob sie gerne radio benutzen fernsehgeräte videogeräte und
        so etwas äh aber zuerst
        e hätte ich auch zwei drei allgemeine fragen äh
        nämlich zu ihrer person was sie so machen so
        i see well that doesn't matter + so er well as far as we can
        and as long as it's fun
        well it's an interview for a radio and television company and er
        we'd like to know what you usually do in your free time
        and whether you like using the radio the t.v. video recorders and things
        like that
        but first er i thought i'd ask you two or three general questions er
        about yourself what you do for instance
    M: ja
        yes
    T: darf ich da einfach mal fragen was/ was machen sie so im
        normalen tag?
        and so can i just ask what/ what do you normally do – every day

By providing signposts of this kind – such as making explicit the
goals and intended structure of an interview beforehand or explicitly
naming the type of shared activity thereby activating the appropriate
'schema' the professional not only steers the expectations of the
learner as the more 'passive' participant in the right direction (thus
creating a background conducive to understanding), but s/he also
contributes towards reducing the asymmetry of interactions of this
kind. In this instance, a new frame is created which sets the interaction on a different footing. Giving the interviewee a clear idea of
what is likely to happen in an encounter is no substitute for helping
her determine its course, but is a minimal prerequisite for participation.

Orientations of this kind are only of limited usefulness, however,
in that they define a particular interactional schema as common

ground but assume that the detail of content can be taken for granted. Thus the social worker in Berta's example above announces 'quelques petites questions', but naturally does not give any indication of what the rules are when responding to questions in Job Centres (cf. the respective sections in Chapter 3 and Chapter 8 on institutional discourse).

As far as the minority worker is concerned, the opening sequence of an interaction is frequently used to orientate the other participant – in this case by drawing attention to one's own inadequate competence and thereby more or less 'eliciting' an adjustment of the way of delivery and formulation from the native speaker. Such a statement usually meets with an immediate reassuring response from the interviewer. An example of this is to be found in the opening we have already quoted from Marcello above. It is even more clear in his Job Centre interview, also in the opening phase:

(1)   M: ich spreche nicht so viel deutsch
              i don't speak so much german
       T: ja das macht nichts wir können uns sicher verständigen
              sie können langsam sprechen sie können sich zeit lassen wie sie
              wollen
(5)   *yes that doesn't matter we're sure to make ourselves understood*
              you can talk slowly you can take your time as you wish

Making new topics salient and their content expectable

As we have seen in our analysis of causes (and this is in line with findings from other studies, see, for example, Long 1983b) unannounced topic switches are almost always associated with understanding problems. So, the more the native speaker can relate a new topic to what has just happened, the greater the minority participant's chance of understanding.

In order to signal the introduction of a new topic, interviewers make use of clear pauses and/or more frequent use of particles. (There are several examples of this in the extract from Angelina's job interview in 7.3 below.) But they can also go further and announce the content of the new topic and link it explicitly to the context of the conversation. Connections of this kind can be made by referring to the purpose of the interaction or its schema as in the following example with Zahra. Here one can see how the native speaker's metadiscursive comment, which is an explanation of why he wants to proceed to the next point, is to act as support to Zahra.

This comment occurs after a 'warm-up' period in the opening phase of Zahra's interview with a doctor. He has just been making polite enquiries about her children, presumably in order to put her more at ease. Before getting down to the business of talking about the illness she has come to consult him about, he signals clearly that now they are going to change topics:

> T: mais enfin nous sommes là pour parler de votre maladie +
> alors qu'est ce que c'est ↑ qu'est-ce que vous avez comme maladie ↑
> *but after all we're here to talk about your illness +*
> *so what is it ↑ what is it what kind of illness have you got ↑*

The next example from a role play shows a different way of 'introducing' the topic: not by metadiscursive comment, but by firmly situating the discourse within the addressee's own experience. Ravinder is at first at a loss to know how to set about his explanation of the fact that the sweater purchased has shrunk in response to the researcher's first, indirect request for more information (1–3). It is not until she takes him back in time and guides him chronologically through the steps of what actually happened (time of purchase (4–5), wearing (11)) that the learner then feels 'situated' in the context sufficiently to start to present his case (lines 18–20), i.e. the sweater was washed and shrunk.

(1)	T:	if there is something wrong with it i can give you your money back
		i expect but it looks okay to me
	R:	i know but + + +
	T:	well you bought it when ↑ on saturday monday tuesday wednesday ↑
(5)		when did you buy it ↑
	R:	+ + +
	T:	what day did you buy it on ↑
	R:	+ + + monday
	T:	on monday ↑
(10)	R:	yeah
	T:	ok and have you worn it ↑
	R:	sorry ↑
	T:	have you had the sweater on ↑
	R:	yeah
(15)	T:	yeah ↑
	R:	two three day
	T:	uhuh
	R:	+ + and wash
	T:	aah mhm

(20) R: and + <   >   <makes gesture with his hands>
      T: i see ↓ you mean it got smaller ↑

Expectability at a local level: left topic dislocation

At the utterance level too there is a way of making new information
more predictable and thus more easily understandable. The topic –
almost as a kind of pre-announcement – is placed in front of everything else.

(1)   T: et des maladies vous avez eu des maladies quand vous étiez
            jeune fille ↑
            quand vous vous étiez/ vous avez déjà été malade à part ces
            grossesses ↑
            and illnesses you had illnesses when you were a young girl
            when you/you had already been ill apart from these pregnancies
       Z: oui toujours + toujours malade
            yes always + always ill

The doctor in this encounter is trying to establish whether or not
she has a history of heart disease and this passage occurs after they
have been talking for several minutes. He has then had time to
assess her competence and in addition to the left topic dislocation
immediately uses a reformulation apparently designed to simplify
propositional content.

As in this example, at the utterance level procedures are often
packed in very tightly, that is, several are intertwined in one contribution. The reason that left-topic dislocation has the effect of
making understanding easier is that the information structure of
the utterance has been changed. This is common to other speech
modifications in reformulations. All procedures of this type are also
used in the process of resolving difficulty with understanding, in
other words in repair as well.

Raising the transparency of one's own speech

When the preceding sections have been more concerned with
the top-down aspect of understanding, this does not mean we
consider those procedures which guide the utterance towards
'optimal bottom-up processing' less important. On the contrary, adaptations on this level again and again turned out to
be the indispensable 'core' of any attempt to facilitate understanding.

We will postpone analysis of examples, however, to the section on resolution of problems with understanding (7.2/7.3.) where these procedures are dealt with in more detail. At this point we will be brief and air the question of whether modifications which aim to maximise understanding can be categorised according to more general principles.

One approach which has been pursued in Foreigner Talk research is that modifications of speech aim at simplifying what is to be said. Intuitively convincing as this argument may appear it is in fact extremely difficult to grasp precisely what is meant by the term 'simplification'. The first difficulty lies in identifying the point of reference of 'easiness'. In other words, what can one take as a yardstick when one is not dealing directly with reformulations that can be compared with the corresponding previous utterance? (This problem already occurred in Chapter 3 when trying to assess degrees of difficulty of an utterance.)

An additional problem is to be found in the fact that one can simplify an utterance on the lexical level by a paraphrase, for example, whilst simultaneously making it more complex on the syntactic level (for a more detailed discussion, see Noyau 1984; Deulofeu and Taranger 1984 for the reverse process). Above all, though,

L'efficacité de la reformulation simplifiée dépend en fait de la bonne **anticipation** par l'autochtone de ce qui, dans la formulation première, n'avait pas pu être décodé, et d'une **évaluation** de ce qui pour l'étranger est plus ou moins difficile. (Noyau 1984: 27).

The effectiveness of a simplified reformulation depends in fact on the extent to which the native speaker is able to **anticipate** *what it was in the original formulation that the learner could not decode and to* **assess** *what it is that the learner finds more or less difficult.* (our translation)

This makes it quite clear that the nature of a successful simplification (which amounts to successful tailoring to the addressee's capabilities) can only – if at all – be fully described for each individual case. On the other hand, the shaping of the comprehension process and of levels of speech connected with it form a guideline for the search for the lowest common denominator of modifications. One aspect which seems an obvious candidate for the differentiation of the term simplification is that of raising explicitness.

So when Gass and Varonis (1985:50/51) give a list of examples of native-speaker modifications aimed at providing greater 'transparency', the principle of 'explicitness' emerges here too on more than one occasion ('implicit information is made more explicit' and 'information becomes specified to a greater degree' where pronouns are replaced by lexical elements or ellipsis is filled in). At the same time this list of 'transparency-modifications' also contains procedures with a different focus, namely that of reduction ('information load per clause is reduced' and 'less information per unit'). It would seem then that 'transparency' is an attractive notion for grouping procedures, but a further internal differentiation might be needed for a more unified concept.

It may therefore be helpful to trace back the way in which transparency for the listener is achieved to two demands which are not only quite separate from each other but may be potentially divergent. This would also explain why it is that transparency is difficult to describe and – for the participants difficult to achieve. We would propose that one could categorise according to *accessibility* on the one hand and *explicitness* on the other. Maximal transparency for the hearer can only be reached by a trade-off between these demands, whereby the respective emphasis depends on context conditions. This conceptualization could – however roughly – be related to the basic duality of processes in language perception and understanding, namely the analysis of the incoming speech (i.e. 'access' or 'form-based' processes), and the syntactic and semantic interpretation of the message to be communicated ('integration' or 'content-based' processes) (cf. Marslen-Wilson 1989:3).

In this approach, analysis of the items heard in an utterance would be supported by *accessibility* on the perceptual level, i.e.

- possibility of segmentation (pauses, lowered tempo etc.)
- salience of the individual elements (volume, articulation, position in the utterance etc.)
- the brevity of the piece to be processed (length of utterance).

The basic premise for raising understandability here would lie – put in simple terms – in 'give little information at a time'.

Explicitness as an important condition for understandability with respect to the 'integration' of meaning would mean organizing one's message in a way that few inferences have to be made by the hearer so as to avoid any kind of 'incompleteness' (see Brown et al 1994). Ellipsis, referential or semantic ambiguity or pragmatic indirectness all ask for an additional effort to 'bridge' missing information. From this perspective understanding is supported by giving all the information the hearer could use for interpretation – and a certain degree of redundancy is surely helpful in this domain. It is clear that this requirement is not in 'natural' harmony with the one of accessibility described above.

It is, however, not only the level of 'information packaging' mentioned above which comes into play here. Another aspect of messages which accounts for degrees of understandability is the *conceptual* difficulty involved (Brown 1989; Esch 1992). Keeping in mind the danger of stretching the term too far, we suggest an extension of the notion of accessibility to include accessibility of meaning (as in distance to the 'here and now'). Analysis in Chapter 7 will show that this in any case is a relevant criterion speakers have in mind when reformulating their utterances in sequences of negotiation.

The overview on means for the facilitation of understanding given below (see p. 180) includes a provisional summary of this conceptualization of transparency through a trade-off between accessibility and explicitness. In Chapter 7 we are going to explore how these two 'opposing players' could be used to describe the demands on understandability in clarifications after non-understanding has occurred.

6.2 RESOLVING OR IGNORING PROBLEMS OF UNDERSTANDING: THE INTERVIEWER'S POINT OF VIEW

In Chapter 4.3 we have already discussed some factors that can influence the decision whether or not to tackle an understanding problem from the perspective of the minority participants. There are some further points to be added if we are going to look now from the opposite angle. Of course the type of activity in which a non-understanding occurs is most important for *both partners* as a background for assessing the need for and likely effects of clarification. In this respect, differences between interviews and conversations are especially salient. Whereas this general distinction between types of discourse is clear for both, in an interview, the majority participants determine its structure and so for them other factors will influence their behaviour.

Length of interaction

It appears that the length of an encounter rather than the degree to which it is goal-oriented influences the choice between two possible general approaches to the clarification of a problem with understanding. In most cases non-understanding is worked through where and when it occurs, directly after it has been revealed and in a way which demands the least effort.

In encounters where the content is of a more complex structure, and where time is at less of a premium some majority participants nonetheless proceed differently. Initially they continue without any attempt at resolution only to return to the unclarified question after a 'diversion'. Frequently a different aspect of the same topic is worked through in the meantime, thus simultaneously improving the basis for understanding. The question is often somewhat modified and usually this type of circuitous clarification is successful. There are several examples of this type of arrangement in Tino's Job Centre counselling session (see the case study in Chapter 5) and in Angelina's interview with a media person. In this interview a long section deals with the question of whether or not Angelina enjoys being a housewife or whether she would prefer to have a paid job. To start with, her response is a general statement and one cannot deduce her personal attitude towards the question. Despite this the interlocutor takes up this shift of topic but does return to his question some turns later, emphasising the fact that he now wants to know her own attitude. In reaction to this Angelina explains how she used to feel about this ('I used to want to go out to work'), which then leads to a side sequence about some biographical details. Only after this, is the question repeated yet again and answered very clearly ('a woman must work; then the day is quick – at home it is slow'). The interviewer characteristically consistently takes up her interpretation of the question first and only after her statement about it is completed (with a good deal of co-construction of meaning) does he return finally to his original question. Another interviewer behaves in a very similar way in her treatment of Çevdet's understanding problems in the counselling interview when they are trying to ascertain what wishes or plans he has with regards to a career.

Besides activity type variability, another factor which comes into play in deciding whether or not and how problems with understanding are resolved, is of course the *type of problem with understanding.* In the two examples just cited the non-understanding is not limited to the linguistic surface of the utterance but goes deeper. While Angelina's only partly relevant replies are accompanied by her wish to evade the question (which is possibly why she interpreted it in her own way) because it put her in a conflict of roles, for Çevdet there is a 'substantive' uncertainty in addition to the difficulties he has with the way the question is formulated. He has not thought enough about his future plans.

In other words, problems of understanding which can be located at the linguistic surface (for example, the minority participant does not yet understand a lexical item) are naturally explained more frequently, more willingly and more 'explicitly' than pragmatic problems which are more strongly linked to the level of relationships (see also Chapter 3) or those problems for which one does not have enough information. Linked to this is the fact that the more narrowly the problem can be defined, the more localised the difficulty is, the easier and less disruptive it is to resolve it (see also next chapter).

Clarification and face

Given the basic asymmetry in most the interactions we have examined it is more difficult for the learner, as the 'weaker' partner, to admit to non-understanding.

This is particularly clear in a job interview where partly explicitly, partly implicitly, the achievements concerned include as good as possible a command of the new language. So, of course, every appearance of problems with understanding amounts to a minus for the applicant. This difficulty does not exist for the interviewer or professional so there are other reasons for the avoidance of clarificatory 'side sequences' on his or her part.

Frequently it is either a real or perceived lack of time, sometimes combined with lack of interest in the detailed exchange. This means that in such encounters, there is a strong tendency to deal with the task in as rational a way as possible.

One reason for overlooking problems with understanding or even ignoring a request for help by the minority participant may be because the interviewer is uncertain of her or his task in the encounter and possibly has little experience of communicating with clients of another language or cultural background. As the interviewer in Angelina's counselling session pointed out in the post-encounter discussion, the content and structuring of a counselling session may place such high demands on the interviewer's attention that there is too little 'capacity' available for additional 'monitoring' of understanding. A more positive consideration is that avoidance of clarification may avoid loss of face for the minority participant. Nonetheless, if one attempts to summarise the different courses interactions follow, then it becomes clear that continuous avoidance of clarification nearly always has a negative outcome. The asymmetry between the interlocutors is heightened, as a result the likelihood of further problems is increased and there is less confirmed shared knowledge which could form the basis of clarification – a vicious circle indeed. By contrast, there are some conversations in the data in which the joint resolution of quite difficult problems of understanding by both parties does not affect the interaction negatively at all, but has a particularly fruitful effect instead. (For examples see Chapters 5 and 7.4.)

Before we turn to the procedures participants use to raise understandability in clarification sequences (Chapter 7 below), a short *summary* in the form of a chart might be useful. It is meant to highlight two points in particular. Firstly, the range of means for preventing problems of understanding encompasses more than linguistic changes. A consideration of the *preconditions* for understanding in terms of knowledge and expectations is of equal importance and this, in turn, is closely related to the possibilities of participation for the minority speaker. Secondly, there is no really simple way of describing what makes utterances 'more understandable1. Instead, there is a tension between potentially differing needs of the hearer which only in some cases can both be satisfied at the same time, but often have to be weighed against each other.

Many of the aspects summarized in the chart will turn up again when we explore sequences of clarification and reformulations in the next chapter, and thus their functioning *in context* will hopefully gain additional clarity there.

NOTES

1. In Gass and Varonis 1987, for example, the native speaker reads out previously formulated questions to the non-native speaker. These even contain firmly prescribed comprehension checks; in Ellis 1985 (see Faerch & Kasper 1986, p.263) the learner does not have to express his or her own intention but has to formulate meaning that has already been prescribed etc.

2. It is clear that an interviewer can opt for other global ways of reducing the difficulty of a communicative task that seems to be unmanageable. One possibility is to change the goals of the interview (e.g. treat topics less thoroughly, avoid certain questions etc.), another to take over the floor all the more and reduce to a minimum what the interviewee is expected to contribute. For a more detailed account cf. Bremer (forthcoming Ch. 3).

PREVENTING PROBLEMS OF UNDERSTANDING

Encouraging participation	Raising expectability	Raising transparency	
		RAISING ACCESSIBILITY	RAISING EXPLICITNESS
open topic management	**discourse**	(a) perceptual:	Full forms instead of:
slow down rhythm for turns	metadiscursive comments	short utterances	ellipsis
if relevant:	on: activity type	salience of elements:	pro-forms
acknowledge language problems	topics	articulation	reduced forms (phonetically)
	shared knowledge	volume	lexicalisation of important information otherwise encoded morphologically
giving room		segmentation	
offer turns	and: *encouraging participation*	pauses	
open questions		rate of delivery	meta-discursive comments on:
allow for pauses	**topics**	chunking	discourse function of utterance
help other with formulations	announce by paralinguistic markers	avoid false starts	discourse structuring
	announce content explicitly		discourse context (e.g. gist summary)
		(b) of lexical meaning	
	locally	high frequency vocabulary	
	left-topic dislocation	recourse to L1/code switching take up of other's items	possibility of re-runs by (modified) repetition
		(c) of conceptual meaning	
		linking of complex topics to the 'here and now'	
		absolute instead of relational reference to time	

Joint negotiation of understanding: procedures for managing problems of understanding

Katharina Bremer with Margaret Simonot

7.0 INTRODUCTION

In several of our analyses so far, we have already broached some of the linguistic means conversational partners use to manage problems of understanding. Our aim in this chapter is to put this aspect of the task of achieving understanding centre stage. The perspective taken here will be complementary to two of the earlier chapters. It relates to chapter 4 in that it explores more systematically how the *majority* speaker *reacts* to some indication of a problem by the minority participant and to Chapter 6 in that it emphasizes the post-hoc aspect of the situation instead of possible 'prevention'.

The specific tension of potentially differing aims in the managing of understanding problems (cf. Chapters 4 and 6 above) is of course relevant here, too. On the one hand, the criteria for making an utterance easy to understand are basically the same as those necessary for preventative procedures. In both cases it is important to use the 'strength' of expectations generated by the context, and to express meaning as *explicitly* as possible in a way *accessible* to the minority speaker. This dual approach offers the best solution for understandable utterances. On the other hand there is always the demand that the means used should be as inconspicuous as possible. Sequences that deal with non- or misunderstanding should therefore not depart too far from what normally happens in conversations: there is a limit to the extent to which the process of solving a particular problem with understanding can be taken. Clarification sequences cannot last indefinitely without becoming unacceptably face threatening to both participants.

The dynamics of the relationship between the interactants also influences the choice of means used to negotiate; some of those are preferred to others depending on what the cause of the problem is assumed to be (cf. Chapter 3 above and Selting 1987). For example repeating an utterance implies that it may only be a problem of not having heard properly. This happens all the time in everyday conversations and is, for this very reason, hardly ever felt to be problematic. It is far more awkward for the relationship if a question remains unanswered even after it has been reformulated several times.

The chance of tackling a problem briefly and effectively naturally depends to a great extent on how good the 'diagnosis' of the problem has been. It is only then that a reformulation can alter, at a first go, the appropriate aspect of the original utterance. This may involve the speed of delivery, the segmentation, the emphasis of 'key words', the meaning of individual words or morphemes, the word order, overall complexity of an utterance or the 'expectability' of its subject matter. In a broader sense of the word, diagnostic work is not limited to finding out at this point in the conversation what it is that makes a particular utterance difficult to understand. Even after something has been reformulated very little has been achieved until the addressee of this new attempt has given some indication of how much more s/he has understood as a result (see also Bange 1987, 1992).

One could therefore say that during the process of clarification two parallel activities have to be managed by the participant. Firstly, there is the job of rephrasing the content, of repackaging the language or concepts of that particular stage of a conversation that needs clarification. Secondly, there is work, usually invisible, around the question of to what extent the listener has understood or, indeed, what they have understood so far. As part of this second thread there is also the implicit negotiation of *responsibility* for clarification. While the participant who encounters a problem (in our data more frequently the minority speaker) is expected to get it solved, here the fact of his or her limited linguistic competence may make it necessary for the 'native speaker' to take over some of the 'monitoring' of how much understanding has been achieved so far. There is even a danger in some cases, however, that the majority speaker may take over too much of it, as we shall see in the following sections. (Cf. also Chapter 4.4 on 'over accommodation'.)

Since the *minority participant's contribution* to the process of solving the difficulty is of major importance for the development of a clarification sequence, this will be our starting point: patterns of joint negotiation are divided into three groups – according to how explicitly or specifically s/he provides information at the outset of the sequence on what s/he has not understood. A negotiation sequence starts off on a different footing if the indication of non-understanding is successful in contributing to 'diagnostic work', and this difference persists even if the linguistic means used in later steps for clarification are similar.

The analyses in the following range of examples aim to draw out the features that clarificatory sequences have in common as well as examining the differences. As we have seen in many of the analyses above, one aspect they have in common is the fact that it is an exception for an understanding problem to be cleared up in one single move (as in the sequence of question – indication of non-understanding (NU) – reformulation – answer). It is instead far more typical that a problem has to be solved in several, even many, steps in which understanding is reached not in a linear fashion but by means of frequent diversions, retracing one's steps and even breaks in the whole process.

7.1 CLARIFICATION FOLLOWING UNSPECIFIC INDICATION OR 'SYMPTOMS' OF NON-UNDERSTANDING

As we have mentioned in Chapter 4 above, both the linguistic means of indicating non-understanding as well as the ability to diagnose the problem oneself, have to be acquired. So the sequences analysed in the following section, that constitute a first 'pattern' of clarification typically show the following constellation: they are above all characteristic of conversations in which particularly wide gaps in understanding have to be overcome and, as a rule, the minority speaker (still) has a very meagre knowledge of the language s/he is communicating in. At the same time, however, there is no possibility of ducking the issue by resorting to easier topics because the interaction revolves around a particular question that has to be clarified explicitly and on which matters of some import rest.

This demands considerable feats of adaptation over quite long stretches of the interaction, which has been described as 'communication exolingue extrême' (Noyau 1984, Porquier 1983, Py 1987). Clarifications of this pattern appear here, as the first in the series, because the whole repertoire of means can, so to speak, be brought to bear in them and thus this gives one a good overview of procedures from the very start.

In these cases – where indications of non-understanding do not include any clues on how to pitch a clarification – the majority participants typically use a *combination of two groups of procedures*, thereby acknowledging that both knowledge and utterance information are needed for understanding:

> they try to make their question retrospectively more predictable by topicalisation and *link back to context*
>
> they aim at making their utterance more 'understandable' by using different types of *reformulations*:
>
> i)   reformulate in order to make the linguistic surface simpler
> ii) reformulate to change the type of question into a 'narrower' one
> iii) make a 'new start' with respect to the formulation, keeping only to the **functional aim** of the original utterance

Since the importance of several levels of contextual resources for understanding have been explored in Chapter 6.1, special emphasis will be put here on different types of reformulations. At some points we shall try to make explicit what speakers achieve with these in terms of the more abstract concepts of *accessibility, explicitness* and *expectability* worked out above.

To illustrate and discuss the characteristic traits of this 'pattern' of clarification sequence, we will look at a somewhat longer excerpt of Berta's interview at the ANPE, which has already been discussed in a case study above (cf. 5.2; see also the excerpt in Chapter 3). The sequence occurs during the first phase of the interview, where the basic facts about Berta's situation and her job preferences have to be settled. Up to this point, the interlocutors have succeeded – with several sequences of negotiation – to establish, that it is a part time job that Berta is looking for and that she would prefer to work in the morning, from about eight a.m. to two p.m. It is within this topic of possible working hours that the interviewer wants to go into more detail:

(1)   N: et si on vous propose un travail plus tôt que huit heures/
             and if you were offered a job starting earlier than eight
             vous accepteriez de le prendre/
             would you accept it
             un travail qui commencerait plus tôt que huit heures du matin/
             a job that would start earlier than eight in the morning
                                                              reformulation

		est-ce que vous a/ est-ce que vous accepteriez de commencer
		would you/ would you accept to start
(5)		plus tôt que huit heures/ avant huit heures
		earlier than eight o'clock/ before eight in the morning
	B:	+ **'lack of uptake': symptom of NU**
	N:	vous comprenez ce que je vous demande/
		do you understand what i'm asking you
	B:	non non + non
		no no + no
	N:	vous ne comprenez pas/
		you don't understand
(10)	B:	non <je *no komprene pa*>
		no i don't understand
	N:	eh + bon vous souhaitez un travail qui démarre le matin vers
		well ok you are looking for a job that starts at about eight
		line back to context
		huit heures +
		in the morning
		mais si je vous propose un travail qui démarre à sept heures ou
		but if i offered you a job that starts at seven o'clock
		reformulation
		à six heures du matin/
		or at six o'clock in the morning
(15)	B:	oui
		yes
	N:	est-ce que vous accepteriez/
		would you accept
	B:	< > <silence>
	N:	de commencer à six heures le matin
		to begin at six o'clock in the morning
	B:	oui
		yes
(20)	N:	vous accepteriez/ **reformulation**
		would you accept
	B:	oui
		yes
	N:	à six heures
		at six o'clock
	B:	oui
		yes
	N:	d'accord + donc vous préfér/ ça vous arrangerait entre huit
		ok + but you would pref/ it would suit you between eight
		resumée
(25)		heures et deux heures de l'après-midi
		o'clock and two in the afternoon
		ratification of understanding

B: oui
     yes

N: mais vous accepteriez de commencer plus tot
     but you would also accept to begin earlier

B: oui
     yes

N: de commencer à six heures du matin
     to begin at six o'clock in the morning

(30) B: <* de akor *>   <d'accord>
        all right

N: c'est bien ça/
     that's fine o.k.

B: *si*
     yes

N: d'accord ++ eh + vous accepteriez d'aller en banlieue (. . .)
     right ++ er would you accept to work in a suburb . . .

The process of actually dealing with the problem of understanding (from line 7 onwards) by referring back to the consensus that both participants reached immediately beforehand is prefaced by several reformulations (1–5) by the advisor of her first question. However, it is not entirely clear whether this is an attempt to produce enough redundancy as a 'preventative' means, or whether Berta has already been 'demanding' help by means of non-verbal signals during this self-paraphrasing of the interviewer. Taking several runs at reformulation right from the beginning might be seen as a complement to the 'wait-and-see' strategy of addressees: to furnish several starting points for understanding in the hope that one of them will be the right one or that several different elements will be combined to make a whole. At the same time, there is always the risk of ending up with too long and too complex turns, especially when the segmentation between single utterances (meant as a reformulation of each other) is not transparent for the minority speaker (see also Chapter 3 above).

It is very clear here, in any case, that the interviewer is already being extremely cautious in her first turn and is very aware of potential problems with understanding. Since Berta, simply by not reacting, indicates that she has not understood, then the issue of whether or not a problem exists has to be clarified (7–10). Even for this, more than one step is necessary. Berta's threefold 'no' (8) appears to be ambiguous for the interviewer and so she *reformulates* her response by repeating it in the negative (9). So even information about understanding itself is prepared in such a way that it only has to be ratified by the minority participant. Berta does this in the form of a confirming repetition (10), which is a more explicit and therefore 'safer' sign of agreement than a simple 'no' on its own.

The transitional step of actually entering into negotiation is marked clearly by a pause and by the discourse marker 'eh + bon' (11). The next turn links the content of what has already been agreed upon with a *reformulation*. This 'link back to the context' also has the function of reinforcing expectations in retrospect. When compared with the original question a number of changes come to light which aim at establishing *accessibility* for Berta without losing *explicitness* :

- the question contains only a *part* of the original content (thanks to a shift in the way the information is distributed across the various units of the utterance – see below); (*accessibility* in quantitative terms)
- instead of using the impersonal 'abstract' expression 'si on vous propose . . .' the reformulated question uses 'si **je** vous propose' and thereby links into the concrete 'here and now'; (*accessibility* in conceptual terms)
- a different base verb is used ('démarrer', see next point) and the verb is no longer in the conditional; (before: 'qui commencer**ait**') (*accessibility* at the morphological level);
- it is structured in a way broadly parallel to that of the preceding utterance (11/12) which 'linked back to the context', and in so doing, the question has the added force of *repetition* which facilitates understanding; (*explicitness*)
- by being placed at the end of the utterance, the time (given) is easily recognisable as a contrast to 'huit heures' by virtue of its parallel position (*predictability* between consecutive utterances);
- the time itself, instead of being relative ('plus tôt que . . ./ avant huit heures') as in the original question is now expressed in absolute terms; by doing this, some of the function words that for minority interlocutors of Berta's level of competence cause difficulties can be chopped (*accessibility*);
- the time in question contains a repetition in the form of the alternative 'à sept heures ou à six heures du matin'. This raises the redundancy (and thereby *explicitness*). At the same time, this alternative is also an indirect means of re-introducing the hypothetical element of the question that had been lost by using the

indicative instead of the subjunctive (i.e. both principles, of *accessibility* and of *explicitness* are brought to bear at the same time and in a balanced way).

Altogether this constitutes a successful attempt by the interviewer to render the utterance more comprehensible in a single step. The solution, though, undergoes a further delay before the difficulty with understanding can finally be clarified. Berta evidently believes that her 'oui' (15) has already answered the question and obviously does not realise that this only answers the final (and redundant) part of the question that has so clearly been broken down into several individual steps (16/17). However, this can be solved by ratifying even smaller units one at a time (18–23).

The third and final phase of this clarificatory sequence consists of a particularly extended sequence of *checking back*. It is not until Berta manages to ratify the suggestions made more explicitly and more independently than by a mere positive response to a yes/no question (by using 'd'accord' (30)) that the interviewer is certain of the result.

While the relative length of the diagnostic phase in this last example is typical of the pattern we describe here, the feature that we have frequently referred to of breaking an utterance down so that each part can be worked through step by step is even more common in our data. This approach takes account, albeit implicitly, of the different tensions involved in rendering something understandable. Although the brevity of the individual steps in the utterance makes them particularly 'accessible', the degree of explicitness does not necessarily have to be limited by this since, where necessary, the entire utterance in all its complexity can be 'de-constructed' to almost as many individual steps as one wishes (cf. also Marcello in Chapter 4.4 and the sequence of Angelina's at the end of this chapter). At the same time this approach ensures a particularly tight control over every step in understanding, since after every step the speaker either waits for confirmation or else demands one by means of a feedback elicitor. On the level of relationships the shared effort put into negotiating can have the effect of compensating for the potential loss of face that threatens both partners in a drawn out clarification sequence. Even if greater effort was made by one rather than the other, both gain in the end. In this way, then, the speakers create a 'modus negotiendi' that combines the different demands on improving comprehensibility in a more or less optimal fashion.

Reformulation: a multifunctional procedure

As in the example with Berta the central element of negotiation in many clarificatory sequences consists of *reformulations*. Similar to the case we have just discussed they are sandwiched in between a context link at the outset and questions that check back (on the degree of understanding) at the end. The term 'reformulation', however hardly explains anything since until now it has acted as an umbrella expression for several different features. It has turned out to be amazingly difficult to define clear boundaries for the changes that exist on a continuum that ranges from a slightly modified repetition, on the one hand, and a totally freshly formulated expression that is only functionally equivalent to the one it is replacing, on the other.

In particular, for those sequences examined in this section in which there is no specific indication from the minority speaker as to what exactly it is that they cannot understand (and they may even be unable to identify this) then the decision about where to pitch the reformulation will depend on the professional. (For reformulations in response to specific indications see section 7.2 below.)

Non-specific indications tend to lead to a series of reformulations at utterance level in which each part may be reformulated in turn by either expansion, reduction or variation. In the case of a series of reformulations, it is not uncommon to find they are punctuated by comprehension checks, and, depending on the degree to which the majority speakers believe themselves able to pinpoint the problem, they may start to suggest answers.

We continue by examining some examples of reformulations used to handle non-understanding in the wake of an unspecific indication that the learner has not understood. We attempt in each analysis to examine two points in particular:

i)   does the reformulation change only the linguistic surface of the original utterance (and if so, how), or is there, in addition to that, a modification or even a change of any of the following?
>   the information provided or required
>   or the basic way of conceptualising the content
>   or the type of question, i.e. the weighting of the information it contains to that which it demands.

ii) within the context of each individual sequence is there any way of explaining why one (type of) reformulation fails whilst another achieves the desired understanding from the interlocutor.

Reformulations changing the linguistic surface of the original utterance

In some cases, a very slight change in the way the utterance is put together on a linguistic level is enough to make it just that bit more understandable. One such case occurs in Gina's job interview when the interviewer changes the tense of the verb from the less familiar imperfect (preterite) form to the everyday perfect:

> N: **waren** sie schon mal beim arbeitsamt ↑
> *were you ever at the job centre* ↑
> G: + +
> N: **sind** sie schon mal beim arbeitsamt **gewesen** ↑
> *have you ever been to the job centre* ↑
> G: <nee>   <erstaunt>
> *<no>   <amazed>*
> N: noch <u>nicht</u> ↓
> *not yet* ↓
> G: nee (. .)
> *no*

One cannot, of course, be absolutely certain about what it was that finally helped Gina to achieve better understanding; simply having more time may have helped her also – to think through different hypotheses that are then confirmed by the reformulation.

One single reformulation in our next example has a similarly economical effect. Ayse, a young Turkish woman, here sees a doctor after having an accident at work. In this case, though, it is not merely the formulation that is changed but a slight shift in perspective appears to make the question easier to understand.

(opening of the conversation; preceded only by greeting)

> (1)   N: sie haben sich am arm verletzt
>   *you've hurt your arm*
>   **wann war das denn** ↑
>   *when did that happen* ↑
>   E: hm ↑
>   N: **wie lange ist das her** ↑
>   *how long ago was that* ↑
> (5)   E: ++ zwei zwei monat ↓
>   *++ two two months*
>   N: vor zwei Monaten
>   *two months ago*
>   E: mhm

N: ist es passiert + und wie ist es denn passiert (. .)
     it happened + and how did it happen (. .)

Reformulations aiming at a 'narrower' question

It is, however, especially in the case of non-specific indications of
NU, often not possible to find a tailor-made reformulation for the
problem. One strategy that is often used in the interviews consists
of *narrowing down the question* in order to shift the balance between
the amount of information the question contains and the amount
it attempts to obtain. This means, for example, replacing an 'open'
question by one which merely demands confirmation or denial.
The question takes possible replies as its starting point. An example of this is to be found in the first part of the Job Centre
interview with Tino where they are trying to establish what work
experience he has had since leaving school. This is immediately
preceded by Tino's statement that he was called up into the army
after school.

(1)   N: und e nach der militärzeit – wie gings dann weiter ↑
           and er after your time in the army – what happened then ↑
      T: + welches ↑ / e <tschuldigung>
           + *which er <sorry>*   <quickly, quietly>
      N: sie ham dann e zweieinhalb jahre militärzeit [absolviert] ↑
           so you served er two and half years in the army ↑
      T: ja (zwei jahre) ja
           yes (two years) yes
(5)   N: und sind sie dann <u>sofort</u> ↑ nach deutschland gekommen
           and did you come to germany <u>straightaway</u> ↑
      T: nein ↓ nein ↓ ts ts ts + + +
           no ↓ no ↓ ts ts ts + + +
           wenn isch habe die militär <u>zu</u> gemacht ↑
           when i have finished military service
      N: mhm
      T: isch habe für fast zwei e fast zwei <u>jahren</u> gearbeitet ↓
           i have worked for almost two er almost two <u>years</u>

The first part of the original question is first of all repeated (line
3) in a single step as a link back to the context. Tino ratifies this
impatiently as something that has already been clarified (simulta-
neous utterance: 4). For the second part of the utterance, however,
the interviewer does not bother to modify her first attempt
although an *explanatory* paraphrase would have been appropriate

when shortening it. Instead of this she offers a possible answer almost as a hypothesis – which as it turns out, in this context is a successful strategy.

More than a reformulation: 'fresh start'

Even where the perspective appears to be shifting, the reformulation moves undertaken in the examples so far have kept fairly closely to the original **content**. We shall now see that the conversation can deviate quite a long way from this without actually involving topic switch. (A topic switch that occurs as a result of an indication of non-understanding in our view would not count as an attempt at negotiation but rather as giving up. From the point of view of the minority participant one could in some cases even speak of a refusal to negotiate; see also section 4.4 on 'overriding'.)

In these cases attempts are made instead to achieve the same goal by different means or via a different route by using a question whose content is different but which fulfills as closely as possible the same function at this point in the conversation. In the following example which is taken from an interview with a young Turkish man, Abdullah, he is applying for an apprenticeship in a garage and the interviewer is just trying to find out more about his motivation for choosing this career.

(1)   N: ja hascht schon mal e irgendwann mit autos zu tun gehabt ↑ +
           have you ever had er anything to do with cars ↑
           damit ( ) sagen kannscht okay das hat dir spaß gemacht ↑
           so that ( ) could say ok you enjoyed that ↑
      B: + ich hab nich verstanden ↓
           + i didn't understand ↓
      N: ja wie kommscht en eben grad an den beruf ↑
           yes how did you come to choose this particular career ↑
(5)   aus was fürm grund möchtest du gern kraftfahrzeugmechaniker
           lernen ↑
           for what reason would you like to train as a motor vehicle mechanic ↑
      B: + ja wir haben ein altes auto
           + yes we have an old car
      N: ja
           yes
      B: wenn etwas kaputt geht ↑ ich kann es e reparieren
           when something goes wrong ↑ *i can er repair it*

In fact, the garage owner had intended at this point to raise a question that verges on the personal, in a more elegant way, by making it more indirect and thereby apparently of no real import. This does not work, though, and in a move that is more of a **fresh start** than a reformulation (ll. 4/5) he opts for greater clarity and directness without relinquishing his immediate aim in the conversation. The example also demonstrates that an unspecific but nonetheless explicit indication of non-understanding by means of a metalinguistic comment (in l. 3) makes the clarification more economic because in contrast to minimal feedback (or other symptoms) it is clearly established that there is a problem with understanding here.

7.2 CLARIFICATION FOLLOWING SPECIFIC INDICATION: EXPLICATION OF LEXICAL MEANING

Most of the non-understandings that are identified and indicated specifically (with respect to their source) by the minority workers centre around the meaning of a single lexical item: a word from the preceding turn is identified and maybe its phonetic form recognized but its meaning is not clear. As the examples below will show, the possibility of distinguishing a lexical item in this way as a source of one's non-understanding is often facilitated by the native speakers' prosodic emphasis on important, i.e. 'key' words (Allwood 1988).

The basic structures of the procedures used to clarify this type of problem are as follows:

A *repetition* of the relevant lexical item as a first step has a double function. It not only confirms the way the form was presented by the minority speaker (if necessary, a correction can be given at this point) but it also acknowledges that it is this item that will now be the centre of attention for both speakers.

An *explication of meaning* for which different linguistic means can be used (cf. Quasthoff and Hartmann (1982), Gülich (1988, 1991), Lüdi (1987); the most important in our data were:

explaining by **synonym**, i.e. replacing the original lexical item by one with similar meaning;

explaining by **definition**, i.e. giving some superordinate or general term / hyperonym and differentiating features of the item;

explaining by **paraphrase**, i.e. naming important characteristics in a descriptive proposition/ description

However, clarification sequences around lexical problems of understanding *differ* in an important respect. They vary in the degree to which they are 'exposed', that is either explication of the meaning of the lexical item is the *only* content of the turn – or it is 'embedded' in a reformulation of the whole utterance or turn that was not understood *because* of the item. The more elaborate an explication is, the more difficult it is for a speaker to integrate into the reformulation of her question. So explanations of meaning in the form of a 'definition' typically form a kind of digression from the current topic which is marked metalinguistically by introductory formulae ('xx – that is a . . .'). It is usually only for clarifying crucial notions in an encounter that speakers decide to invest so much effort.

This is the case for example for the term 'Ausbildung' (training) in Tino's Job Centre interview (see also case study in 5.4). During the session there are three phases where understanding rests on the meaning of this lexical item. First, when it has to be established whether Tino had some training; then, later on the interviewer wants to know if Tino would consider taking a training course; and finally, near the end of the encounter this question is brought up again when the interviewer wants to conclude the interview. It is, therefore, very important for Tino to understand what 'Ausbildung' means.

The following excerpt is taken from the second occasion. At the first attempt, the interviewer had given up and switched topic. After both speakers have realized that without training of some kind it will be very difficult for Tino to find a better job, the question has to be tackled again:

(1)   N: ja ham sie denn sich schon mal überlegt ob sie nich ne
              <u>ausbildung</u> machen wollen ↑
              well have you ever thought of starting a training course
              + hier in deutschland
              + *here in germany*
       T: entschu/ <u>ausbildung</u> ↑
              sorr/ training ↑
       N: <u>ausbildung</u> + äh
              training
(5)   am anfang unseres gesprächs hab ich ja – schon mal äh – des
              angeschnitten ↓
              in the beginning of our conversation i have mentioned er it already

ausbildung das heißt also wenn jemand einen beruf <u>lernen</u>
möchte +
training that means if someone wants to learn a trade
drei jahre lang ↓ + eine <u>lehre</u> macht ↓ drei jahre lang
during three years ↓ + follows a course ↓ during three years

T: mhm
     mhm

N: und dann isch man äh hat/ hat man ein' <u>gesellenbrief</u>
     and then you are er have/ have a certificate

(10)   wenn man fertig ist mit der lehre
     when you have finished the course
     <u>sowas</u> mein ich + verstehen sie mich nicht ↑
     that's what i mean + you don't understand me ↑

T: <mnm>   <= no>
     mnm

N: + nicht ↑ äh-+ möchten sie was lernen ↑
     + no ↑ er + you want to learn something ↑

T: <u>ja</u> <u>aah</u>
     yes

(15) N: jetzt verstehen sie [wenn/ möchten sie]
     now you understand if/ you want

T: [eine/ ein etwas (besong)] ein arbeit besonde
     a/ something (special) a special job

N: ein <u>beruf</u> lernen
     to learn a job

T: beruf *professione* ja
     *job *professione* yes*

N: ja
     yes

(20) T: ja
     yes

In her question the interviewer had already tried to made clear
that 'Ausbildung' is of central importance here: it is emphasized as a
key-word. In his indication of non-understanding in (3), Tino takes it
up with questioning intonation. The counsellor starts her explanation
of meaning with a third reprise of the word – which is at the same
time a ratification of Tino's 'try' with the non-understood item and
an introduction to a longer explicative phase. Her next step (5/6) is a
link back to the context of the interaction which precedes the actual
explication. This is framed by a metalinguistic comment: 'Ausbildung
that means . . .'. In (6) 'profession' and 'learning' are named as the
defining features of the expression, and after a small pause the usual
duration of such a course is given as an additional characteristic.

Since Tino still does not signal understanding at this point, she adds a further explication in (7). It consists of a modified repetition of her first attempt, this time using 'Lehre' as a *synonym* for 'ausbildung'. But even further information on the term in the form of describing the kind of certificate one gets in the end is not successful (9) – a fact that both interlocutors agree on very explicitly in (11/12). Finally it is a *reformulation* (13) of the original question in words that turns out to be the best way to make at least part of the lexical meaning of 'Ausbildung' accessible for Tino. Compared to the more 'technical' semantic components she tried to explain before, this is a simplification (to some degree) – 'lehre' is a specific type of training, with a fixed course, duration and certificate, whereas 'to learn something' has a much wider range of meanings.

Another example where the understanding of a single lexical item is of crucial importance for the whole encounter is Abdelmalek's Job Centre interview. A long stretch of the conversation centres around the term 'preuves' (papers), where the clerk of the national unemployment agency (ASSEDIC) tries to make clear to Abdelmalek why these papers are so important for an adequate handling of his case.

(1) N: heu + bon + alors euh + vous avez apporté le euh/ le papier
         well ok + you have brought the er/ the paper
         les preuves de la recherche d'emploi
         the papers concerning your search for a job ↑
     A: non < >   <laughs>
         no
     N: vous n'avez pas apporté [les preuves de la recherche d'emploi ↑]
         you did not bring [the papers concerning your search for a job ↑]
(5) A: [(xxxx)]
     N: alors comment je vais faire ce dossier moi ↑
         and now how am i going to put together your file ↑
     A: carte de séjour ↑
         residence permit ↑
     N: non vous savez + je euh vous êtes au chômage vous êtes obligé de /
         no you know + i er you are unemployed you are obliged to/
         je vous ai donné un papier ou on vous a donné un papier
         i had given you a paper or a paper was given to you
(10)   sur lequel il fallait voir [les employeurs]
         which you should have shown the employers
     A: [ah]

N: et puis ils écrivent monsieur abdelmalek est venu demander du
     travail
     and then they write mr abdelmalek was here to ask for a job
     et mettre le cachet + ça c'est ce qu'on appelle les preuves\
     and put the stamp + that's what one calls the papers
     A: \ouais ouais les preuves
     yes yes the papers
(15) N: vous les avez apportées
     have you brought them
     A: non pas < porte> hein
     no not bring

The relevant item 'preuves' has been mentioned already twice
(1/2) when it finally becomes clear that Abdelmalek does not
understand what it means – or at least not well enough for the
purpose of the interview. His hypothesis of 'carte de séjour' (7)
functions here as a sort of indirect indication of non-understanding. As in the example above, the interviewer uses an
introduction to her extended explication: 'vous savez' (you
know) can be seen as a colloquial announcement that he is going
to explain something. This is followed again by a *link back to the
context*, this time stating explicitly the 'essentials' of Abdelmalek's
situation ('vous êtes en chômage', 8). After some self corrections
the interviewer then explains 'preuves' by naming the general
notion (a paper) and its specific features (in a relative clause: in
which . . .). A metalinguistic comment (13, 'that's what one calls
. . .') includes a further reprise of the explicated item and closes
the clarification. Only when A. has indicated his understanding
(14), the original question is taken up again ('have you brought
them . . .').

In these two examples speakers have taken a considerable
amount of time to try and really expand on the 'general' meaning
of the relevant lexical item – while postponing a clarification of the
actual question at hand. In many cases however, they attempt to
solve both tasks simultaneously by integrating the explication of
the lexical concept with a new, modified formulation of their original statement. A certain shift in the purpose of an explanation is
then adequate or sometimes even necessary: to make understandable just that part of the lexical meaning of an item which is needed
in the actual context of the utterance.

An example of this type of procedure for clarifying a lexical problem can be found in the same encounter with Abdelmalek:

(1)   N: si je vous/ comprenez s'il n'y a pas de preuves#
            if i understand you if there are no papers
        A: #ah oui ↓
            oh yes ↓
        N: la commission paritaire elle va pas vous reconduire dans vos droits +
            the joint commission will not renew your right to stay +
            vous allez perdre vos droits [et si vous]
            you will lose your rights and if you
(5)   A: [droits]
            rights
        N: perdez vos droits vous allez avoir très peu d'argent par jour hein
            lose your rights you will have very little money each day hm
        A: ah <u>pauvre</u>
            oh poor
        N: eh oui c'est ça (. .)
            yes that's it

When Abdelmalek indicates (5) that he does not understand the term 'droits' (rights) the interviewer here chooses not to explain what 'rights' mean in general but sticks to the relevant verb phrase (to lose one's rights). This is first repeated (6) and then explained – not abstractly, but by making explicit the *consequences* this would have for Abdelmalek. (One could call this type of explication a 'functional' paraphrase.) And as Abdelmalek's own re-phrasing shows (7), he understands perfectly now what 'perdre ses droits' would mean for him.

A similar procedure – i.e. offering a kind of 'functional para-phrase' for the meaning of a term – is used in the next example, where Madan is asked at the post office about a parcel he wants to send and does not know the word 'value':

(1)   N: what's the value ↑
        M: sorry ↑
        N: the value + what's the value
        M: what value ↑
(5)   N: the cost
            how much did you pay for them ↓
        M: + + in india ↑
        N: no no here how much did you pay for them ↑
            whats the value ↑
(10)   M: er this (xxx)
        N: this/ this the things here
        M: erm shop

N: no no how much was it ↑
M: oh how much er only five pound shirt (..)

The first attempt to clarify the lexical meaning of 'value' here is by giving a *synonym* ('cost', 5) which is then immediately followed by a colloquial paraphrase (6). The second attempt (9) emphasises the concrete situation of Madan buying the clothes (. . .'did you'). And after solving another misunderstanding (10/12), a third reprise of this paraphrase (13) is finally successful. In all of her attempts, the English speaking interlocutor sticks to her question while explaining the (contextual) meaning of 'value' at the same time.

7.3 MAXIMAL USE OF PROCEDURES – AN EXAMPLE

We close this description of the various means that can be used to manage problems with understanding with the analysis of a particularly extensive clarificatory sequence. Its length and complexity make it a 'telling' rather than a 'typical' case (Ellen 1984) and it is for this reason that we have chosen it.

Firstly, the majority speaker makes use of a whole range of means in order to clarify one single question and this can then be viewed in *context*. The individual procedures used and the relationship between the process of resolution and the dynamics of the encounter (in other words motivation for resolution, its *dénouement*, success and effect on the rest of the conversation) seem to be a good way of summing up the results so far.

Secondly, it gives some impression of the way in which extreme difficulties with understanding can nevertheless be solved assuming that the interlocutors are prepared to invest the appropriate degree of patience, perseverance and co-operation.

Angelina has enquired about job vacancies in a large firm and there are several possibilities: office work, kitchen work and on the shopfloor. Her interlocutor is an engineer employed by the company who is usually involved in job interviews (though as a rule for the more highly qualified posts). He also has experience of applicants of different nationalities and a basic knowledge of Italian (about one third of the workforce are Italians). At this time Angelina has been in Germany for just over one and a half years but has had little contact with Germans and for this reason her command of the new language is minimal.

The example comes from the end of the first part of the encounter. To start with, Angelina is asked first about her education and previous work experience. They establish that office work is not suitable for her for the time being and as an alternative she is offered work in the kitchen or dining-room. This whole first part is beset by difficulties with understanding and is constantly interrupted by 'side sequences.' Angelina is exclusively in the role of answering questions, or listening. But at this point (line 1 below) her interlocutor, Mr. B., tries to hand over the initiative to her and get her to ask him about aspects of the job that interest her. This has been directly preceded by a short description from Mr. B. about the two areas of work in the canteen, which now follows in a slightly shortened version. For the sake of clarity the sequence is divided into four sections each followed by an analysis of the procedures used.

Section A: in which the problem surfaces and a first attempt at clarification is unsuccessful.

(1)   N: in der kantine gibt's <u>küchen</u>arbeit ja ↑ +
           in the canteen there's work in the kitchen yes ↑
           und dann gibt's e <u>saalarbeit</u> +
           and then there's er dining room work +
           in der <u>küche</u> ↑ + müssen (. . .) kochen ↓ + vorbereiten ↓ ja
           undsoweiter mm (xx)
           in the kitchen ↑ (. . .) have to cook ↓ prepare you know ↓ and so on (xx)
      A: < >   <laughs>
(5)   N: und im <u>saal</u> ↑ das ist servieren ↓ (. .)
           and in the dining room ↑ it's serving ↓ (. .)
      N: gut ↓ <u>ham sie fragen</u> da ↑ + ham sie fragen +
           good ↓ have you got any questions there ↑ have you questions +
           <u>frage</u> ↑
           question ↑
      A: fragen (küche)
           questions (kitchen)
      N: verstehn' sie frage ↑
           do you understand question ↑
(10) A: frage <u>ja</u>
           question yes
      N: ja ↓ haben sie fragen über <u>küche</u> und <u>saal</u> ↑
           yes ↓ do you have questions about kitchen and dining-room ↑
      A: e küche
           er kitchen
      N: ja
           yes

A: küche
      kitchen

(15) N: haben sie fragen ↑ *do/ domanda* haben sie *domanda* ↑
         do you have questions ↑ *domanda* do you have *domanda* ↑

A: E <u>warum</u> e isch e in küche ↑
      er why er i in kitchen ↑

N: nein nein <sie verstehen nicht>   <quietly>
      no no   <you don't understand>

As far as one can tell from what she says, Angelina assumes throughout this whole excerpt that it is she who is *being asked* a question. She understands the word 'frage' (question) and obviously tries to link it to the immediately preceding conversational context. It is, however, not clear whether her reply (l. 8) is actually meant as a reply. When the alternatives kitchen vs. dining room are taken up again in (11) it seems that Angelina only has the three emphasised keywords (question, kitchen, dining room) on which to construct meaning. She forms a hypothesis about the question – 'whether she would prefer to work in the kitchen or dining room' – and decides on kitchen (12/14). When Mr. B. then goes on asking (15) Angelina checks back. She puts forward a hypothesis for confirmation which could be paraphrased as 'do you want to know why I've decided on kitchen?' for which there are no grounds in Mr. B.'s reply (15) but which from her point of view could be a (perhaps the only) logical continuation of the question, i.e. a best-guess.

The clarification procedures used by Mr. B. in this phase are unsuccessful mainly because they deal with a different problem from the one which is really present. Mr. B. does not (yet) understand what it is that Angelina does not understand. His efforts centre on the lexical item 'question' which he takes as not understood. It is thus taken out of the question as a whole in the first step of 'de-construction' (7) and his understanding is first implicitly (by intonation) and then explicitly (8) expressed. Neither does Mr. B. trust the clarification of this point (10) since in his *reformulations* (15) it is again the word 'question' which is being simplified, this time by means of Angelina's mother tongue.

Section B: in which a second attempt at clarification fails and Mr. B. really wants to give up

(18) N: <es gibt die arbeit in küche oder saal in der kantine ja ↑>
        there is work in the kitchen or dining-room in the canteen ok ↑
           <loudly, clearly>

A: mhm
      mhm
(20) N: und jetzt <u>möchte</u> ↑ <u>ich</u> <u>wissen</u> ich möchte wissen ob sie <u>fragen</u>
           haben +
           and now i'd like to know ↑ i'd like to know whether you have questions
           ja ↑ sie fragen <u>mich</u> ob e die arbeit <was weiß ich>
                                                              <speeded up>
           yes you ask me whether er the work <i don't know what>
           <u>schwer</u> is ob das <u>lang</u> ist ob das + <u>heiß</u> ist
           is heavy if its long if its hot
           verstehen sie was ich meine ↑
           do you understand what i mean ↑
A: <nein>   <quietly>
      no
(25) N: verstehn sie nicht + ja
           you don't understand + well

After they have clarified that there is no lexical problem, Mr. B. introduces his second attempt by explicitly recreating the *frame* for his question. He links his utterance to the conversational context (18) and makes sure of the shared basis of knowledge (ja? mhm, 18/19) before he goes on to a new reformulation of the first part of his question. Although this *reformulation* (20) is more explicit (as far as the 'subject' of the question is concerned) in comparison to (1) it is however syntactically more complicated and retains the stress on the word 'frage' (question) which, as we have seen, is still apparently important for Angelina's understanding.

His feedback elicitor ('ja?' (21)) remains unanswered. The fact that he shifts the emphasis onto the new keyword 'mich' (me), i.e. to the addressee of the question (thereby focussing on the real problem for the first time) but still without success is presumably accounted for by Angelina's not knowing this pronoun. He then continues by suggesting answers – in this case, possible questions. Even that does not help, perhaps because of the indirect formulation. In other words, his examples are not recognisable as *questions* for Angelina.

The renewed failure of yet another attempt to work out the problem is explicitly documented (23/24); Mr. B. undertakes no further attempt at clarification ((25): pause, yes) but seems to have come to the end of his resources.

Section C: now Angelina takes the initiative after which the first part of the question is clarified

(26)   A: \<eine frage\>   \<quite loudly\>
             a question
       N: ja
             yes
       A: verstehsch ↓
             understand ↓
       N: frage
             question
(30)   A: ein frage *una domanda*
             a question *una domanda*
       N: ja gut und jetzt ↑ haben <u>sie</u> fragen ↑ a/ hab/
             yes good and now ↑ do you have any questions ↑
             haben <u>sie</u> fragen an mich
             have <u>you</u> any questions for me
       A: \<*ah io una domanda a lei*\>   \<lively, loud\>
             oh i a question to you
       N: genau ja +
             yes exactly

Angelina is obviously unhappy to leave the problem unresolved and so initiates a new phase of working the problems through: she too starts by explicitly confirming what has already been agreed on (26/28) and supports this by her translation (30). This then provides the basis for a fresh reformulation in which the addressee of the question is given emphasis ('Sie' [you], 31) and this is a lexical item with which Angelina is familiar. Angelina now understands and makes this unequivocally clear through her spontaneous translation and expression of relief (33).

Section D: in which the second part of the question is also finally cleared up and Angelina really does start to ask questions

(35)   N: haben sie fragen <u>über</u> die arbeit ↑
             have you any questions about the job
       A: + \<habe sie frage ↑ \>   \<quietly\>
             have you questions
       N: \<<u>über die</u>\> a/ arbeit   \<very clearly\>
             about the job
       A: *sul lavoro*
             about the job

N: ja + ja haben sie fragen *sul lavoro* ↑
       *yes + yes have you any questions *sul lavoro* ↑*

(40)   A: *una domanda a lei devo fare*
       shall i put a question to you ↑

N: ja
       yes

A: e +

N: verstehn sie tippen und so nix ↓   ja ↑   aber kantine <u>küche</u> +
       you understand typing and that kind of thing ↓ yes but canteen
       <u>kitchen</u>
       große küche un dann <u>töpfe</u> ja
       big kitchen and then <u>pans</u> yes

(45)   A: mhm

N: un dann <u>heiß</u> ja un dann undsoweiter ↓ und jetzt <u>fragen</u> sie mich +
       and then <u>hot</u> yes and then and so on and now you <u>ask</u> me
       was sie <u>wissen</u> wollen ↓ + was wollen sie wissen über küche ↑
       what you want to <u>know</u> ↓ what do you want to know about the kitchen ↑

A: e + + e de arbeide in küje is e e + + is e *pesante*
       *er + + er the work in kitchen is er er + + *pesante**

N: schwer
       heavy

(50)   A: schwer
       heavy

N: die arbeit in der küche <u>is</u> schwer ↓
       the work in the kitchen <u>is</u> heavy ↓

A: ja
       yes

N: ja
       yes

A: is schwer + warum ↑
       is heavy + why ↑

On the basis of what has now been achieved ('have you got any questions' has at last been clarified) Mr. B. can now deal with the clarification of the second part – here he first simplifies from the particular back to the general: 'about the kitchen and the dining room' becomes 'about the job'. Although this seems to be too much at one go for Angelina, she is now able to identify her lack of understanding, that is, to narrow it down by indicating *which part* of the utterance she has not understood (36). In this way the reformulation in l. 37 can concentrate on the problematic part of the second part of the question. It is the combination of this continued simplification and the heightened clarity of articulation which finally leads to success and Angelina demonstrates her understanding once again through a translation which is simultaneously a confirmation check (38). We can assume that her renewed checking back (40) and her hesitation (42) can only have the function of gaining time and is not intended to indicate non-understanding. She first has to think of a question, and formulation is still difficult for her. Now Mr. B., who has been made unsure of himself by events so far, feels the necessity to sum up by a repetition in which he goes from the more general concept 'job' back to the more specific 'kitchen'.

In constructing this illustrative scenario he makes syntactic simplifications of a type he has never used before. In order to exemplify the situation about which he is trying to prompt questions, he lists one keyword after another (big, kitchen, pans, hot) linking them only by 'dann' (then) and emphasising them through intonation (44/46). A final *paraphrase* ('wissen wollen' – 'want to know' instead of 'have questions') is added onto this, the redundancy is increased by the repetition and the extension 'und Saal' (and the dining room) omitted for strategic reasons.

Angelina now starts with her question. She needs a lot of planning time which Mr. B. allows her as well as furnishing a German equivalent for the Italian word *pesante*. But the question which Angelina then constructs with her interlocutor (48/50) is not marked as a question either by syntax or intonation. In order to eradicate any trace of doubt as to whether or not he has understood her properly, B. uses intonation (l. 51) to make it especially clear that his utterance is an *answer* – the answer to Angelina's identical question.

Angelina's first independent question is the first of a whole series of questions which determine the conversation from then on almost to the end. She enquires about the size of the company, working hours, pay etc. Understanding in this following section is considerably less problematic than in the opening phase where she had a very passive role. The effort expended, by both sides, on clarifying one single question was in the end worthwhile. Angelina makes good use of her newly-won conversational role and she accepts the offer of taking more control which raises her chances of understanding. At the same time her taking the initiative is, as far as B. is concerned, the best possibility (if not the only one) of getting a conversation going and thereby achieving (some of) his goals. 'In reality' the entire sequence lasted just under three minutes!

The analysis of this example illustrates the following points:

- Through the use of a broad range of procedures, understanding can even be achieved in the face of considerable obstacles such as the minority participant's extremely limited command of the language spoken combined with the fact that the demands placed on her (to ask questions about the job) were totally beyond her horizons of expectations. In other words, the limits of understanding can always be extended further.
- Understanding problems can only be resolved by *joint* efforts. Without Angelina's contribution, indicating as best she could, with the very limited means at her disposal, what had been understood and what was still problematic, even the most experienced interviewer would find it difficult to make progress in such an encounter.
- Successful clarification presupposes correct 'diagnosis' of the problem. As soon as a procedure tackles the right point then the problem can be speedily cleared up.
- The assessment of the cost-benefit relationship of such a drawn-out clarificatory sequence depends on the importance of the lack of understanding for the encounter as a whole. One can only assume that the fact that Angelina apparently does 'take off' and makes a series of pertinent questions in the succeeding section redeems this initial and laborious, even if co-operative, section.

EIGHT

Taking stock: contexts and reflections

Celia Roberts

8.0 INTRODUCTION

This chapter draws on current ideas in interactional sociolinguistics and critical theory to revisit and critique aspects of the theory, methodology and methods underlying the work on 'understanding' in this volume. This critical review throws up some suggestions for future work on intercultural communication. We have placed this more theoretical and critical perspective at the end of the book since some readers will be more interested in the data and analysis of earlier chapters, while others, we hope, will wish to take things further by reading to the end.

Revisiting any work a few years after the so-called final report has been written is rather like a mid-life crisis. There is a sense of missed opportunities, of working from one perspective and now finding one has another, surely wiser one, of wanting to retrieve, relive and accomplish something rather different. So this chapter draws on theoretical influences which, during the project, were only general rumblings at the back of our minds. These influences would have affected our methodology and to some extent, specific methods, if we were to start the project now. But our critique of the project is also affected by what we learnt from our informants and to this extent it is like any undertaking: it is only as it draws to a close that we realise how we could have done it.

A good example of this is the role of institutional discourse in the lives of migrant workers. A social perspective on adult second language development must, as we have suggested in Chapter 1, situate minority workers in a marginal position within a white dominated society. The critical perspective implied by such an approach we would argue needs to be much more explicit and worked through in any detailed linguistic analysis. Social theory and interactional sociolinguistics (see below) helps to make the connections between issues of power and knowledge and the fine-grained detail of negotiating understanding and resources in face-to-face encounters.

Although we were very aware of the limited opportunities our informants had to participate in the majority society (Jupp, Roberts and Cook-Gumperz, 1982, Allwood and Simonot 1984), it is still easy to underestimate the extent of the limitations. For most informants, apart from the data collection conversations with researchers, their only extended face-to-face encounter with native speakers from the majority groups was in bureaucratic and service encounters.

In addition, informants were often aware of the complexities and difficulties of such institutional encounters. For example, Ergün, commenting on the housing officer interviews remarked

> Bu çeşit konuşmalar bize zor geliyor. bize hep zor konular, ev alacağım, satacağım gibi laflar. yani bize normal bir şey sorsalar %75 bilirim. böyle ancak %50 biliyorum. bu çeşit konularla sık sık karşılaşsaydım, tabii ki daha iyi cevap verebilecektim.

> *This type of conversation on difficult subjects is for us very hard. It relates all difficult subjects: housing application, selling etc. Look if they would ask me about normal subjects, then I would know 75% of it, now I know only 50%. If I would come across more often these difficult subjects, then I would be able to give better answers.*

We discuss, below, the impact of these issues on identities, relationships with the majority and motivation to learn the new language.

The nature of institutional discourse as a learning environment and as the mediation between a minority group and the majority takes on a particular significance. Methodological considerations and data collection need to reflect this. In particular, the relationship between situated interpretation in interactions and the wider sociopolitical consequences of being a minority worker can only be illuminated through collecting data of naturally occurring and, if necessary, re-created bureaucratic encounters.

One of the great challenges of this study was to work in an interdisciplinary way, drawing on the epistemologies and methodologies of second language acquisition and those of sociology, anthropology, educational development and, latterly, social theory and its critical perspective. This raises important questions about what justification we have for staking out our piece of social territory as a knowledge base, how we set about defining this knowledge and how we represent this knowledge. A social SLA perspective is caught between positivistic and experimental paradigms, on the one hand, and, on the other, an interpretive and more critical methodology. This affects issues of data collection and analysis but also of representation.

Much SLA work is represented within a positivistic tradition in which the discourse strives to be 'objective'. The euphemism of 'untutored' SLA is a good example of this. The descriptor 'untutored' distances the reader from the reality of struggling to communicate and learn in a hostile environment. The language of this 'objective' approach is clinical, the underlying orientation is to the authority of fact, hypotheses have to be proved or disproved.

By contrast, within the phenomenological tradition, knowledge is represented through the relating and patterning of concepts derived from observed behaviour. For example, within conversation analysis, the phenomena of 'adjacency pairs', and 'side-sequences' key the reader into the orderly sequencing of conversations. Here, the appeal is to the authority of concepts. Again, in contrast to this, much current anthropological and ethnographic work uses metaphor to illuminate, and in some way, translate concepts and data. It also puts emphasis on the voices of the informants themselves and on the writers' reflexive awareness of themselves as part of the social world they study (Hammersley & Atkinson 1983). Within this tradition, the authority is in the writing itself, the rhetorical strategies of the ethnographic text (Clifford and Marcus 1986, Atkinson 1992). Methodologically, there is the obvious contrast between deductive, experimental and hypothesis-testing paradigms and the interpretative approaches of phenomenology and ethnography.

	Positivistic	Phenomenological	Ethnographic
Knowledge base	Objective reality, capable of fragmentation & of being studied independently	Situated behaviour	Holistic interpretations within wider socio-political context
Representation	Authority of facts	Authority of concepts	Authority in the voices of participants and rhetoric of the writing
Methodology	Hypothesis testing	Interpretive analysis	'Thick description'

In methodology, methods and representation we have had to reach a compromise. In the next section we discuss in more detail the issues of data collection and analysis introduced briefly in chapter one. This is a discussion of a process which is still continuing, here and beyond, as we develop our theoretical orientation, analytical skills and awareness of the epistemologies in our own writing of texts.

8.1 FACING UP TO OUR METHODS

We have described, in Chapter 1, the methods of data collection used on the project. As data was collected and the process of analysis began, it became increasingly clear that our social perspective on the understanding process would problematise our data and our approach to analysis. So, in this section, we aim to critique these methods.

Aaron Cicourel (Cicourel 1992) argues for an explicit and honest account of how data is collected and the circumstances under which it is collected. He argues that tape-recordings and analysis of naturally occurring data without understanding and taking account of the broader context within which they are embedded can result in a purely formal analysis:

> Verbal interaction is related to the task at hand. Language and other social practices are interdependent. Knowing something about the ethnographic setting, the perception of and characteristics attributed to others, and broader and local social organisational conditions becomes imperative for an understanding of linguistic and non-linguistic aspects of communicative events.
>
> (Cicourel 1992:294)

He also argues that in both field research and laboratory experiments, the researcher may well be constructing social practices and levels of awareness which are not part of informants' routine lives. (see also Briggs 1986, Silverstein 1992). In other words, as researchers we must be much more reflexive about how we use data and much more aware of the limitations of our data in accounting for informants' practices. In the spirit of honesty and explicitness that Cicourel asserts, we will now review our methods of data collection and analysis.

As we have outlined in Chapter 1, the data for 'understanding' was limited to naturally-occurring encounters in the field, institutional simulations and conversations with researchers. Data collected in more experimental elicitation procedures was excluded, in order to focus on data which most nearly represented some of the possible social interactions of the informants. Each of these data collection methods has its own difficulties. The field data was collected by accompanying the informant on a series of outings – for example to the shops, to the railway station, to the estate agent – and tape-recording their encounters. As far as possible informants chose activities or were asked to carry out tasks which were necessary or useful as part of their everyday lives. In many instances, their encounters were so routine and limited that little data was collected. There was the added factor that these were not naturally-occurring events in any real sense, but prearranged sorties for the purposes of collecting data.

Simulated gatekeeping interviews as data are clearly open to the criticism that they are set up. Considerable experience of using videoed and audioed role-plays in analysing inter-cultural communication (Roberts, Davies and Jupp 1992) suggests that linguistic features at or below the level of sentence are not very susceptible to change in role-played situations. However, social relationships, the emotional tone or key of the encounter and the lack of life-determining outcomes are all likely to be affected by the fact it is a role-play. As far as possible, the institutional simulations were with real gatekeepers such as housing officials, work supervisors and so on, who interviewed informants on issues that were of genuine concern to them. The implications of using such data in looking at intercultural discourse are that local features tend to be looked at rather than global ones and that many of the interactions, as we have indicated in Chapter 2 above, either progressed more smoothly or had a more positive outcome than is likely in similar, naturally-occurring events. Although some of the interviews were videoed, there was not a sufficient data base for the purposes of this book. The lack of any analysis of non verbal communication or of the relationships between speech and non verbal communication in constructing context is clearly a weakness and one which future studies will need to rectify.

Conversations with researchers had ethnographic as well as linguistic significance. Through regular visits over the two and a half year period usually to the home of informants or researchers, trusting relationships were established. The details of informants' lives and experiences gradually emerged and at the same time data was gathered on how they managed informal conversations covering narratives about previous jobs, daily routines, their aspirations and so on. It must be said, however, that such researcher-initiated conversations constrain the social relationships and speaker rights of informants. In fact, since for many informants the data collection events were the only occasions in which they communicated in the new second language, these researcher conversations were often used as 'pedagogic conversations' by them, as we have suggested above (Roberts and Simonot 1987).

The methods used in the ESF project go some way towards answering Cicourel's criticism of much discourse analysis. Ethnographic data on perceptions and characteristics was collected and the regular feedback sessions held with researchers who shared the same first language in which informants commented on the tape-recorded interaction, meant that analysts' interpretations could be triangulated with informants' (Denzin 1978). This process of triangulation allows different data sources to be compared and contrasted. This afforded at least a partial solution to the criticism levelled at conversation analysts that their formal analysis is, implicitly, based on assumptions of shared sociocultural knowledge. In other words, they allow in ethnographic evidence, by the back door, so to speak, while denying the necessity for it.

Triangulation of data sources contributes to making the analysed data more 'credible' (Lincoln and Guba 1985). However, post-hoc commentaries on data create their own problems Their usefulness depends on the extent to which informants are able and willing to discuss all aspects of the interaction. For example, the Turkish worker, Mohammed, saw the feedback sessions only as an attempt to discuss his grammatical errors. Also, as Silverstein (1981) and Gumperz (1992a) discuss, moment-by-moment inferencing is highly context sensitive and made at a subconscious level so that asking informants to recall their interpretive processes has its own limitations and may cause reinterpretations.

> Situated interpretations are intrinsically context-bound and cannot be analysed apart from the verbal sequences in which they are embedded. Moreover, inferences are subconsciously made so that . . . they are not readily accessible to recall. It is therefore difficult to elicit information about the grounds upon which particular inferences are made through direct questions.
>
> (Gumperz 1992a:232)

However, in the analysis of intercultural texts, where speakers have very limited use of the majority language, sole reliance on turn-by-turn analysis of the data leaves enormous interpretive gaps. For those reasons both in-depth analysis and ethnographic elicitation were used, although neither singly nor in combination could they provide a total solution to the problem of understanding in intercultural contexts, as we have suggested in Chapter 3. Finally, the data collection routines of the project meant that there were many similar encounters to compare both across informants within a country and cross-linguistically from the five participating national groups. This meant that data analysis could draw on broadly similar sequences from other encounters to enrich possible interpretations at a local level. This gave at least some partial compensation for the difficulties encountered.

In other respects, as we have suggested above, the data could be criticised for lacking what Cicourel has called 'ecological validity'. Our increasing concern with the critical and contextualising issues mentioned above, which puts more emphasis on collecting naturally occurring data within a broader ethnographic framework, raises questions about any type of elicited data.

But there are other reasons why ecological validity is so difficult to achieve. These are largely to do with ethical and practical concerns. It is extremely difficult to collect institutional data unless the researcher is working in that institution already. Also, as we have suggested most informants had little contact with the white majority and so naturally occurring data was difficult to collect. These practical limitations also had an ethical dimension. There are ethical difficulties in audio and video recording naturally occurring gatekeeping interviews. Such interviews have real-life consequences for interviewees and the additional pressure of being recorded can obviously have a negative impact.

Similarly, it is unethical to put pressure on informants to engage in what they may see as stressful interactions and so the outings had to be restricted to the types of routine activities with which they felt comfortable, but which produced very little data. We were caught, therefore, in a paradoxical situation. We wanted to be more ethnographic in order to be more ecologically valid. But respect for informants is a central principle of ethnography (Cameron et al 1992) and we were forced therefore to substitute less ecologically-valid data collection methods in order not to exploit or put additional demands on people whose conditions at work and home were already immensely pressurising.

As with data collection, issues surrounding data analysis raise many problems. Most SLA research is concerned with general developmental trends. The type of context free generalisations aimed at, for example, the development of past tense markers over time, assume that it is possible and worthwhile to isolate some aspects of language, and isolate language use from the language user, in order to trace through the acquisition of a particular feature. This positivistic approach is at odds with the phenomenological and ethnographic paradigms in which all interpretations are contextually bound and only the conceptual or theoretical constructs drawn from the data have any potential for transfer.

Another feature of positivistic research is the assumption that there is a direct and often single relationship between a cause and an effect. Interpretative research on the other hand, sees no simple one-way relationship between cause and effect but sees 'all entities in a state of mutual shaping' (Lincoln and Guba 1985). And for this reason, as we have indicated in Chapter 3, it is not possible to find a single cause for an understanding problem.

The complexity both of our informants' lives and of the institutional discourse data collected challenged both the assumptions about the isolatable and fragmentable nature of language use and any causal model which sought clear-cut correlations between socio-biographical information and language development.

A holistic and interpretative approach to second language research is, therefore, not concerned with general developmental trends of particular features but with *understanding* the nature of intercultural communication and the conditions under which a measure of shared interpretation and language development may take place. So, the data was analysed in an in-depth way, drawing, methodologically, on some aspects of conversation analysis and interactional sociolinguistics in that each piece of data was analysed, turn-by-turn as an interactional whole but each case study was also used to draw out general patterns of interactive behaviour at a conceptual level. The chapters on managing understanding from a minority perspective (Chapter 4), on causes (Chapter 3) and on joint negotiation (Chapters 6 and 7) are attempts to combine an increasing awareness of the power of contextualisation with ethnographic insights and the need to seek general patterns in the data in a way which made us accountable to that data. This can be summed-up as follows:

(i)   the interaction was analysed as a joint construction by native and non-native speakers.
(ii) ethnographic information was actively taken into account in the analysis of data.
(iii) specific attention was paid to the institutionalised nature of gatekeeping interview data and proper recognition of this made in terms of the impact of unequal power relations on topic, topic control, speaker rights, especially the right to indicate problems with understanding, and issues of face.

This approach contrasts with a hypothesis driven approach in which data are submitted to the imperatives of a hypothesis. For example, a hypothesis such as 'in early stages the learner is more likely to use silence to mask non-understanding than for any other reason' raises many difficulties of the type described earlier in the book. To take one example the function of silence is difficult to identify, and may well vary across activity types and its role in enabling or avoiding understanding is impossible to quantify.

Scanning data for evidence to support or disconfirm a hypothesis is an altogether different task from drawing concepts out of data in the spirit of grounded theory (Glaser and Strauss 1967). The situated and provisional nature of all processes of inferencing make it impossible to work in any other but a qualitative way.

One final area of difficulty which we raise is the issue of data types. As we have suggested, the nature of institutional discourse creates a very different environment for understanding and managing non-understandings than informal conversation. Different kinds of data produces different results and to some extent different theories and vice versa. So, for example, opportunities for minority speakers to select and lead on a topic or 'the room to speak' phenomenon will be different in interviews and conversations, as our data examples in previous chapters have shown (and see remarks on Institutional Discourse below). However, a social perspective on 'understanding' should be capable of developing a conceptual framework which illuminates the interactional work required to negotiate understanding within power relations across a range of settings.

If we had our time over again, what would we do? Firstly, we would seek to collect more institutional data, particularly more videoed data, both of specific interaction, and of the organisation more generally and also collect data of minority speakers from different linguistic backgrounds communicating in the majority language. (For example, as Michael Clyne and his colleagues in Melbourne and the National Centre for English Language Teaching and Research in Sydney are doing in Australian workplace contexts, Clyne, Ball and Neil 1991, Willing 1992.) Secondly, we would concentrate our efforts, from the start, on qualitative approaches to the data and focus more on certain contextualisation cues, such as prosodic features. Thirdly, we would collect more and focus more on ethnographic data and bring to it a more explicit critical theory. To sum up, we would sharpen up our qualitative research methods and anchor language development studies within the well established tradition of qualitative social science research.

8.2 SOCIAL AND DISCOURSE PERSPECTIVE ON SECOND LANGUAGE DEVELOPMENT

As we have tried to show throughout the book, in contrast to most SLA work, the theme of 'understanding' was treated as a social phenomenon. Studies in education, sociology, social psychology, anthropology, sociolinguistics and the philosophy of language assert the indisputably social nature of learning and language learning. Language socialisation (Ochs and Schieffelin 1983), is a more accurate description than language acquisition for the process whereby individuals become culturally competent members of society.

A social perspective also puts those developing a new language, in this case, minority ethnic workers, centre stage. This emphasis on the social actors struggling to use a second language, rather than on the process of language development itself, tries to reflect the social reality of recently arrived migrant workers, constructed by society as 'the lowest of the low' (Wallraff 1988). Although a highly restricted and goal-orientated competence in the second language may be necessary to gain some of the basic essentials of life in a new society, for most workers enduring difficult, sometimes appalling, physical conditions at work, coping with domestic concerns and managing the conflicting identities of being part of a minority group are likely to press down unremittingly in a way that issues of second language and language development will not. The case studies in Chapter 5 give some evidence of this.

For example, Tino's main concern is to find a job which involves fewer hours than at present and which would give him a wage which would allow him to rent a room of his own. Similarly, Berta had to cope, for the first six months after arriving in France, with living in a refugee centre with her three young children. In the longer term, however, all the informants developed at least some level of second language competence and several became fluent. But for nearly all of them in the early stages of learning and for many at the end of the period of data-collecting, formal institutional and service encounters were the only occasions on which they interacted with members of the white majority. For this reason detailed studies of face-to-face interaction are central to an appreciation of the complex ways in which accomplishing understanding (or not) feeds into socially and racially stratified societies and into individual and group motivation to learn.

Informants gave detailed examples of how interactive experiences feed into motivation and attitudes and how these in turn promote or discourage contact and interaction. The contrasting narratives of the two young Turkish workers in Germany, Çevdet and Ilhami, illustrate this well. Both of them received combined language and skills training in metal work and both worked, subsequently, in hard labouring jobs. But their experiences with fellow workers and supervisors were markedly different. Çevdet had good relationships with his supervisors whereas Ilhami had direct experience of racial discrimination which thrust him into a negative cycle of rejection, limited interaction, misunderstandings and little progress in German.

The history of our informants over the two to three years of the project illustrates well that there is no simple causality between motivation and competence, between initial language/vocational training and subsequent work prospects or between a willingness to communicate and take part in the project and linguistic proficiency. The picture is more complex than any such correlations suggest.

From a macro perspective, minority workers are located in the lowest strata of society and there is no obvious escape from this 'lived experience', in any of their encounters with the majority group. And yet encounters have a life of their own and the interactional consequences of different encounters feed into the differing experiences and behaviours of individuals.

A social perspective on understanding, therefore, focusses on the interplay of local and individual experiences and motivations on the one hand, and wider social theories of power and stratification, on the other. For this reason we turn to two major theoretical areas: critical perspectives within social theory and interactional sociolinguistics to capture something of the relationship between wider sociopolitical formations and the detailed life of interactions.

8.3 A CRITICAL PERSPECTIVE

The notion of 'criticalness' has colonised many disciplines – for example, critical ethnography, critical social psychology as well as linguistics itself, for example, critical discourse analysis (Fairclough 1989, Fowler, Hodge, Kress and Trew 1979), feminist linguistics (Cameron 1993), sociolinguistics (Rampton 1995) and applied linguistics (Phillipson 1992, Pennycook 1994) and the conflict model in the study of bilingualism (Martin-Jones 1989).

A critical perspective raises important issues both conceptually and methodologically for those engaged in intercultural communication and second language development. A social perspective on the face-to-face contact between minority workers and white gatekeepers cannot avoid a critique of social relations within a given society. The marginal position of minority workers within the socioeconomic and political structures is daily acted out in the harsh experiences of physical labour, poor living conditions and education, and lack of connection with the political life of the majority group at national or local levels. Added to this are the frequent racist attacks and the racist discourse of much of the media and, now, explicitly even of political parties.

In addition to a general critical perspective on processes of understanding in 'unequal encounters' (Fairclough 1989, Thomas 1983, François 1990) it is important to work through the detail of how an interaction both reflects and sustains unequal power relations, as those working in 'critical linguistics' have started to do. In other words, merely to describe how minority workers negotiate a level of understanding tells us little about how that interaction feeds into and reinforces existing social relations of inequality or how these social relations and the knowledge of them brought into interaction further constrain opportunities for learning.An example from this is the contrastive encounters that

Andrea and Santo experience in gatekeeping encounters (see Chapter 2).

Social theory, particularly the work of Habermas, Gramsci, Foucault and Bourdieu, engages with power relations and the connection between knowledge and power. Power is exercised in modern society not by force but by discourse. The dominant discourses of society use ideology to construct and maintain power but also to mask and conceal from people the way in which such ideology works. This 'concealed communication' prevents the goal of open communication and understanding (Habermas 1984) and ensures that ordinary people collude in their own domination (Gramsci 1971).

We can see this collusion at work, in the data examples collected in the field. For example, Abdelmalek's reference to being particularly polite to get a favourable response from the most racist of his interlocutors and in the feelings of guilt and self-deprecation expressed by informants. In similar examples we can see how power is exercised through discourse, either in overtly oppressive ways as in Berta's experience at the hospital where her daughter was taken after an accident (and see Paula's experience below) or in more indirect ways as in Tino's interview with the job counsellor where it is *her* interactional style which constructs him as incompetent. It is this kind of discursive practice which feeds into wider discourses on minority groups and out of which the relationship between face-to-face encounters and stereotypes develops.

Both Foucault and Bourdieu are concerned with the relationship between everyday practices and the socio-historical and economic conditions which shape them. The power struggles within discourse are conceptualised by Bourdieu as part of the political economy. All practices, he suggests, are to do with the struggle over capital – both economic and symbolic (Bourdieu 1991). To Bourdieu, communication is a form of cultural capital and language use, or discourse, functions within a 'linguistic market place': 'linguistic exchanges are economic exchanges' (op cit: 66).

Like others working within a critical perspective, Bourdieu takes a broadly deterministic view of power relations based on the political economy of the market place. Within this market economy, symbolic, cultural and therefore communicative power rests with the dominant group. Since this group establishes the norms and conventions of the institutions which it controls, its members tend to gain material, symbolic and cultural capital from the institutions which both represent such capital and offer it. By contrast, a mutually reinforcing negative cycle of low status and low communicative power keeps dominated groups on the social and economic periphery.

Within this framework, the minority workers are disadvantaged in three ways. They are structurally positioned at the bottom of the socioeconomic ladder. Even those who were skilled or professional workers in their own country, are identified in the new one, by their largely unskilled and marginal jobs or increasingly, their unemployed status. Secondly, their inexperience in the new language means that they lack even the communicative power, or linguistic capital, of the indigenous working class. Thirdly, they are oppressed by the ideology of common sense (Gramsci 1971), that learning the language of the new country should take precedence over maintaining their own language and community ties. This is well illustrated in Marcello's interview in the Job Centre (see Chapter 3) when the interviewer tells him not to speak to his fiancée any longer. He then replies 'we have to forget'. This ideology of the majority, which also permeates the minority groups, masks the problematic and conflictual nature of the language learning process, and has led many working in communication theories to interpret misunderstanding and miscommunication in terms of models of linguistic and pragmatic failure or mis-attribution of group norms and motives.

There is considerable evidence in our data that minority workers are persistently positioned, interactionally, as dependent and marginal. But there is also evidence of individual agency and creativity in their use of resources both to function effectively and resist or attempt a resistance to social practices they will not submit to. (Santo's and Berta's interactions are good examples of this and see Chapter 4.)

Even in these most unequal of encounters, there is evidence of creativity and assertion in the detailed responses of informants both in institutional interaction and in discussion afterwards. As Schenke (1991:53 quoted in Pennycook 1994) argues, it is important to be: '. . . more responsive to the capillary effects of power and more attuned to smaller, less "heroic" acts of resistance and personal/social change.'

A more complex picture in which a determined social world is fractured and destabilised by the possibilities of individual agency and resistance is closer to Foucault's view of power and discourse as the complex of signs and practices that control our lives. Here the competing gatekeeping discourses of racism, of liberal professionalism and of individualism contest or coincide with discourses of instrumentality, victimisation, integration and resistance on the part of minority workers. There is no simple understanding of 'understanding' as between dominated and dominant, but nor can power relations ever be ignored. This more complex view is well illustrated in our key data of simulated interviews. Here the professionals have given up their time to work on the project and there are many instances of considerable time and effort taken to accomplish understanding.

And yet the type of institutional discourses that minority workers are subject to tend to construct them in a simple and essentialist way as dominated. Not only are they interactionally disadvantaged but the prevailing discourses about them, among the majority, produce a social reality of them as inadequate, difficult and a threat to the fabric of society. These discourses also fix the way institutions operate as normal and stigmatise those who cannot or will not insert themselves into institutional routines. The complexity of the relationships between local practices and broad societal trends suggests how important it is to relate detailed data analysis to general social analysis.

Most work however within the critical and social theory tradition has been general and abstract and singularly lacking in any data or data analysis. There are exceptions, for example in the ethnographic studies of the Birmingham Centre for Contemporary Cultural Studies (Willis 1977, McRobbie 1978, 1994) and recent studies in critical ethnography (Thomas 1993, Denzin 1989, Manning 1992).

Critical ethnography uses ethnographic methodology for emancipatory and action-research goals (Thomas 1993). In other words, ethnography involves participants in reflective practices which contribute to changing their lives. The use of critical ethnography in second language development research would lift it beyond developmental patterns and learner strategies to an understanding of the role of second language development in the lives of a particular group, would contribute to an insider's perspective on attitudes and motivation and help to account for the detail in the speaker's struggle to understand, in terms of the way in which cultural practices enter into interaction. So it would help to show how encounters between the majority community and minority workers are constitutive of the social reality of such workers' lives – only a part of which is the language struggle. As Bourdieu says 'what speaks is not utterance, the language, but the whole social person' (Bourdieu 1977 quoted in Hinnenkamp 1991).

Social theory, as we have said, has focused on wider social structures rather than on the detailed processes of how such structures come about – the structuring element (Giddens 1976, Fairclough 1985, Mehan 1979). To find data and discussion of these structuring processes we can turn to interactional sociolinguistics and to the work of Gumperz and his associates.

8.4 CONTEXT AND CONTEXTUALISATION

This articulation of detailed interactional life and social identity and cultural practices is most suggestively described in recent work on context and contextualisation (see Chapter 2 for a preliminary discussion). Until the 1970s the notion of context was occasionally used to provide an imaginary setting for isolated sentences or at best, was divided into linguistic and social context and seen as a determinant of the meaning of language in use.

Since the 1970s, thanks to work in pragmatics and to the approaches discussed briefly in Chapter 2, context has become an increasingly complex and fascinatingly problematic notion (see Duranti and Goodwin (eds) 1992 for a useful overview). The term 'contextualisation' with its active verb-like nuances, also has a new and influential lease of life, most notably through the work of John Gumperz and his associates (Auer and di Luzio (eds) 1992). Auer describes 'Contextualisation' as comprising 'all activities by participants which make relevant, maintain, revise, cancel any aspect of context which in turn, is responsible for the interpretation of an utterance in its particular locus of occurrence' (1994:4). In other words, contextualisation cues are the means by which speakers and listeners construct local meaning together and connect it to wider knowledge sets and experiences.

These cues draw on 'brought along' social knowledge but function, at the particular moment at which they are used, to channel the semantic information into a message which is relevant in a rich way. By this we mean that it resonates with the preceding utterances, fits the conventional ordering of the activity and is expectable in terms of what is to come. So, the message indexes a whole world of interactional experiences which it is assumed both sides share.

For example, in the training counselling interview between Abdelmalek and a trainer, discussed briefly in Chapter 3, the trainer shifts topic from eliciting Abdelmalek's work history to thinking of his future:

(1)   N: hein + c'est bien ça + + bon eh hem +
              et maintenant quel type de + travail vous aimeriez faire la
              and now what kind of a job would you like to do there
       A: comme le travail
              as a job
       N: hem
(5)   A: ah parce que travail pas + le chômage
              ah because don't work unemployment

Abdelmalek, as we have suggested in Chapter 3, misses the hypothetical mode of the verb 'aimeriez', but there is a great deal of contextualisation work in this section of the interview which would cue a native speaker into the purpose of the question. Firstly, there is the formulaic, closing comment, 'c'est bon ça' to indicate that it is time to shift topic. Together with this comment are the hesitation and perturbation phenomena which often mark the shift to a new topic. Secondly, there is the placement of 'maintenant' up front to give thematic focus to the temporal shift from past to present. This may be particularly confusing for Abdelmalek since 'maintenant' refers to his present wishes about the future and not to his present job situation. Thirdly, the contextualisation work of the interviewer assumes the 'brought along' context of typical counselling interviews in which the job-seeker's preferences are discussed, in however a perfunctory way. And, as we have discussed in Chapter 3, it is commonplace for minority ethnic workers to have understanding problems when asked about personal hopes and aspirations. Finally, a majority language speaker in the context of this kind of interview, unlike Abdelmalik, is likely to know how to respond to the notion of 'kind of job' since they would be familiar with the ways in which work is categorised in that society and what would be the convention in responding to this type of question in an interview as opposed to, for example, a chat with friends. So, context may include any or all of the following: the discourse task, the specific activity, the speech act, mood, topic, participants' roles, social relationships and modality.

In practice, Gumperz has worked with a more defined list of contextualisation cues: code switching, prosody, formulaic expressions,
choice of lexis and syntax, openings and closings and sequencing
strategies.

In the Abdelmalek example above, prosody, formulaic expressions, choice of lexis and syntax and opening and closing
phenomena are all used to contextualise the question on preferred
future work. These are the means whereby a situated assessment of
intent can be made, in contrast with what Gumperz calls context
free semantic information. The assumption, here, is that interactants are familiar with the semantic content or referential meaning
of utterances but need contextualisation cues in order to channel
the semantic/referential information along the appropriate interpretive lines at that point in the interaction.

Recently, Gumperz has expanded on the nature of contextualisation cues (1992a). He stresses that they cannot be assigned stable,
core lexical meanings but that they function relationally. In other
words, it is in their relation to other features of the interaction and,
particularly in contrast to them, that they guide or channel relevant
meaning. For example, in the interview with the Job Centre counsellor, Tino does not immediately cue into the context implied by
the counsellor who starts in a top-down way to establish a
detailed picture of his education, training and work experience
(see Chapter 5).

The impersonal formulation that she uses 'how many years was
the school?' presupposes that Tino completed his elementary
schooling and that all Italian children would. In other words she
brings along a schema that assumes a set number of years of compulsory schooling which all children will have experienced. Tino
has to check that she is asking about *his* schooling, not schooling in
general. Her intended meaning is in relation both to her schematic
knowledge and to the particular context of the kind of gate-keeping
interview in which personal information is often elicited indirectly.

The detailed means by which contextualisation functions show
how the power/knowledge nexus of institutional discourse
works in largely indirect ways. The conventionalised questions
about preferences in a labour market in which any job is difficult
to get and the indirectly conveyed assumptions about 'educational capital' not only create misunderstandings and so
interactional discomfort, but also mask the material facts of high
unemployment and assumptions about what is 'normal' and

'natural' – in this example, a set number of years of compulsory schooling.

In communication and miscommunication among native-speakers and in intercultural communication generally, the theory of contextualisation cues has considerable explanatory power. It can be extended to intercultural communication with minority workers with limited second language competence in order to highlight the problematic nature of such communication. With inexperienced speakers of the majority language, even lexical and grammatical items lack stability and their misuse and misinterpretation may also function relationally. In other words, the contrast between the native and the non-native speakers' use of lexical items may be frame creating in the ways that contextualisation cues are in intra and intercultural communication more generally. This is well illustrated in the example from Berta's interview (see Berta's case study in Chapter 5) where 'do' in this particular context is problematic.(see also below on the nature of Institutional Discourse).

In this interview, the interviewer is trying to establish what level of responsibilities and skills she has in her job in the kitchen:

(180) N: ah ah d'accord et là qu'est ce que vous faites alors?
           ah ah ok and there what do you do then
      B   qu'est ce que tu/ eh la personne del chef que *el* me explique
           + el m'explique eh que je prépare de manger
           what do you/eh the person of the head who he explains to me
           + he explains to me eh what i prepare to eat

This type of unspecific questioning, 'qu'est ce que vous faites' is typical in job counselling interviews and a relevant response depends crucially on the interpretation of 'do' which has a relatively stable meaning in these contexts but it is not one which minority speakers can easily interpret appropriately. Berta interprets it, referentially, and describes the detailed routine in the kitchen rather than describing and evaluating her job responsibilities.

So, in these types of intercultural encounters any lexical grammatical, phonological or non-verbal item may function as a contextualisation cue, triggering a whole new set of inferences, for either side, which, subsequently may be found to have little or no connection with the specific business at hand. Ergun's misunderstanding about his future wife's pregnancy is a good example of this.

Another feature of contextualisation cues is the fact that they often cluster together in order to frame a whole activity or channel a specific response. For example, gaze, postural change, prosodic features and a particular lexical choice may all work together to evoke a particular response. Again, speakers, like the informants in this study, may cue into any feature that, plausibly, could help them. This may mean they may only pick up on one feature but it will not be strong enough to channel an interpretation or they may not pick up on any of them (a possibility also in any intercultural communication), thus illustrating the generally precarious nature of such communication, given that the native speaker will routinely be relying on them.

For example, in the interview with Angelina in which she is asked about a typical day at home (see Chapter 3) she can only cue into some of the contextualising work done by the interviewer:

> N: wie/ + wie ist so ein arbeitstag äh was machen sie zuerst
>   morgens
>   *what/+ what is a working day like er what do you do first thing*
> A: \<zu essen\> was ↑   \<laughing, amused\>
>   *to eat what* ↑
> N: \<mhm\>   \<confirms\>

As we have noted, Angelina attempts to make an on-topic contribution by guessing that the interviewer wants to know what she does about eating. It is not clear whether she thinks the interviewer wants to know what she eats or how she organises her eating arrangements. Certainly, if it was the former, such a question would be more appropriate in a medical or health interview where issues of diet were being discussed. The difficulty here, and it is a commonplace one, is that minority speakers have no way of knowing how intrusive or personal majority interviewers consider they have the right to be (see Abdelmalek in the travel agent in Chapter 2). So their contextualisation cues, which in intracultural communication would both frame the whole activity and elicit a particular local response, here are reacted to either by an impromptu guess or by a further clarification question.

These examples suggest that the methodology and analytic techniques used in interactional sociolinguistics can be extended to studies of intercultural communication where minority workers have limited experience of the majority language. We have found that the contextualising process is, problematic at every turn, for both majority and minority speaking participants. Not only are the majority speakers' contextualising strategies often uninterpretable by their interlocutors, but the contextualising function of basic semantic information is frequently lost. In addition, where a non-understanding is identified and a clarificatory sequence initiated, this, in turn, produces a new context within the larger frame of the whole activity.

There is a strong case for bringing the rich interpretive tools of contextualisation analysis to the kind of data illustrated in this book, both to deepen our understanding of intercultural communication and, practically, in contributing ideas to improve second language teaching and the development of intercultural competence.

For both purposes the value of contextualisation theory in making connections between detailed interpretations and wider sociopolitical processes must not be underestimated. As Silverstein argues, from a theoretical perspective, a narrow view of 'contextualisation', which is concerned with assigning intentionality in a linear way to an interaction as it unfolds, relies heavily on individual rational consciousness. He proposes a wider view of 'contextualisation' which 'seeks to know how language use . . . indexes – brings into contextual reality, – those implicit values of relational identity and power that . . . go by the name of "culture"' (Silverstein 1992:57). So, in discussing the problem of the indeterminacy of 'contextualisation' (when is enough, enough?) he suggests 'we can see that anything, any aspect of experienceable reality of some cultural group, can be made relevant to the achievement of interactional text by being introduced as a presupposable in the real time course of discursive interaction' (op cit: 69). Of course, precisely what is selected as relevant is not random and will depend upon the speakers' location in and orientation to a particular social and cultural world.

So, Silverstein asserts, with Gumperz, the primacy of notions of power and identity in understanding how cultural practices both enter into and are constitutive of interaction. The relationship between power, identity and contextualisation has been underplayed in discussions of John Gumperz's work. There is a tendency to assume, wrongly, that those who deal in the fine-grained detail of interaction are relatively unconcerned with larger social theories, their contingent power relations and the values implied by such concern. However, Gumperz's work has consistently tried to show that in complex multi-ethnic urban societies, there is a linguistic dimension to racial discrimination. In this respect, his work relates closely to Bourdieu's concept of the 'linguistic market place' (Bourdieu 1991) and to Foucault's 'orders of discourse' (Foucault 1971) which put constraints on what is allowable. An example from an aspect of contextualisation illustrates this well.

As Auer points out (Auer 1992:34) a single contextualisation cue often has a double indexing role: both a social role schema and a management schema. A cue may trigger what is perceived as allowable, for example in a job or housing interview, and it may also serve to allocate speaker/learner roles. If the minority worker misses the cue, (either they are unable to process it or they are not aware of the precise background knowlege which is indexed by it) they may be rapidly and negatively evaluated in two ways. Firstly, they may be judged as socially incompetent, because they have failed to follow the norms of conversational involvement and secondly as morally suspect because they have ignored the constraints on what is allowable in a typical gatekeeping encounter. This is what Gumperz means by the interpretive weight of contextualisation in which non-recognition of contextualisation cues is seen as a matter of attitude, 'a social faux pas.' As E M Forster drily puts it in his classic study of intercultural communication, *A Passage to India*: 'Tangles like this still interrupted their discourse. A pause in the wrong place, an intonation misunderstood, and a whole conversation went awry.' (Forster 1936:267).

In the wider sociopolitical context, the 'brought-along' experiences of previous intercultural contact feed into the processes of inferencing which texture the interaction and contribute to its evaluation. The 'brought-away' perceptions from such interactions may not necessarily be negative, although they frequently are.

Some informants talked explicitly of racism. For example, Paula and other parents from the refugee centre had decided to go to the school principal because all the children from the centre were having problems with the other children in the school. Paula also talked about the type of routine racism which she experienced, for example, in shops:

(1)   P: je entre et je vu une madame et do do do personnes *mas* eh
            plus et + je le + je le viens eh ++ de an question *por*
            un un radio-cassette + elle me di que ah je oblié que
            je suis tres nerviou pasque madame je le vi le
(5)   face(mimique)

I entered and I saw a woman and two two two persons more
er more and + i + i come to them er ++ with a question for a recording
radio-set + she told me that ah i forgot that i am very nervous because
madam i saw them their face (mimic)

N: hm (essaie d'interpreter la mimique) c'est-a-dire ↑ sérieux ↑
hm (trying to interpret paula's mimic) that is to say ↑
serious ↑

P: oui oui eh je/
yes yes eh i/

N: qu'est-ce que tu veux dire par sérieux ↑ c'est-à-dire euh
what do you mean by 'serious' is it er . . .

P: eh méch/ comment ↑ méchant
eh nast/how is it ↑ nasty

(10) N: méchante donc tu l'as trouvée mechante ↑
nasty so you thought she was nasty ↑

P: oui oui et je suis très nervou
yes yes and i am very nervous

N: ah oui
so

P: elle appelle son mari
she call her husband

N: oui
yes

(15) P: et le me dit ah madame quelle nationalité ↑
and her told me ah madam what nationality ↑

N: tu disais que il a fait hm une expression du visage il a eu une
expression du visage qui t'a/
you were saying that he made mhm an expression, he had an
expression on his face which did not

P: oui
yes

N: qui t'a pas plu ↑
which did not please you ↑

(20) P oui
yes

As potentially damaging, are the differential evaluations of encounters where, for example, the minority ethnic worker may feel an interview went well whereas the gatekeeper is negative. An interesting example in the data is Andrea's reaction to the clerk in the building society (see Chapter 3). Despite the clerk's unhelpful and unclear contributions, Andrea, in the feedback session, thought she had been kind. Such difficulties in evaluating native speakers' contributions may, cumulatively, lead to perceptions of miscommunication and unfair treatment, and perceived discrimination can be as damaging as real discrimination. For example, if the minority worker rates the professional as kind and helpful, but the encounter results in no progress or a negative response from the institution, then the whole institution may be perceived as discriminatory.

In future research of this kind, there is a strong case for working in considerably more depth and more systematically on informants' perceptions, both of recorded interactions and of their encounters, more generally, with the majority community. Insights from this data can then be used to undertake more detailed work on contextualisation than has been possible in this study.

8.5 INSTITUTIONAL DISCOURSE

The critical and interactional sociolinguistic perspectives come together in the study of institutional discourse. For the great majority of informants, as we have indicated, institutional encounters represented the only occasion of extended contact with the white majority. And paradoxically, those with the least communicative power are those who are required, most frequently, to deal with the bureaucracies of the social, housing and employment services. This study has focussed on these encounters because they are crucial to people's lives and because they are extended encounters. Other studies have begun to look at workplace interactions (Candlin and Lucas 1986, Clyne, Ball and Neil 1991, Clyne 1991, Roberts et al 1992, Willing 1992, Cope and Kalantzis 1994). Further studies are needed on majority-minority interaction, on inter-minority interaction and on the construction of social identity and reality within specific communities (see Hewitt 1986 and Rampton 1995).

At a theoretical level, the discourse of institutions is about the control and distribution of power and knowledge. Institutional discourse is enacted on a daily basis, as if it was normal and natural (Fairclough 1989, 1992a & b), as if it was the only way in which institutional life could be carried out. The discourse itself prevents questions being asked about its validity or the right of the institution to carry out its business the way that it does (Habermas 1984, Foucault 1971).

At the level of interaction, 'the discourse analysis' level, this control and distribution of power is routinely carried out through the structure of the interaction and by the gatekeeper authorised to exercise it. (Erickson and Shultz 1982, Drew and Heritage 1992, Agar 1985, Fisher and Todd 1986, Tannen and Wallat 1986, Fairclough 1992a, Gumperz 1982a & b, Mehan 1979, Philips 1982, Shuy 1984.) Although these gatekeeping encounters are jointly constructed, most of the analysis has been from an institutional perspective. However, in our studies, our focus has been as much on the minority workers themselves and on their experience of institutional discourse. Their relative inexperience in the target language means that they are even less likely to pick up on the institutional frames of the interaction than native speakers. In addition, they face fundamental difficulties in both interpreting the questions they are typically asked and creating space for themselves to convey their intentions. Such questions are: information questions, usually expecting short answers and often presented as slot-fillers, for example 'you live in a . . .', confirming questions, usually made as statements with an intonation change and often with a tag,'is that right?', and open questions allowing space for some opinion. Frequently, as we have illustrated, a combination of such questions is presented in one turn by the interviewer.

In addition to processing these questions, the minority workers have to do a great deal of knowledge work, interpreting institutional lexis that indexes, paradoxically, both a precise and a vast, ambiguous world and all within the time constraint of bureaucratic encounters. This ambiguity is all the more evident as institutional gatekeepers are trained to be more 'user-friendly'. (Fairclough 1992a). The multi-voiced nature of bureaucratic talk, mixing formulae, technical jargon and informal conversation, both creates problems of 'footing' and masks the controlling nature of such talk. The minority worker is doubly muted, she cannot use her own language and she cannot use her own voice, since it is the gatekeeper's categories of discourse that must prevail. And yet, despite the weight of the dominant discourse pressing down on them, the minority workers in our study develop the capacity to be active participants in the interactions and jointly construct a level of shared meaning together.

Minority workers may bring along schemata about bureaucratic encounters concerning what is allowable to say (and the boundary between public and private life may be drawn differently) and what is the participant's status in the interaction and likely goals.

But such, apparently, fixed scripts are only a partial explanation for the schema illustrated in the data.

Presuppositions about what bureaucratic encounters can achieve in the new country may be brought along, together with experiences of previous interactions since arrival. A generalised and over-optimistic notion that institutions can help clients is common and is often at odds with the precise fitting of a client's situation into bureaucratic categories which is perceived by the gatekeeper as their role (as in the Tino case study).

One of the most significant findings from our data is the degree of similarity in the gatekeeping encounters in all five European countries, and in the strategies used by the gatekeepers. These relate, broadly, to:

– the type of activity and underlying ideological schema
– issues of face and footing
– preventative and post-hoc attempts to resolve understanding problems

As we have suggested above, understanding problems can result from schema mismatch and the schemata themselves index a set of institutional ideologies. The gatekeeping encounter, in crosslinguistic comparative perspective, shows that interviewers share assumptions about its organisation, topic inclusion (what it is allowable to talk about) and goals. So, for example, the categorisation of work experience in terms of responsibilities and skills, discussions of personal preferences and detailed questions about personal and private matters were routine to the gatekeepers, problematic to their clients.

A typical outcome in such a situation is a revisiting of the same topic by the gatekeeper in order to elicit a more satisfactory response. This is what occurs, for example, in the Berta interview (see case study 5.1) when the interviewer, some twelve turns later, again asks Bertha what she does in the kitchen. But as is so often the case, the preferred response is only implicit in the question.

Indirectness, and open or vague questions are characteristic of such institutional discourse and are a major strategy for coping with issues of face. The gatekeepers' concern is with their own face and, to some extent, especially in the simulated interviews which form much of our data, with the face needs of their clients.

For the gatekeeper, it is one thing to tolerate listening to a range of syntactic variations and accents, but it is quite another to tolerate not being understood. If after many attempts, routine questions still elicit an inadequate response, the professional's own skills may be put into question and their own face wants need attending to. It is for this reason that, in the simulated interviews, there are so many protracted attempts to come to some level of shared agreement about the substance of the encounter.

Such protracted encounters, especially when they reduce the interaction to focussed interrogatory sequences, may lead to attempts to repair damaged face work and re-establish the interaction with a different alignment between participants, or a different 'footing'. The conflict between bureaucratic practice and friendly relations is often attempted to be resolved through gestures of positive face and solidarity. Openings may begin with the assertion that this is 'a little chat' or that 'quelques petites questions' (some little questions) will be asked. A much more substantial example is in the Ergün case study where there are two attempts by the Dutch worker to de-emphasise the official relationship by introducing a humorous voice into the interview. In the first instance he jokes about the fact that Ergün does not yet need a house for the elderly and then he closes the difficult problem-solving section about whether Ergün's future wife is pregnant or not, with a comment on the gestation period of elephants!

Their attempts at solidarity in gatekeeping encounters are complemented by the more general strategy of asking vague and general questions so as not to impose an interpretation on the client. However, this is a highly conventionalised strategy, since the gatekeeper has a circumscribed set of acceptable responses which fit her schema. The minority speakers' problems with understanding frequently manoeuvre the majority speaker into having to be more direct (as in the case of the Ilhami interview in chapter 3). For example 'what do your children do?' 'what does your job involve?' do not elicit the expected detailed, relevant response. As a result, the gatekeepers have to probe explicitly in what are perceived by them as delicate areas.

The management of politeness and face issues in these institutional encounters can also be interpreted in a more critical way. If we take Bourdieu's market place metaphor (1991) then politeness and face are forms of censorship based on market constraints (op cit pp. 77–8). Gatekeepers' efforts, therefore, are not simply interpreted as personal, friendly gestures but as part of the ritual of institutional control in which those with relatively more power can afford to manipulate politeness strategies to achieve institutional goals.

Chapters 6 and 7 have looked at ways in which preventative strategies and joint negotiation are used in institutional discourse and similarities, cross-linguistically, were illustrated. In some instances, attempts at prevention cause further complexity, as in Ergün's interview with the housing officer, which, in turn requires strategies of clarification. However, what is significant in the simulated interviews is the amount and sophistication of strategies used to overcome problems. We have indicated that naturally-occurring gatekeeping data (both from this project and elsewhere) suggest that the dominant speakers may not, generally, make the efforts evidenced in the simulated data. It may be useful, therefore to use this type of data as exemplary material, illustrating the kind of effort and adjustments that can, and need to be, made if intercultural encounters are to be more satisfying to both sides.

The patterns of presentation and response evident in the data must be set within the context of local variety highlighted in Chapter 2. In looking at common patterns we do not want to iron out the variability and individual life of each encounter. However, taking a critical perspective on institutional discourse and allying it to the issues of contextualisation discussed above, it is possible to see a constant interplay between dominant language and ideology and locally negotiated solutions to problems.

These examples of institutional discourse illuminate the struggle over meaning at many different levels. Because the clients have limited experience of the dominant language, any item within an utterance may, as we have suggested, lack stability and create new and confusing contexts. But at a more macro level there is also the struggle over what counts as meaning: what the gatekeeper considers she has the right to know and what counts as adequate and relevant evidence. In other words, whose cultural capital will prevail and indeed what counts as cultural capital at all? In this sense we must go beyond the notion of encounters as jointly constructed to Bakhtin's notion of language as a struggle for voice: 'A word is territory shared by both addresser and addressee (Voloshinov 1973: 86) but, like any other territory, it is the site for potential conflict over ownership. Discourse becomes a political act through which meanings and relations are defined and in which there is always the potential for mutual misunderstanding.

The potentiality for destabilisation lies, therefore, not only in the ongoing creation of context, but in the fact that any encounter brings in a whole history of social and political experiences which charge the encounter with particular meaning. So, as social interaction 'pumps energy from a life situation into the verbal discourse, it endows everything linguistically stable with living, historical momentum and uniqueness.' (Voloshinov 1976:106).

This brief discussion of patterns of intercultural communication in institutional discourse across several western European countries suggests that it is worthwhile putting forward some practical recommendations which could be effective across these countries. And in the spirit of both allying theory with practice and drawing on the imperatives of critical ethnography and pedagogy, this type of research must include an action which could help to bring about change. So we will end the book by looking at some practical implications.

8.6 SOME PRACTICAL IMPLICATIONS

It is not surprising that there has been so much focus on institutional and gatekeeping discourse since, as we have indicated, it often represents the only contact, beyond the passing remark or exchange, that minority workers have with the majority. These encounters also represent rich pickings for the analyst. And our own role in foregrounding their importance, because they provide fascinating data, has to be admitted. But it would be wrong to concentrate practical efforts in improving intercultural communication and language education only on gatekeeping encounters, although they are so significant in terms of social justice.

Those informants who rapidly developed competence in the new language and/or created a life for themselves in the new country which at least to some extent met their aspirations, were those with opportunities for daily and sustained contact with the majority. These contacts provided the environments for learning over time, rather than the demanding, stressful and complex gatekeeping encounters so well illustrated in our data.

There are, therefore, three major implications for practitioners arising from this study. The first concerns more awareness-raising among the majority community, particularly gatekeepers, of the experience of being a minority and the language and intercultural skills that the majority group needs to develop if they are to be competent professionals in a multi-lingual society. Our data has also well illustrated that the degree of participation and the effort involved in joint negotiation requires such encounters to be given more time. This has organisational implications for institutions which impose a flat rate on professionals for each interview – such as five minutes for a patient in a doctor's surgery or ten minutes for an employment interview.

The second implication concerns the opportunities for sustained contact with the majority community. As we have indicated in Chapter 1, at least on the level of lexical richness, informants, opportunities to interact with the wider community were a significant factor, whereas formal language training was not. (This is hardly surprising and accords with recent work comparing mono-lingual and bilingual children's lexical knowledge, Verhallen and Schoonen 1993.) This does not imply that language tuition is inef-fective for adults, since the extent and the quality of what was on offer has not been taken into account, but it does suggest that any formal tuition needs to be orientated towards maximising sustained contact, and so use of the new language, outside the cocooning classroom. In other words, classroom learning needs to be comple-mented by structured opportunities outside the classroom for minority workers to interact with speakers of the dominant lan-guage. And experiences from such encounters can then be used to develop critical awareness (using the first or majority language) of the ways in which discourses are used to reproduce dominant groups and how the majority language can be expropriated by the minority for their own purposes.

Together with these efforts, there needs to go a more concerted programme in first language maintenance and support to, as Fishman argues, 'reverse language shift' (Fishman 1991). This would contribute in part to resolving some of the conflicting identi-ties and sense of loss of community experienced by any migrant group.

The third implication concerns the teaching of 'understanding'. There is a mass of evidence in the data to show that understanding is an active, interactive endeavour. This calls for two strategies. The first is the encouragement of support groups among minority workers themselves from both the same and different language backgrounds, so that they can raise consciousness of issues and achieve a measure of solidarity among themselves. The second covers the role of the majority speaker. Understanding is best developed through opportunities for joint negotiation with a native speaker skilled in making their contribution as transparent as possible. In classroom settings, this usually means the teacher. He or she also has a responsibility to help students find successful ways of responding to understanding problems. As we have suggested, these are highly context-specific.

Ways of responding to understanding problems are also variably successful, depending, of course, on context. Nevertheless, there are some general patterns which suggest that higher order inferencing processes, and explicit markers of non-understanding are particularly helpful. This, therefore, raises the question of whether a specific programme of teaching these responses would be helpful to learners.

Such a programme might include:

(i)   a focus on the use of explicit responses to understanding problems e.g. metalinguistic comments and the use of partial repetition to distinguish the non-understood elements

(ii) a strong encouragement to formulate hypotheses, to develop, in other words, high inferencing capacities in the struggle for understanding

(iii) awareness raising of the strategic use of different responses to an understanding problem which fits the particular local context

(iv) awareness of issues of face in conveying problems of understanding and in mitigating face-threats to gatekeepers

(v) encouragement to take initiatives in topics as a way of reducing some frame and schema difficulties in understanding.

. Finally, there is also a case for using language awareness sessions to raise and discuss explicitly causes of understanding problems (Auerbach and Wallerstein 1987, Fairclough 1992b, van Lier 1995).

The theoretical and practical implications arising from this study are based on the idea of a social linguistics. The recent work on context and on critical linguistics assumes a 'language and . . .' perspective in which the collocation with language is one of a list that might include: power, social relations, discrimination, disadvantage, ideology, cultural studies or cultural politics, identities and so on. The call for a study of language and language development embedded in the social might seem rather stale. After all,

Hymes made a similar plea 20 years ago (Hymes 1972 and see Gee 1990, 1992). And yet most recent work on SLA, on intercultural communication within a social psychological tradition and language learning more generally has failed to engage with 'the whole social person' (Bourdieu 1991) or to view language as indexing 'those implicit values of relational identity and power . . . that go by the name of culture' (Silverstein 1992).

Because this study was about minority ethnic workers, our responsibilities and priorities as social linguists were particularly pressing. Being, however inadequately, participant observers in the lives of a small group of minority workers 'abandoned to the clutches of a foreign language' (Canetti 1976) we had to look at 'understanding' as embedded in their everyday lives. It would be impossible now to look at linguistics and language development in any other way, either theoretically or practically. And just as, as researchers we have been drawn into lives far removed from our own comfortable environments, so as ordinary people, constructed within a particular moral universe, our concern for social justice must permeate our work and our attempts to contribute to a social and critical linguistics and inform programmes and activities that develop understanding in intercultural encounters and acknowledge the power relations within which they are formed.

Appendix A

Abdelmalek

Abdelmalek arrived in France from Morocco in the autumn of 1981, at the age of twenty. In Morocco he had had only elementary education and he had no qualifications. He had picked up a little Spanish in Spain but produced only one-word utterances in French on his arrival at Marseille. He became a fisherman but suffered a very bad accident in 1984 after which he attempted to get the compensation owed to him. He had stayed single, and as such he lived in rented accommodation for workers where mostly foreign workers live. He was an active interactant and used sessions to extend his skills as communicator. At the end of the project, he had become a very competent communicator, but his linguistic system had not developed beyond the noun-verb form distinction.

Andrea

Andrea is an Italian in his mid-thirties. He came to England, leaving his wife and their son behind in Italy. He had finished the *scuola media* and obtained a professional qualification as a technician. In London he had several jobs, mainly as a barman or a waiter and his colleagues and friends were mainly Italian. He started attending English classes at the start of the project but because of the pressure of his new job (split shift in a bakery) he had to stop. Finally, his wife and son joined him in London. He had few contacts with English-speaking people except for service encounters (job, car, estate agent, school, doctors . . .) which explains that, despite his efforts to take advantage of most of the programme encounters and the considerable progress he had made, he still remained a non-assertive and cautious interactant.

Angelina

Angelina came from Naples to Germany. She was married and had two young children. In Italy she had attended primary school and three years of secondary school. When she arrived in Germany she had no German and, as she worked at home looking after her children and did not attend any language course, she had very few opportunities to acquire it. Her Italian husband spoke better German than she did. So he did the shopping and dealt with the official contacts. Their relatives and friends were Italian. So she had very few opportunities to use her German. Given her extremely restricted means she was successful in understanding and making herself understood, but needed a friendly relationship with her interlocutors and, even at the end of the project, some interpreting was still necessary.

Berta

Berta came to France from Chile to join her Chilean husband who had been in the country as a political refugee for a year. She was in her thirties and had had eight years of primary and secondary education in Chile. She had no professional training and no knowledge of French when she arrived. For the first six months, she lived in a refugee centre with her husband and three children aged seven to fourteen, and then they settled in a flat of their own outside Paris.

Her first months in Paris were very difficult for her but she had the will to fight, help her children and better her own social status. From the beginning, Berta seized every opportunity offered to her to work and follow courses in French and vocational training. Her children adapted rather well at school and her sister-in-law having joined them in Paris married a French man. In these conditions, Berta focused on French more and more and her competence gradually improved.

Çevdet

Çevdet emigrated to Germany when he was fifteen years old after eight-and-a-half years' schooling. He first arrived in a hostel with his father and received a little German tuition from a social worker. Then he started a vocational course in metalwork including German classes. After the course, he worked in a paint-removing plant where he learnt more German but worked in very hard conditions. Then he changed jobs twice. He also belonged to a mixed Turkish-German sports team, so his linguistic contacts were comparatively intensive and his German became very good. When his elder brother and mother finally joined them in Germany they rented a flat together. By that time, although a little shy, Çevdet achieved a near native-like competence.

Ergün

Ergün was seventeen when he came to Holland to join his family. In Turkey, he had had five years of primary school and started work as a motor-mechanic. He lived with his parents, got a job in a textile factory, played in a Turkish football team and had occasional contacts with Dutch speakers. He then moved to a city in the North of Holland where he spoke more Dutch than before because there were few Turkish people living in the city. He played in a Dutch football team. He also had a Dutch girlfriend.

Ergün was a very good communicator. He indicated his understanding problems and was willing to find solutions. In this way he created learning opportunities for himself through a continuous effort to maintain smooth and native-like interactions.

Fatima

Fatima came to Holland from Morocco to join her husband. She was twenty-five and had been a very successful needle woman in Morocco. She had had only two years of primary school and ten months after her arrival her proficiency in Dutch was almost zero. But she had started a basic course in Dutch at the community centre. She worked in the kitchen of a motel with other Moroccan and Turkish women. So, her contacts with Dutch speakers were very limited. Apart from a period when her husband was abroad, she relied on him in all encounters with officials. Then, she had a baby and, therefore she had more contacts with Dutch mothers and health officials.

In spite of these new circumstances, Fatima's communicative competence remained very low. She understood very little and was a very low participator – a role appropriate to an Arabic woman in public. When her husband was absent she was much more outgoing and she had positive attitudes towards learning Dutch. But still she progressed very little.

Gilda

Gilda came to France from Colombia, following her Colombian husband and bringing her two young children with her. She was about thirty and had had only primary education in her home country. The family had problems finding housing accommodation and they eventually settled in a very small apartment, in a house where Gilda's brother lived with his family, in the suburbs of Paris. But they went on looking for better housing. Gilda found a job as a cleaning-woman and the children went to school where they made good progress and were happy.

Except for the school and health contacts (teacher, her childrens' friends' parents, doctors), Gilda met relatively few French-speaking people. Her husband, who was a very active communicator and met a lot of French people, took care of most administrative contacts and was willing to keep the Spanish language at home. Completely devoted to her children, Gilda was not very communicative. She made a little progress but she continued to mix up the two languages, French and Spanish.

Gina

Gina came from Italy to live in Germany at the age of eighteen to join her parents. She first attended a language course provided by the Centro Italiano in Mannheim where she mainly met other Italians. She then found work as a cleaner. Practically all her colleagues were Italians so that the opportunities for learning German were relatively limited. Contact with Germans was not encouraged at home, and her engagement to an Italian living in Italy did little to help her progress in German. On the contrary, her interests centred on Italy and the prospect of her setting up a future there.

In such circumstances, one understands Gina's low interest in extending her knowledge in German. In the encounters, she often avoided indicating non-understanding or dropped the message when she could not get it through. She was quite satisfied to 'manage' with the means available and the majority speaker's help.

Ilhami

Ilhami had seven years of schooling in Turkey and then, on his arrival in Germany, he joined a vocational course. He did not get on with his father, so he moved to a private hostel. He was an occasional labourer, then he found a job in a refrigerating firm where his contacts with German speakers were very limited. The working conditions were bad but he was even more embittered by his experiences of racial discrimination and, although his circumstances became less stressful, he consciously kept at a distance from life in Germany and the Germans.

Ilhami's difficult experience and, as a consequence, his negative attitude towards Germans and Germany explains why he often remained aloof and less willing to show politeness and construct understanding and accounts for the slowing down of his development.

Madan

Madan arrived in England at the age of twenty-five, for his arranged marriage to a Punjabi woman of British citizenship who had lived in that country for eighteen years. He was born in India and spoke the Mawlai dialect of Punjabi. He completed six years of primary school, had three years of Hindi and one year of English as a foreign language. Then he spent varying lengths of time in Afghanistan, Jordan and Syria as a labourer. In England, he found a job as a press operator in a factory, where he used English and Punjabi. Although or because his wife speaks English very well, they do not use it at all at home where they live with his wife's sister's family.

Madan's linguistic competence remained very limited but, in the project encounters, he made efforts to cooperate and his confidence considerably improved.

Mahmut

Mahmut came to the Netherlands to join his wife who had been living there for four years. In Turkey, he had had primary education and had worked as a car mechanic. After a year of unemployment, he found a job in a meat factory. His contacts with the Dutch were restricted to colleagues, authorities and hospital when he had an operation. Although, as a former mechanic, he met a lot of people in second-hand car markets, he mostly spent his spare time with Turkish friends and relatives. Mahmut was very much aware of his shortcomings in Dutch and of the importance for him to improve his language competence. He made progress in his ability to understand and be understood. He ended up being promoted at work, buying a car and a home of his own.

Marcello

Marcello came from Italy to Heidelberg to live with the Italian family of his girl-friend. She was born and grew up in Heidelberg and spoke German like a native speaker. The language spoken in the family was Italian, but nevertheless the 'standard' of acquisition was set for him, and in later stages he would readily ask for words, grammatical rules, etc. The family's attitude towards Germany and the Germans was quite positive and they expected Marcello to learn.

In such a context, Marcello's motivation was very strong. He wanted to find a better job and, for this he needed to improve his German. As his working hours did not allow him to take a language course, he took advantage of all the contacts he had with Germans. He was a very active interactant, indicating non-understanding and understanding, establishing a good relationship with his interlocutor. And he made good progress.

Mohamed

Mohamed came from Casablanca with his family to join his father who had been living in the Netherlands for almost fourteen years. He had attended primary school and had been trained as a car mechanic. On his arrival, he found a job as a factory worker. He was nineteen years old and he lived in a small town with relatively few immigrants. So he had a lot of contact with Dutch speakers. He found himself a Dutch girlfriend and moved in with her in her parents' house. Not surprisingly Mohamed quickly became an accomplished speaker of Dutch. However, he was a low contributor and was less and less motivated to participate in the programme encounters.

Paula

Paula came from Chile where she attended school until the age of fifteen. She arrived in France at the age of thirty-two as a political refugee, with her Chilean husband who had been imprisoned and tortured and two teenage children. Her husband had to spend some time in the hospital and Paula felt very lonely and anxious. Her daughter had psychological problems and did not feel well at school. Paula had no contact whatsoever with French people and only a few with Latin Americans. She dared not go out alone and she had terrible headaches. This situation explains why Paula was a very insecure interactant. She had a lot of understanding problems but, when she felt encouraged, she could make herself understood. Although she kept hesitating and using her Spanish, she gained a little self-confidence, improved her understanding and made progress in expressing herself in French.

Ravinder

Ravinder came to the UK at the age of twenty, from a small village in the Punjab where he had received basic schooling. Shortly after arrival he was married to a girl who had grown up and been educated in the UK and who therefore spoke native-speaker English. However, she and Ravinder communicated mainly in Punjabi. Ravinder's main contact with the English language was through customers in his brother-in-law's shop where he worked and through social visits to pubs in the area. Although he was shy, he was motivated to learn the language. His minimal contact with English gave him sufficient self confidence to enable him to pass the driving test and to deliver goods for his brother-in-law. At this point, he seemed to feel that his knowledge of English was now adequate for his purposes.

Santo

Santo came from the Neapolitan region and spoke the Neapolitan dialect. He completed eight years of schooling in his home country and, at the age of twenty-five, he came to England expecting to stay indefinitely. He rented a room in a house shared by people of various nationalities. He found a job in an Italian restaurant and found himself an Italian-speaking girlfriend. So, his contacts with English-speaking people were rather sparse. Nevertheless, his speaking and listening skills in English were judged to be 'quite good' mainly because he was a very active interactant. But despite becoming more proficient, his repertoire did not develop much over the period of observation.

Tino

Tino came from Southern Italy where he attended school for eight years. He had no professional training and was unemployed until, at the suggestion of a friend, he first came to Germany and worked in a pizzeria. Then he returned to Italy and came back to Heidelberg a year later and stayed. He worked as a waiter in an Italian restaurant. He had regular and frequent contacts with Germans and a German girlfriend with whom he lived for a while. Due to his relatively intensive contacts, Tino made rapid progress and by the end of the observation period he was speaking fluently.

Zahra

Zahra came to Marseille from Morocco to join her husband. She was thirty-two years old. In Morocco, she received no formal education but in France she attended a French course twice a week for a short period. She is married and has four children who settled reasonably well into the education system. In France she worked as a kitchen assistant, then as a cleaning lady, then as a seamstress in the clothing workshop where her husband worked.

Despite being a low participator Zahra made slow but steady progress. But, at the end of the observation period, she still only had limited fluency in French.

Appendix B

PRESENTATION OF TRANSCRIPTS

For this book, data excerpts originally transcribed according to different 'systems' had to be harmonized. This was one of the reasons for our decision that good *readability* should be the guiding principle for the (re)presentation of transcripts as well as for the English translation.

Two general traits of the layout ensue from this:

Speakers are transcribed orthographically throughout. As a rule, non-standard pronunciation or dialect features are *not* represented in the transcriptions. Exceptions are made in those cases where such features are the basis for understanding problems.

Turns are rendered line by line, which in many cases involves a segmentation into chunks of speech that had been much less perceptible in the original conversation.

For the same reason of readability the transcription chosen attempts to minimize the use of conventions, limiting these to the following features:

use of L1 (or other (third) language):	*bbbbb*
short, longer pauses:	+, ++, +++
stress on word(s):	bbbbbbb underlined
self-corrections:	/
overlap:	A:bbb bbb[bbbbb] bbbb
	B: [ccc]
inaudible parts of words or utterances:	bbbb bbbb(xxx) bbb
interruptions:	A: bbbb # (xx)
	B: # cccc
question intonation:	bbbb ↑
falling intonation:	bbbb ↓ (used only when especially salient)

additional comments on way of speaking etc.:   <bbbb>   <low voice>
unclear utterances: (xxx)

N = the majority speaker throughout
The minority speaker is represented by the initial of their (anonymised) name.

English *translations* of the minority speaker´s contributions attempted to avoid two extremes: to sound overly 'strange´ on the one hand, or, on the other hand, to iron out the individual characteristics (e.g. lexical or syntactic) of their speech, because these are important for an understanding of the data. This meant that in some places we had to re-invent non-standard formulations, which cannot always be done in a wholly satisfactory way.

References

Agar, M. (1980) *The Professional Stranger: an informal introduction to ethnography*, New York: Academic Press.

Agar, M. (1985) 'Institutional Discourse', *Text* **5**, 147–68.

Agar, M. (1992) The 'Biculture in Bilingual', *Language and Society* **20**, 167–81.

Allwood, J. (1988) *Feedback in adult language acquisition*, Strasbourg/Göteborg: European Science Foundation (Report II).

Allwood, J. and Abelar Y. (1984) 'Lack of understanding, misunderstanding and adult language acquisition' in G. Extra and M. Mittner (eds), pp. 27–55.

Allwood, J. and Simonot, M. (1984) 'Understanding, misunderstanding and breakdown', in C. Perdue (ed.), pp. 68–94.

Andersen, R. (ed.) (1983) *Pidginisation and creolisation in second language acquisition*. Rowley: Newbury House.

Apfelbaum, B. (1991) 'Formes de réflexion linguistique dans des tandems franco-allemands: le cas des séquences déclenchées par le partenaire natif'. 1er colloque international *'Analyse des interactions'*, Aix-en-Provence.

Aston, G. (1986) 'Trouble-shooting in interaction with learners: the more the merrier?' *Applied Linguistics* **7**, 128–43.

Atkinson, M. and Heritage, J. (eds) (1984) *Structures of Social Action*. Cambridge: Cambridge University Press.

Atkinson, P. (1992) *Understanding Ethnographic Texts*. London: Sage.

Auer, P. (1992) 'Introduction: John Gumperz' approach to contextualization', in P. Auer and A. di Luzio (eds), pp. 1–53.

Auer, P. and di Luzio, A. (eds) (1992) *The contextualization of language*. Amsterdam: Benjamins.

Auerbach, E. and Wallerstein, N. (1987) *ESL for action: problem posing at work*. Reading, MA: Addison Wesley.

Bakhtin, M. (1978) *Esthétique et théorie du roman*. Paris: Gallimard.

Bakhtin, M. (1981) *The Dialogic Imagination*. Austin: University of Texas Press.

Bakhtin, M. (1984) *Esthétique de la creation verbale*. Paris: Gallimard.

Bange, P. (1987) 'La régulation de l'intercompréhension dans la communication exolingue', Communication à la *Table Ronde du Réseau Européen Acquisition des Langes*, La Baume-les-Aix.

Bange, P. (1992) *Analyse conversationelle et théorie de l'action*. Paris: Hatier-Didier.

Bateson, G. (1972) *Steps to an ecology of mind*. New York: Ballantine.

Bateson, G. (1979) *Mind and Nature. A Necessary Unit*. New York: Dutton.

Becker, A. and Perdue, C. (1984) 'Just one misunderstanding: a story of miscommunication', in G. Extra and M. Mittner (eds), pp. 57–82.

Bennet, T., Martin, G., Mercer, C. and Woollacott, J. (eds) (1981) *Culture, ideology and social processes*. London: Batsford.

Blanc, H., le Douaron, M. and Véronique, D. (eds) (1988) *S'approprier la langue de l'autre*. Paris: Didier Erudition.

Blommaert, J. and Verscheuren, J. (eds) (1991) *The Pragmatics of International and Intercultural Communication*. Amsterdam: Benjamins.

Bourdieu, P. (1977) *Outline of a theory of practice*. Cambridge: Cambridge University Press.

Bourdieu, P. (1991) *Language and symbolic power*. Cambridge, Mass.: Polity Press.

Bremer, K., Broeder, P., Roberts, C., Simonot, M. and Vasseur, M.-T. (1988) *Ways of Achieving Understanding: Communicating to Learn in a Second Language*. Final Report to the Steering Committee of the European Science Foundation Additional Activity 'Second Language Acquisition by Adult Immigrants' Strasbourg.

Bremer, K., Broeder, P., Roberts, C., Simonot, M. and Vasseur, M.-T. (1993) 'Ways of achieving understanding', in C. Perdue (ed.), *(Volume II)*, pp. 157–200.

Bremer, K. (forthcoming) *Verständigungsarbeit. Problembearbeitung und Gesprächsverlauf zwischen Sprechern verschiedener Muttersprachen*.

Briggs, C. (1986) *Learning how to ask*. Cambridge: Cambridge University Press.

Broeder, P. (1991) *Talking about people. A multiple case study on adult language acquisition*. Amsterdam: Swets and Zeitlinger.

Broeder, P. (1992) 'Learning to repeat to interact: Learner's repetitions in the language acquisition process of adults', *Journal of Intercultural Studies*, **13**, 19–35.

Broeder, P. (1993) 'Learning to understand in interethnic communication', *Issues in Applied Linguistics* **4**, 57–89.

Brooks, D. and Singh, K. (1979) 'Pivots & Presents' in Wallman, S. (ed.).

Brown, G. (1989) 'Making sense: the interaction of linguistic expression and contextual information', *Applied Linguistics* **10**, 97–108.

Brown, G. and Yule, G. (1983) *Discourse Analysis*. Cambridge: Cambridge University Press.

Brown, G, Malmkjaer, K., Pollitt, A. and Williams, J. (eds) (1994) *Language and Understanding*. Oxford: Oxford University Press.

Brown, P. and Levinson, S. (1987) *Politeness: Universals in Language Usage*. Cambridge: Cambridge University Press.

Bruner, J. (1986) *Actual minds, possible words*. Cambridge, Mass.: Harvard University Press.

Buechler, H. and Buechler, J. (eds) (1987) *Migrants in Europe: the Role of Family, Labour and Politics*, Westpont, Connecticut: Greenwood Press.

Cameron, D. (1993) [2nd edition] *Feminism and Linguistic Theory*. London: Macmillan Press.

Cameron D., Frazer, E., Harvey P., Rampton, B. and Richardson, K. (1992) *Researching language: issues of power and method* London: Routledge.

Canale M. and Swain, M. (1980) 'Theoretical Bases for Communicative Approaches to Second Language Teaching and Testing', *Applied Linguistics* **1**, 1–47.

Candlin C. and Lucas, J. (1986) 'Interpretations and explanations in Discourse: models of advising in family planning', in Ensink, T. et al. (eds).

Canetti, E. (1976) *Das Gewissen der Worte*. München/Wien: Hanser.

Canetti, E. (1980) *Histoire d'une jeunesse, la langue sauvée*. Paris: Albin Michel.

Cicourel, A. (1992) 'The interpenetration of communicative contexts: examples from medical encounters' in A. Duranti and C. Goodwin (eds).

Clahsen, H., Meisel, J. and Pienemann, M. (1983) *Deutsch als Zweitsprache: der Spracherwerb ausländischer Arbeiter*. Tübingen: Narr.

Clark, H. and Schaefer, E. (1989) 'Contributing to discourse', *Cognitive Science*, **13**:259–94.

Clark, H. and Wilkes-Gibbs, D. (1986) 'Referring as a collaborative process', *Cognition* **22**, 1–39.

Clarke, J., Hall, S., Jefferson, T. and Roberts, B. (1976) 'Subcultures, cultures and class: theoretical overview in S. Hall and T. Jefferson (eds) *Resistance Through Rituals*, London: Hutchinson.

Clifford J. (1990) 'Note on (field)notes', in R. Sanjek (ed.).

Clifford, J. and Marcus, G. (1986) *Writing culture*. Berkeley, California: University of California Press.

Clyne, M. (1991) 'Patterns and intercultural communication in Melbourne factories: some research in progress', *Language and Language Education* **1/1**, 5–30.

Clyne, M., Ball, M. and Neil, D. (1991) 'Intercultural communication at work in Australia', *MultiLingua* **10/3**, 253–75.

Cohen, A. (1987) 'Using verbal reports in research on language learning', in K. Faerch and G. Kasper (eds).

Cole, P. and Morgan, J. (eds) (1975) *Syntax and Semantics*, vol. 3: *Speech Acts*, New York: Academic Press.

Cook, V. (1991) *Second Language Learning and Language Teaching*. London: Edward Arnold

Cope, B. and Kalantzis, M. (1994) 'Making diversity work: the changing culture of Australian workplaces', in D. Headon and D. Hall (eds).

Coupland, N., Giles, H. and Wiemann, J. (eds) (1991) *Miscommunication and problematic talk*. Newbury Park: Sage Publications.

Crawley, R., Stevenson, R. and Tallerman, M. (eds) (1986) *Proceedings of the Child Language Seminar*, Trevelyan College, University of Durham.

Cutler, A. (1989) 'Auditory lexical access: where do we start?', in W. Marslen-Wilson, (ed.), pp. 342–56.

Dascal, M. (1985) 'The relevance of misunderstanding' in M. Dascal (ed.), pp. 441–59.

Dascal, M. (ed.) (1985) *Dialogue: an interdisciplinary approach*. Amsterdam: Benjamins.

Dascal, M. (1989) 'On the roles of context and literal meaning in understanding', *Cognitive Science* **13**, 253–7.

Dausendschön-Gay, U. and Krafft, U. (1989) 'Formes d'interaction communicative dans des situations de contact entre interlocuteurs francais et allemands', in D. Kramer (ed.), pp. 391–404.

Dausendschön-Gay, U., Gülich, E. and Krafft, U. (eds) (1991) *Linguistische Interaktionsanalysen. Beiträge zum 20. Romanistentag.* Tübingen: Niemeyer.

Day, R. (ed.) (1986) *Talking to Learn: conversation in second language acquisition.* Rowley, Mass.: Newbury House.

Dechert, M. and Raupach, M. (eds) (1989) *Interlingual processes.* Tübingen: Narr.

Denzin, N. (1978) [2nd edition] *The research act: a theoretical introduction to sociological method.* New York: McGraw-Hill.

Denzin, N. (1989) *Interpretive Biography.* Newbury Park, California: Sage.

Denzin, N. (1992) *Symbolic interactionalism and cultural studies: the politics of interpretation,* Oxford: Blackwell.

Deulofeu, J. and Taranger, M. (1984) 'Relations entre le linguistique et le culturel-microscopie de quelques malentendues et incompréhensions', in C. Noyau and R. Porquier (eds), pp. 99–129.

Dietrich, R. (1989) 'Communicating with few words. An empirical account of the second language speaker's lexicon', in R. Dietrich and F. Graumann (eds), pp. 233–72.

Dietrich, R. and Graumann, F. (eds) (1989) *Language processing in social context.* Amsterdam: North Holland.

Dietrich, R. and Klein, W. (1986) 'Simple Language', *Interdisciplinary Science Reviews* **11/2**, 110–18.

Drew, P. and Heritage, J. (eds) (1992) *Talk at Work: interaction in institutional settings.* Cambridge: Cambridge University Press.

Duranti, A. and Goodwin, C. (eds) (1992) *Rethinking context: language as an interactive phenomenon.* Cambridge: Cambridge University Press.

Eco, U. (1979) *The role of the reader: explorations in the semiotics of texts.* London: Hutchinson.

Ehlich, K. (1980) 'Fremdsprachlich Handeln: Zur Pragmatik des Zweitspracherwerbs ausländischer Arbeiter', *Deutsch Lernen* **1**, 21–37.

Ehlich, K. (1992) 'Kommunikationsbrüche – Vom Nachteil und Nutzen des Sprachkontakts', *Zielsprache Deutsch* **23**, 64–74.

Ellen, R. (ed.) (1984) *Ethnographic Research: a guide to general conduct.* London: Academic Press.

Ellis, R. (1985) *Understanding second language acquisition.* Oxford: Oxford University Press.

Ellis, R. (ed.) (1987) *Second Language Acquisition in Context.* London: Prentice-Hall International.

Ellis, R. (1994) *The study of Second Language acquisition.* Oxford: Oxford University Press.

Ensink, T., van Essen, A. and van der Geest, T. (1986) *Discourse analysis and public life.* Dordrecht: Foris Publications.

Erickson, F. (1982) 'Talking-down: some cultural sources of miscommunication in inter-racial interviews', in A. Wolfgang (ed.).

Erickson, F. and Shultz, J. (1982) *The counsellor as gatekeeper: social interaction in interviews.* New York: Academic Press.

Ericsson, K. and Simon, H. (1987) 'Verbal reports on thinking', in K. Faerch and G. Kasper (eds).

Esch, E. (1992) *Native/non-native interaction: Foreigner-Talk*. Doctoral dissertation, Open University, Milton Keynes.

Evans, M. (1986) 'The effects of different interview styles on the quality of child language data', in R. Crawley, R. Stevenson and M. Tallerman (eds), pp. 297–325.

Extra, G. and Mittner, M. (eds) (1984) *Studies in Second Language Acquisition by Adult Immigrants*. Tilburg: Tilburg University.

Faerch, K. and Kasper, G. (1986) 'The role of comprehension in second language learning', *Applied Linguistics* 7, 257–74.

Faerch, K. and G. Kasper (eds) (1987) *Introspection in second language research*. Clevedon: Multilingual Matters.

Fairclough, N. (1985) 'Critical and Descriptive Goals in Discourse Analysis', *Journal of Pragmatics*, 9: 739–63.

Fairclough, N. (1989) *Language and power*. London: Longman.

Fairclough, N. (1992a) *Discourse and social change*. Cambridge: Polity Press.

Fairclough, N. (ed.) (1992b) *Critical language awareness*. London: Longman.

Felix, S. (ed) (1980) *Second language development. Trends and issues*. Tübingen: Narr.

Fetterman, D. (1989) *Ethnography: step by step*. Newbury Park, California: Sage.

Fiksdal, S. (1989) 'Framing uncomfortable moments in cross-cultural gatekeeping interviews', in S. Gass, C. Madden, D. Preston and L. Selinker (eds), pp. 190–207.

Fisher, S. and Todd, A. (1986) *Discourse and Institutional Authority*. Norwood, New York: Ablex.

Fishman, J. (1991) *Reversing Language Shift*. Clevedon: Multilingual Matters.

Flores d`Arcais, G. (1988) 'Language perception', in F. J. Newmeyer (ed.), *Linguistics: The Cambridge Survey*. Vol III: *Psychological and biological aspects*. Cambridge: Cambridge University Press, pp. 97–123.

Forster, E.M. (1936) *A passage to India*. Harmondsworth: Penguin.

Foucault, M. (1971) *L'Ordre du discours*. Paris: Gallimard.

Fowler, R., Hodge, K., Kress, G., and Trew, T. (1979) *Language and Control*. London: Routledge and Kegan Paul.

François, F. (1982) 'Ebauche d'une dialogique', Langage et situations, *Connexions* no. 38, ed. EPI, 63–87.

François, F. (1990) *La communication inégale: heurs et malheurs de l'interaction verbale*. Paris: Delachaux et Niestlé.

François, F., Hudelot, C., et Sabeau-Jouannet, E. (1984) *Conduites linguistiques chez le jeune enfant*. Paris: Presses Universitaires de France.

Fritz, G. (1991) 'Comprehensibility and the basic structures of dialogue', in S. Stati, E. Weigand, and F. Hundsnurscher (eds), pp. 3–24.

Garcia, O. and Otheguy, R. (eds) (1990) *English across Cultures*. Berlin: Mouton de Gruyter.

Garfinkel, H. (1967) *Studies in ethnomethodology*. Englewood Cliffs, New Jersey: Prentice Hall.

Gass, S., Madden, C., Preston, D. and Selinker, L. (eds) (1989) *Variation in second language acquisition*. Clevedon: Multilingual Matters.

Gass, S. and Varonis, E. (1985) 'Variation in native speaker speech modification to non-native speakers', *Studies in Second Language Acquisition* 7, 3–58.

Gass, S. and Varonis, E. (1987) 'The effect of familiarity on the comprehensibility of nonnative speech', *Language Learning* 34, 65–88.

Gass, S and Varonis, E. (1991) 'Miscommunication in non-native speaker discourse', in Coupland, N., Giles, H. and Wiemann J. (eds), *Miscommunication and problematic talk*. Newbury Park: Sage Publications, pp. 121–45.

Gee, J. (1990) *Social Linguistics and Literacies: Ideology in Discourses*. London: Falmer Press.

Gee, J. (1992) *The Social Mind: Languages ideology and social practice*. New York: Bergin and Garvey.

Geertz, C. (1973) *The interpretation of cultures*. New York: Basic Books.

Giacomi, A. and de Hérédia, C. (1986) 'Réussites et échecs dans la communication linguistique entre locuteurs francophones et locuteurs immigrés', *Langages* 84, 9–24.

Giacomi, A., Houdaïfa, E. and Vion, R. (1984) 'Malentendus et/ou incompréhensions dans le dialogue interculturel: "à bon entendeur salut!"', in C. Noyau et R. Porquier (eds), pp. 79–99.

Giddens, A. (1976) *New rules of sociological method: a positive critique of interpretative sociologies*. London: Hutchinson.

Glaser, B. and Strauss, A. (1967) *The discovery of grounded theory: strategies for qualitative research*. Chicago: Aldine Publishers.

Goanach, D. (ed.) (1991) *Acquisition et utilisation d'une langue étrangère. L'Approche cognitive, Le Français dans le monde*. Paris: Hachette.

Goffman, E. (1974) *Frame Analysis: an essay on the organisation of experience*. New York: Harper and Row.

Gramsci, A. (1971) *Selections from the prison notebooks*. (ed. and trans. by Q. Hoare and G. Nowell-Smith). London: Lawrence and Wishart.

Gramsci, A. (1981) 'Culture', in T. Bennet, G. Martin, C. Mercer and J. Woollacott (eds), *Culture, ideology and social processes*, pp. 193–97.

Grice, H. (1975) 'Logic and Conversation', in P. Cole and J.L. Morgan (eds).

Grillo, R. (ed.) (1989) *Social Anthropology and the politics of language*, London: Routledge.

Gülich, E. (1986) 'L'organisation conversationelle des énoncés inachevés et de leur achèvement interactif en `situation de contact', *Documentation et recherche en linguistique allemande contemporaine-Vincennes* (DRLAV) 34/35, 161–82.

Gülich, E. (1988) 'Handlungsschema und Formulierungsstrukturam Beispiel eines Beratungsgesprächs ("Das Zeitungsabonnement"). Ein Diskussionsbeitrag', *Sprache und Pragmatik (Lund)* 8, S. 43–66.

Gülich, E. (1991) 'Pour une ethnométhodologie linquistique: Description de séquences conversationelles explicatives', in U. Dausendschön-Gay, E. Gülich, and U. Krafft (eds), pp. 325–64.

Gülich, E. and Kotschi, T. (1987) 'Reformulierungshandlungen als Mittel der Textkonstitution. Untersuchungen zu französischen Texten aus mündlicher Kommunikation', in W. Motsch (ed.), pp. 199–261.

Gumperz, J. (1982a), *Discourse strategies*. Cambridge: Cambridge University Press.

Gumperz, J. (ed.) (1982b), *Language and social identity*, Cambridge: Cambridge University Press.

Gumperz, J. (1984) 'Miscommunication as a resource in the study of second language acquisition: a discourse analysis approach', in G. Extra and M. Mittner (eds), pp.139–44.

Gumperz, J. (1992a) 'Contextualization Revisited', in P. Auer and A. di Luzio (eds).

Gumperz, J. (1992b) 'Contextualization and Understanding', in A. Duranti and C. Goodwin (eds), pp. 229–52.

Gumperz, J. and Hymes, D. (eds) (1972) *Directions in Sociolinguistics: The ethnography of communication*. New York: Holt, Rinehart and Winston.

Gumperz, J. and Roberts, C. (1991) 'Understanding in intercultural encounters', in J. Blommaert and J. Verschueren (eds), pp. 51–90.

Habermas, J. (1984) *Theory of communicative action*. London: Heinemann.

Hamburger, F. (1989) 'Auf dem Weg zur Wanderungsgesellschaft – Migrationsprozeß und politische Reaktion in der Bundesrepublik Deutschland', *Deutsch lernen* 1, 3–35.

Hammersley, M. and Atkinson, P. (1983) *Ethnography: principles in practice*. London: Tavistock Publication.

Hatch, E. (1978) 'Acquisition of syntax', in J. Richards (ed.).

Hatch, E. (1980) 'Conversational analysis: an alternative methodology for second language acquisition studies', in R. Shuy and A. Shnukal (eds), pp. 182–96.

Hatch, E. (1983) 'Simplified input and second language acquisition', in R. Andersen (ed.).

Hatch, E. (1987) *Second language acquisition*. Rowley, Mass.: Newbury House.

Headon, D. and Hall, D. (1994) *The Abundant Culture*. Sydney: Allen Unwin.

de Hérédia, C. (1986a) 'Intercompréhension et malentendus. Etude d'interactions entre étrangers et autochtones', *Langue Française* 71, 48–69.

de Hérédia, C. (1986b) 'Asymmetric communication in bilingual exchanges', *Studies in Second Language acquisition* 8, 369–89.

Hewitt, R. (1986) *White talk black talk*. Cambridge: Cambridge University Press.

Hinnenkamp, V. (1989) *Interaktionale Soziolinguistik und Interkulturelle Kommunikation. Gesprächsmanagement zwischen Deutschen und Türken*. Tübingen: Niemeyer.

Hinnenkamp, V. (1991) 'Talking a person into interethnic discourse: An analytic case study', in J. Blommaert and J. Verschueren (eds).

Hinnenkamp, V. (1992) 'Comments on Christian Heath's: Gesture's Discreet Tasks', in P. Auer and A. di Luzio (eds).

Hörmann, H. (1981) *Meinen und Verstehen. Grundzüge einer psychologischen Semantik*. Frankfurt/M: Suhrkamp.

van Hout, R. and Strömqvist, S. (1993) 'The influence of socio-biographical factors', in C. Perdue (ed.), pp. 164–72.

Hymes, D. (1972) 'Models of the interaction of language and social life', in J. Gumperz and D. Hymes (eds).

Jansen, B., Lalleman, J. and Muysken, P. (1981) 'The alternation' hypothesis: acquisition of Dutch word order by Turkish and Moroccan foreign workers,' Language Learning, **31**: 315–36.

Johnson, P. (1981) 'Effects on reading comprehension of language complexity and cultural backgrounds of a text', *TESOL Quarterly*, **15**, 169–81.

Jupp, T., Roberts, C. and Cook-Gumperz, J. (1982), Language and disadvantage: the hidden process, in: J. Gumperz (ed.), pp. 232–56.

Kellerman, E. (1991) 'Compensatory strategies in second language research: a critique, a revision and some (non)implications for the classroom', in Phillipson et al. (eds).

Kleifgen, J. (1989) 'Communicative inferencing without a common language', in S. Gass, C. Madden, D. Preston and L. Selinker (eds).

Klein, W. (1984) *Zweitspracherwerb. Eine Einführung*. Königstein: Athenäum.

Klein, W. (1986) *Second language acquisition*. Cambridge: Cambridge University Press.

Klein, W. and Dittmar, N. (1979) *Developing grammars*. Berlin: Springer.

Klein, W. and Perdue, C. (eds) (1988) Utterance structure. *Final report of the European Science Foundation Project: Second language acquisition by adult immigrants (Volume VI)*. Strasbourg: ESF.

Klein, W. and Perdue, C. (eds) (1992) *Utterance structure: Developing grammars again*. Amsterdam: Benjamins.

Kramer, D. (ed.) (1989) *Actes du 18éme congrès international de linguistique et philologie romaines*, Universität Trier 1986, Tübingen: Niemeyer.

Kress, G. (1985) *Linguistic processes in sociocultural practice*. Victoria: Deakin University.

Lakoff, G. and Johnson, M. (1980) *Metaphors we live by*. Chicago: University of Chicago Press.

Larsen-Freeman, D. and Long, M. (1991) *An introduction to second language acquisition research*. London: Longman.

Leech, G. (1983) *Principles of pragmatics*. London: Longman.

Levinson, S. (1979) 'Activity types and language', *Linguistics* **17**, **5/6**, 356–99.

van Lier, L. (1988) *The Classroom and the language learner*. London: Longman.

van Lier, L. (1995) *Language Awareness*. London: Penguin.

Lincoln, Y. and Guba, E. (1985) *Naturalistic Inquiry*. Beverly Hills, California: Sage.

Linell, P., Gustavsson, L. and Juvonen, P. (1988) 'Interactional dominance in dyadic communication: a presentation of initiative-response analysis', *Linguistics* **26**, 415–42.

Locke, J. (1690) *Essay concerning Human Understanding*. Ed. by P.H. Nidditch, Oxford: Clarendon Press 1975.

Long, M. (1980) 'Inside the "black box": methodological issues in classroom research on language learning', *Language Learning* 30, 1–42.

Long, M. (1981) 'Input, interaction and second language acquisition', in H. Winitz (ed.) *Native Language and Foreign Language Acquisition*. Annals of the New York Academy of Sciences 379.

Long, M. (1983a) 'Linguistic and conversational adjustments to non-native speakers', *Studies in Second Language Acquisition* 5, 177–93.

Long, M. (1983b) 'Native speaker/non-native speaker conversation and the negotiation of comprehensible input', *Applied Linguistics* **4**, 126–41.

Long, M. (1989) 'Input and second language acquisition theory', in S. Gass, C. Madden et al. (eds).

Lüdi, G. (ed.) (1986) *Devenir bilingue – parler bilingue Actes due 2e Colloque sur le bilinguisme,* Université de Neuchàtel, 20–22 septembre 1984; Tübingen 1987: Niemeyer.

Lüdi, G. (1987) 'Travail lexical explicite en situation exolingue', in G. Lüdi (ed.), *Romania igeniosa': Festschrift für Gerold Hilty zum 60. Geburtstag,* Bern u.a.: Lang, pp. 463–91.

Lüdi, G. and Py, B. (eds) (1986) *Devenir bilingue, parler bilingue.* Tübingen: Narr.

Manning, P. (1992) *Organizational communication.* New York: de Gruyter.

Marslen-Wilson, W. (1989) 'Access and integration: Projecting Sound onto Meaning', in W. Marslen-Wilson (ed.) *Lexical representation and process,* Cambridge, Mass.: MIT press, pp. 3–24.

Martin-Jones, M. (1989) 'Language power and linguistic minorities: the need for an alternative approach to bilingualism, language maintenance and shift', in R. Grillo (ed.).

McLaughlin, B. (1987) *Theories of Second Language Learning.* London: Edward Arnold.

McRobbie, A. (1978) Working class rules and the culture of femininity in Womens' Studies Group, Women Take Issue: CCCS/Hutchinson.

McRobbie, A. (1994) *Postmodernism and popular culture.* London: Routledge.

Mehan, H. (1979) *Learning Lessons.* Cambridge: Harvard University Press.

Meisel, J. (1980) 'Linguistic simplification: a study of immigrant workers' speech and foreigner talk', in S. Felix (ed.), pp. 13–40.

Mishra, A. (1982), 'Discovering connections,' in: J. Gumperz (ed.), pp. 57–71.

Moerman, M. (1988) *Talking Culture: ethnography and conversational analysis,* Philadelphia: University of Pennsylvania Press.

Motsch, W. (ed.) (1987) *Satz , Text, sprachliche Handlung,* Berlin: Akademie.

Naiman, N., Fröhlich, M., Stern, H., and Todesco, A. (1978) *The good Language learner.* Research in Education series no. 7, Toronto: The Ontario Institute for Studies in Education.

Newmeyer, F. (ed.) (1988) *Linguistics: The Cambridge Survey, Vol. III: Psychological and biological aspects.* Cambridge: Cambridge University Press.

Noyau, C. (1984) 'Communiquer quand on ignore la langue de l'autre', in C. Noyau and Porquier, R. (eds), pp. 8–36.

Noyau, C. and Deulofeu, J. (eds) (1986) *L'acquisition du Français par des adultes migrants.* Langue Française 71.

Noyau, C. and Pourquier, R. (eds) (1984) *Communiquer dans la langue de l'autre.* Paris: Presses Universitaires de Vincennes.

Ochs, E. (1979) 'Introduction: What child language can contribute to pragmatics', in E. Ochs and B. Schieffelin (eds), *Developmental Pragmatics,* New York: Academic Press.

Ochs, E. and Schieffelin, B. (eds) (1983), *Acquiring conversational competence.* London: Routledge.

Pennycook, A. (1994) 'Incommensurable Discourses?', *Applied Linguistics* **15/2**: 115–38.

Perdue, C. (ed.) (1982) *Second language acquisition by adult immigrants: A field manual*. Strasbourg. European Science Foundation.

Perdue, C. (ed) (1984) *Second Language Acquisition by Adult Immigrants. A field manual*. Rowley: Newbury House.

Perdue, C. (1986) 'Understanding and misunderstanding in adult second language acquisition: Recent work in the ESF project', in G. Lüdi (ed.).

Perdue, C. (ed.) (1993a) *Adult language acquisition: cross-linguistic perspectives. Volume I Field Methods*, Cambridge: Cambridge University Press.

Perdue, C. (ed.) (1993b) *Adult language acquisition: cross-linguistic perspective. Volume II The results*, Cambridge: Cambridge University Press.

Philips, S. (1982) *The invisible culture*. New York: Longman.

Phillipson, R. (1992) *Linguicism*. Oxford: OUP.

Phillipson, R., Kellerman, E., Selinker, L., Sharwood-Smith, M. and Swain, M. (eds) (1991) *Foreign/Second language pedagogy research*. Clevedon: Multilingual Matters.

Pica, T., Young, R. and Doughty, C. (1987) 'The impact of interaction on comprehension', *TESOL Quarterly* **21**,

de Pietro, J., Matthey, M. and Py, B. (1989) 'Acquisition et contrat didactique; les séquences potentiellement acquisitionnelles dans la conversation exolingue', in D. Weir and H. Fugier (eds), pp. 99–124.

Porquier, R. (1983) 'Communication exolingue et apprentissage des langues', in B. Py (ed.), pp. 17–47.

Py, B. (ed.) 1983 *Acquisition d'une langue étrangère III*, Paris/Neuchàtel: Presses Universitaries de Vincennes et CLA Neuchàtel.

Py, B. (1987) 'Making Sense: Interlanguage's Intertalk in Exolingual Conversation', *Studies in Second Language Acquisition*, **8/3**, 343–53.

Py, B. (1991) 'Les stratégies d'acquisition en situation d'interaction', in D. Gaonach (ed.).

Quasthoff, U. and Hartmann, D. (1982) 'Bedeutungserklärungen als empirischer Zugang zu Wortbedeutungen. Zur Entscheidbarkeit zwischen holistischen und komponentiellen Bedeutungskonzeptionen', *Deutsche Sprache* **2**, 97–118.

Rampton, B. (1987) 'Stylistic variability and not speaking normal English: some post-Labovian approaches and their implications for the study of interlanguage', in R. Ellis (ed.).

Rampton, B. (1990) *Communication strategies revisited: General survey and commentary*. Paper presented at the 9th AILA World Congress, Thessaloniki, Greece.

Rampton, B. (1995) *Crossing: Language and ethnicity among adolescents*. London: Longman.

Richards, J. (ed.) (1978) *Understanding in second and foreign language acquisition*. Rowley, Mass.: Newbury House.

Richards, J. and Schmidt, J. (eds) (1983) *Language and Communication*. London: Longman.

Roberts, C., Davies, E. and Jupp, T. (1992) *Language and discrimination. A study of communication in multi-ethnic workplaces*. London: Longman.

Roberts, C. and Simonot, M. (1987) '"This is my life": How language acquisition is interactionally accomplished', in R. Ellis (ed.), pp. 133–48.

Rost, M. and Ross, S. (1991) 'Learner use of strategies in interaction: Typology and teachability', *Language Learning* **41**, 235–73.

Rubin, J. (1975) 'What the "good language learner" can teach me', *TESOL Quarterly* **9**, 41–51.

Russier, C., Stoffel, H., and Véronique, D. (eds) (1991) *Interactions en langue étrangère*. Publication de l'Université de Provence.

Sacks, H. (1971) Unpublished lecture notes. University of California.

Sacks, H., Schegloff, E. and Jefferson, G. (1974) 'A simplest systematics for the organisation of "turn-taking" for conversation', *Language* **50**, 696–735.

Sanjek, R. (ed.) (1990) *Fieldnotes: the making of anthropology*. Ithaca, New York: Cornell University Press.

Sarraute, N. (1980) *L'usage de la parole*. Paris: Gallimard.

Schegloff, E. (1984) 'On Some Questions and Ambiguities in Conversation', in M. Atkinson and Heritage (eds).

Schegloff, E. (1987) 'Some sources of misunderstanding in talk-in-interaction', *Linguistics* **25**, 201–18.

Scholtes, R. (1983) *Textual power*. Yale University Press.

Schmidt, R. (1994) 'Deconstructing consciousness in search of useful definitions for applied linguistics', *AILA Review* **11**.

Schumann, J. (1978) *The pidginization process: a model for second language acquisition*. Rowley: Newbury House.

Scollon, R. (1976) *Conversations with a one year old Honolulu*. Honolulu: University of Hawai Press.

Scollon, R. and S. Scollon (1983) 'Face in interethnic communication', in J. Richards and J. Schmidt (eds).

Selting, M. (1987) *Verständigungsprobleme. Eine empirische Analyse am Beispiel der Bürger-Verwaltungs-Kommunikation*. Tübingen: Niemeyer.

Shuy, R. (1984) 'Linguistics in other professions', *Annual Review of Anthropology* **13**, 419–45.

Shuy, R., and Shnukal, A. (eds) (1980) *Language use and the uses of languages*. Washington: Georgetown University Press.

Silverstein, M. (1981) 'The Limits of Awareness in Sociolinguistics', *Working Paper* **84**, Austin, Texas.

Silverstein, M. (1992) 'The indeterminacy of contextualization. When is enough enough', in P. Auer and A. di Luzio (eds).

Simonot, M. (1983) 'Communicating to learn', Paper presented at Dutch Association of Applied Linguistics Annual Conference, September 1983.

Sperber, D. and Wilson, D. (1986) *Relevance*. Oxford: Blackwell.

Stati, S., Weigand, E. and Hundsnurscher, F. (eds) (1991) *Dialoganalyse III. Referate der 3. Arbeitstagung Bologna*, Tübingen: Niemeyer.

Stern, H. (1983) *Fundamental Concepts of Language Teaching*. Oxford: OUP.

Tannen, D. (ed.) (1993) *Framing in Discourse*. Oxford: OUP.

Tannen, D. and Wallat, C. (1986) 'Medical Professionals and Parents: a linguistic analysis of communication across contexts', *Language in Society* **15**, 295–311.

Taylor, J. (1986) 'Do you understand? Criteria of understanding in verbal interaction', *Language and Communication* **6**, 171–80.

Taylor, T. (1992) *Mutual Misunderstanding: scepticism and the theorizing of language and interpretation*. London: Routledge.

Tedlock, D. (1983) *The Spoken word and the work of interpretation*. Philadelphia: University of Pennsylvania Press.

Thomas, J. (1983) 'Cross-cultural pragmatic failure', *Applied Linguistics* **4**, 91–112.

Thomas, J. (1984) 'Cross-Cultural communication as "unequal encounter": towards a pragmatic analysis', *Applied Linguistics* **5**, 226–35.

Thomas, J. (1993) *Doing Critical Ethnography*. Newbury Park: Sage.

Trévise, A. (1984) 'Les malentendus: effets de loupe sur certains phénomènes d'acquisition d'une language étrangère', in C. Noyau and R. Porquier (eds), pp. 130–52.

Tyler, A. and Davies, C. (1990) 'Cross-linguistic communication missteps', *Text* **10**, 385–411.

Varonis, E. and S. Gass (1985) 'Non-native/Non-native Conversations: A model for Negotiation of Meaning', *Applied Linguistics* **6/1**, 71–90.

Vasseur, M.-T. (1988) 'La collaboration entre les partenaires dans les échanges entre locuteurs natifs et apprenants étrangers: formes, développement, variations', in H. Blanc, M. le Douaron and D. Véronique (eds).

Vasseur, M.-T. (1989) 'La gestion de l'intercomprehension dans les échanges entre natifs et non-natifs', *L'Interaction*, Paris: Association des Sciences du Langage, pp. 36–55.

Vasseur, M.-T. (1991) 'Solliciter n'est pas apprendre: initiative, sollicitation et acquisition d'une langue étrangère', in C. Russier, H. Stoffel & D. Véronique, D. (eds), pp. 49–66.

Verhallen, M. and R. Schoonen (1993) 'Lexical Knowledge of Monolingual and bilingual children', *Applied Linguistics* **14/4**, 344–63.

Verschueren, J. (1990) 'English as object and medium of (mis)understanding', in O. García and R. Otheguy (eds), *English across cultures*.

Vion, R. (1985) 'Compréhension et comportement communicatif', in D. Véronique (ed.) *GRAL/Papiers de travail*, Aix-en Provence: Université de Provence.

Vion, R. (1986) *Les diverses phases d'une interaction*. Paper presented at ESF meeting on Understanding, London, March 1986.

Vion, R. and Mittner, M. (1986) 'Activité de reprise et gestion des interactions en communication exolingue', *Languages* **84**, 25–42.

Voionmaa, K. (1984) 'Lexikal overföring och rationaletet', *Papers presented to the 4th Scandinavian Conference on Bilingualism*, Uppsala.

Voloshinov, V. (1973) *Marxism and the philosophy of language*. Cambridge, Mass: Harvard University Press.

Vygotsky, L. (1978) *Mind in society: The development of higher psychological processes*. Cambridge: Cambridge University Press.

Wallace, C. (forthcoming) *Reading*. Oxford: Oxford University Press.

Wallman, S. (ed.) (1979) *Ethnicity at Work*. London: Macmillan.

Wallraff, G. (1988) *Lowest of the Low*. London: Methuen.

Watson-Gegeo, K. (1988) 'Ethnography in ESL: Defining the essentials', *TESOL Quarterly* **22/4**.

Weird, D. and Fugier, H. (eds) *Actes du 3ème colloque regional de linguistique*, Strasbourg: Université Science Humaines et Université Louis Pasteur.

Wells, G. (1987) *The meaning makers. Children learning language and using language to learn*. London: Hodder and Stoughton.

Wenden, A. (1991) *Learner Strategies for Learner Autonomy*. New York: Prentice Hall.

Werner, O. and Schoepfler, G. (1989) *Systematic Fieldwork*. Vol. 1., California: Sage

Werth, P. (ed.) (1981) *Conversation and Discourse*. London: Croom Helm.

Willing, K. (1992) *Talking it Through*. Sydney: National Centre for English Language Teaching and Research.

Willis, P. (1977) *Learning to Labour: How working class kids get working class jobs*, Saxon House.

Wilpert, C. (ed.) (1988) *Entering the working world*. Aldershot: Gower.

Wilson, A. (1978) *Finding a voice: Asian Woman in Britain*. London: Virago.

Wilson, D. and Sperber, D. (1981) 'On Grice's theory of conversation', in P. Werth (ed.).

Winitz, H. (ed.) (1981) *Native Language and Foreign Language Acquisition*. Annals of the New York Academy of Sciences, 379.

Wolff, D. (1985) 'Verstehensprozesse in einer zweiten Sprache', *Studium Linguistik* **17/18**, 162–74.

Wolff, D. (1986) 'Unterschiede beim muttersprachlichen und zweitsprachlichen Verstehen', *Linguistische Berichte* **106**, 445–55.

Wolff, D. (1989) 'Identification of text-type as strategic device in L2 comprehension', in M. Dechert and M. Raupauch (eds), pp. 137–49.

Wolfgang, A. (ed.) (1982) *Research in non-verbal communication*. New York: Academic Press.

Name index

Index